—THE—
EAST COAST
MAIN LINE
1939-1959

D1556525

—THE—
EAST COAST
MAIN LINE
1939-1959

B.W.L. BROOKSBANK
AND PETER TUFFREY

FONTHILL

This work is dedicated to the management and staff of the LNER whose professionalism and devotion to duty enabled the ECML to play its triumphal part in the Second World War, and especially to those railway personnel who were killed or injured in the conflict.

Fonthill Media Limited
Stroud House
Russell Street
Stroud GL5 3AN

Fonthill Media LLC
12 Sires Street
Charleston SC 29403

www.fonthillmedia.com
office@fonthillmedia.com

First published in the United Kingdom
and the United States of America 2017

British Library Cataloguing in Publication Data:
A catalogue record for this book is available from the British Library

ISBN 978-1-78155-551-4

Typeset in Minion Pro 10pt on 13pt
Printed and bound in England

Contents

Acknowledgements

We are grateful to the assistance from the following people: Marian Crawley, Peter Jary, Catherine Mather, Hugh Parkin, Bill Reed, Tristram Tuffrey.

Foreword

This is an account of the East Coast Main Line and connecting lines, during the last years of the London and North-Eastern Group of the Big-Four consolidated and privately- owned railways of the 21 inter-war years, and continues into the first 12 years following the Nationalisation of the railway companies on 1 January 1948. For the 'Big Four' and for the nascent British Railways these were the years of triumph over the adversities of the Second World War and both the difficulties and the decline that followed. Hence the title given by one of us (BWLB) to his original book published in 1997, *The original Triumph & Beyond: the East Coast Main Line, 1939–1959*, part one, which was subsequently followed up by a part two, *The Route of the Flying Scotsman* and a part three, *Infrastructure, Traffic & Staff*, published 2002 and 2006 respectively.

That series was the outcome of many years of research into primary sources, principally at the National Archives (formerly the Public Record Office), with the invaluable encouragement and help freely given by numerous people, experienced as authors and of railway administration, who also provided most of the illustrations. The acknowledgement to these men is detailed in the original Part One.

The present volume arises from the interest shown in the original book by writer Peter Tuffrey, who is both a Railway Enthusiast and a well-known author of many years of experience with over 90 books to his credit B. W. L. Brooksbank is immensely grateful to his undertaking to do a minimally condensed re-write of *Triumph & Beyond* and providing many new illustrations. By the generous agreement of our publisher, Alan Sutton (Fonthill Media), it is proposed presently to publish a Part Two, in which will be incorporated the more important sections of the original Parts Two and Three.

Introduction

Technological progress and the industries of man have radically altered our surroundings. Nowhere is this more evident than in the transport industry. In the space of two generations the part once played by the railways in Britain, moving merchandise, raw materials, and people, has been shifted to the roads, and the importance of the railway system is vastly reduced.

In 1938, although road transport had shown a phenomenal growth during the interwar period, in terms of ton-miles, some 41 per cent of the freight traffic was still being carried by rail, 17 per cent by coasting vessels, 4 per cent by canal, but 42 per cent by road, the railways carrying 16,266 million ton-miles of which half was coal class traffic. In 1939, 95 per cent of the 230 million tons of coal was conveyed by rail in 740,000 wagons—most of them privately owned, and these constituted 57 per cent of the fleet of 1.3 million running on the railways. The four main line railway groups owned 19,700 locomotives, and the total mileage of the railways was 20,000. In 1939 there were about 2.03 million motor-cars and 0.42 million goods vehicles on Britain's roads.

In little more than one generation, a network of motorways has been constructed in Britain at outrageous cost in public money. The new roads duplicate and often displace the railways that serve the same basic purpose of providing a track for rapid movement of people and goods. Yet, the building of roads consistently fails to keep pace with the increase in the number of private motor vehicles and seems merely to generate more traffic and more congestion.

It would almost appear that the underlying factors that weigh so drastically against the railways are psychological. People love their motor vehicles that they drive themselves and which bring them so many basic benefits and satisfaction vis-à-vis public transport. They are not only obviously far more convenient and private than a bus or a train, but they nurture a sense of potency in driving a powerful vehicle and an image of social superiority.

The protagonists of road transport were already in the ascendant in the 1930s. Between the wars the number of private cars on Britain's roads had risen from 110,000 in 1919 to 2,034,000 in 1939; motor-cycles from 115,000 to 488,000; buses, coaches and taxis from 44,000 to 90,000 and goods vehicles from 62,000 to 418,000.

There was an enforced withdrawal from the roads during the war, but soon afterwards pre-war trends returned more strongly than ever once the nation's wealth revived. By the end of the 1950s the share of the railways of the sum total of passenger miles[1] by all modes (including the private car) had fallen to 15.6 per cent. In 1938, at 20,000 million their share had been 28 per cent, and near the end of the century it was down to under 6 per cent. In 1938, passenger-miles in Britain by private car were about 25,000 million or 35 per cent of the mileage by all modes. A different lifestyle has evolved based on the motor vehicle, with dispersal of both homes and work out of towns and cities and a tendency for community life to disintegrate. Whereas in 1951 only 14.5 per cent of British households had regular use of a private car and only 1.2 per cent had more than one, towards the turn of the century two thirds had a car and one fifth had more than one car. After the war there had been an opportunity for the State to integrate freight transport by confining road vehicles to the distribution from railheads of merchandise carried by rail over the longest distances, and under the 1947 Transport Act for the Nationalisation of transport the long-distance hauliers had been gradually taken over by the new Road Haulage Executive. However, their lorries were decontrolled under the Conservative 1953 Act and there was positive encouragement of traders to use their own private transport unreservedly. 'C' licence vehicles, which had not been brought under state control, then proliferated enormously, and came to do more harm than anything else to rail freight revenue. The whole concept of a unified transport policy was thrown to the winds, and the BTC was left in the impossible position of still having to balance its books while the railways were left at the mercy of unfettered road competition and starved of adequate funds to modernise. Furthermore, the construction of the motorway network and the acceptance of ever larger and faster lorries has been accompanied by the drastic elimination of not only rail freight depots but also rail access to factories—and the erection of most new factories and distribution depots beside motorways and well away from railways. A vicious circle in the freight transport industry was started which left British Railways scarcely transporting any merchandise at all.

Instead, the employment of separate small units for transport, albeit essential for strictly local journeys, has been allowed to become the predominant mode for longer distance journeys and even to a large degree for bulk overland movements.

The reader will rightly conclude that this account is written from the viewpoint of enthusiasts for railways. The last two generations have never known the degree of comfort and convenience offered by the—privatised—railways before the Second World War, and the elderly remember only the relative privations of rail travel after the war. Here an attempt is made to sketch these pre-war circumstances, before going on to describe how they were in wartime and afterwards—and before 'Beeching,' using the ECML of the London & North Eastern Railway (LNER) as an example. In doing so it is inevitable that many facets of the operation of lines connecting with the ECML are encompassed and that the fortunes of the LNER as a whole and of British Railways are relevant to the story.

The 'Big Four' railway groups were joint-stock companies of tremendous resources, some of the greatest privately financed corporations in the world. Yet, they were struggling hard long before the war to remain profitable. The LNER had not been able to pay a dividend on the ordinary shares since 1926, and in 1938 could not even pay any on the first preference stock. The LNER was the second largest of the 'Big Four', and actually the least profitable. In 1938 it had a total route mileage of 6,258, and some 1,962 stations, a staff of about 177,000, and possessed 6,518 locomotives (almost all steam), 19,600 coaching stock vehicles (12,300 of which were passenger coaches, with seating for 683,000 people) and 258,000 wagons. Total freight carried was 130 million tons (5,600 million net ton-miles) per year, and passenger traffic amounted to 4,700 million passenger miles per year.[1] The spine of the LNER system was the ECML: London–Doncaster–York–Newcastle–Edinburgh. The ECML was, and still is, one of the prime trunk routes, and much of the LNER system depended on the operation of this spine. It carried a substantial proportion of the LNER's traffic, and when we study the ECML we are in many ways studying the LNER—and its successor regions of British Railways. The trains and the installation of the ECML were both big business and an institution.

In the 1930s, a mystique associated with the ECML had grown up, not only with railway enthusiasts but also among railway staff and the general public. This was principally as a result of the LNER's development of the great expresses from King's Cross to Yorkshire, the North East and Scotland, of unsurpassed speed and comfort, hauled by some of the largest and fastest steam locomotives ever seen in Britain.

The romance of the ECML expresses has ensured the publication of numerous books and countless articles about them. Relatively little however has been recorded about the more mundane operations and the layout of the ECML as a working railway and how the rest of the railway system interconnected with it. The present account aims to fill the gap.

Considered in the wider context of those memorable years of the 1940s and 1950s and examined in depth, the delineation of the ECML, its centres and their operations, is a big subject. In this book, an outline is offered of the ECML and its principal centres. There follows a survey of the background history of the railways of Britain during the twenty years and three months between the outbreak of the Second World War and the end of 1959, with a section about how the LNER and the ECML were affected. After that, particulars are tackled—the train services and ancillary facilities provided on the ECML for passengers, and the yards and services for freight. Special attention is paid to the Second World War, with accounts of passenger and freight operations during the conflict, also on war damage and on accidents, lists of military establishments and private sidings.

No attempt is made to record the history of the ECML either before 1939 or after 1959. Instead, the concern here is with what happened in the war, in its aftermath and in the earliest years of Nationalisation.

1

The East Coast Main Line (ECML) in the late 1930s: an outline

The ECML has always been a coherent and integral operating system, but it cannot be studied in isolation. When looking later at the traffic, and trains, and operations on the line the wider context of the national network will have to be recognised and account taken of the services that fed into the ECML.[1] Often under examination will be facts and fortunes of the LNER as a whole—sometimes of its three distinct areas, and in the post-Nationalisation era the Eastern, North Eastern and Scottish Regions of British Railways (ER, NER and ScR of BR). In presenting and discussing traffic statistics for example, the more global figures will be noted and taken as the basis for the assessment of trends, while estimating that about two thirds of the LNER's traffic involved the ECML in whole or in part. After Nationalisation, this trunk route, still operated as a unity, was divided commercially and administratively between the ER, NER and ScR, and this will have to be borne in mind in assessing the relevance of facts and figures to the situation on the ECML itself. The Scottish Area of the former LNER, of which the ECML was a relatively small part, was absorbed into a much larger ScR that also comprised the former LMS lines in Scotland while—from February 1949—the ER included the London, Tilbury & Southend section of the former LMSR. In April 1950 a few more former LNER lines passed into the London Midland Region (LMR), while the NER gained considerable stretches of the former LMSR in Yorkshire—albeit not until 1957 its operating functions. In February 1958 more profound changes of regional organisation were instituted, with the abolition of 'penetrating lines'. These administrative changes may complicate the interpretation of statistics to some extent, but it had little effect on the unitary framework of the ECML around which this account revolves.

In 1938 the LNER had been in existence for a mere 15 years, formed in 1923 by the agglomeration of six great companies: the Great Northern (GN), Great Central (GC), North Eastern (NE), North British (NB), and Great North of Scotland (GNS) Railways. The LNER was still divided administratively, and in spirit, into three relatively autonomous areas—Southern (Western and Eastern sections), North Eastern, and Scottish. Traffic agreements had long since established a close cooperation between the GNR, NER and NBR to provide an integrated London–Edinburgh express passenger and freight service. The three railway companies had together built coaching stock, the East Coast Joint Stock, especially for these services. The GNR itself had 'ended in a field' near Shaftholme Junction, four miles north of Doncaster, where an end-on union was made with the NER, but it had running powers into York—and reciprocally the NER had running powers into Doncaster.[2] Over the border, the NER had running powers over the NBR from Berwick-upon-Tweed to Edinburgh (Waverley). Thus ECML expresses came to be worked by GN locomotives to York where the NE engines took over (occasionally at Doncaster instead) and worked trains through to Edinburgh.

Arlesey station is viewed from the crossing on 3 June 1956. Facilities were removed only four years later, but on 3 October 1988 were reinstated with four running lines and a bridge replacing the crossing. *Picture: R. Stephenson/B. W. L. Brooksbank Collection*

Freight traffic on the ECML in the 1930s remained relatively regionalised. A few through-freight, also parcels, and particularly fish trains ran right through between London and Scotland, far more only from York and Newcastle to Edinburgh etc., but the great bulk of the ECML freight and mineral traffic was staged: basically, London–Peterborough–Doncaster–York–Newcastle–Edinburgh. In addition, much of this traffic fed on to and off the ECML and used it only in part. Thus on the freight side the ECML was far less a unity than it was on the passenger side, and in a sense this made the traffic that much more interesting, while the nature—and often the motive power, of the freight trains differed radically at the major centres down the ECML.

The ECML was certainly not one of the easiest trunk lines to operate. There were a number of stretches of double track even at its southern end, the first coming just 10 miles from King's Cross, and only 122 miles (138 from 1942 and 140½ from 1959) out of the 393 route miles from King's Cross to Waverley were provided with four tracks. Some operating convenience was gained on the southern section of the route as a result of the former GNR's rather unusual segregation on four track sections of tracks 'by direction' instead of the more usual segregation 'by use' (*i.e.* Down Slow, Down Fast, Up Fast, Up Slow), and by the provision of a few flying junctions (at Holloway, Finsbury Park, Wood Green, and Langley), and also separate signal boxes for Down and Up directions which interacted little with each other. However, segregation by direction caused added difficulties for empty stock and light engine movements. Nevertheless, with such a preponderance of double track, if there had not been roughly parallel alternative routes over which freight traffic could be directed, it would have been impossible to run trains of a wide range of speeds, from high-speed expresses to lumbering coal trains. As it was, the two track stretches acted as severe bottle-necks that forced the scheduling of expresses in batches, with long intervals to allow the coal trains to be worked through. These were: New Barnet (Greenwood Box) to Potters Bar, and Welwyn (Digswell) to Woolmer Green Box (each 2½ miles),[3] through Arlesey and Sandy stations, and Huntingdon North to Yaxley (13½ miles—but mitigated with Up or Down goods lines part of the way). In addition, the layouts of King's Cross, Peterborough North, and Grantham also to

Sandy station (*right*) and the former Bedford & Cambridge Railway buildings (later LNWR, open 1862–1968) have been pictured from Potton Road bridge on 3 June 1956. *Picture: R. Stephenson/B. W. L. Brooksbank Collection*

a large extent those at Doncaster, Darlington and Newcastle, not being segregated by direction were very awkward for operating staff. Due to junctions and curvature there were very severe speed restrictions at Peterborough North, Selby, York, Durham, Newcastle and Morpeth, with less severe limits at most of the other major junctions and over several important bridges on the route. Officially, the overall speed limit was 90 mph, but for various reasons such a speed was prohibited over much of the ECML; thus the limit was somewhat less between Retford and Selby and from Darlington to north of Newcastle, owing to the threat of mining subsidence, and in the London suburban area.

It was therefore no mean feat to run not only the 'Flying Scotsman' non-stop (in summer) from King's Cross to Edinburgh (with corridor tenders to allow changeover of crews), but also—as was done in the late 1930s—to run (on Mondays to Fridays) three high-speed trains which for their time were among the fastest in the world. These were: the 'Silver Jubilee' (King's Cross–Newcastle in just 4 hours at an average speed of 67. 1 mph, with one stop at Darlington); the 'Coronation' (King's Cross–Edinburgh in just 6 hours, 65.5 mph, with stops at York and Newcastle); and the 'West Riding Limited' (King's Cross–Leeds in 2 hours 43 minutes, 68.4 mph non-stop, then Bradford in 3 hours 5 minutes). Thanks to the powerful Class A4 streamlined Pacifics, these trains could be scheduled at those relatively high speeds in spite of restraints of the route referred to, for the ECML had no stiff or long banks comparable to those on most other trunk routes; the steepest of any length was the 4½ miles at 1-in-96 of Cockburnspath Bank facing Up trains.

For the pleasure of using the 'Silver Jubilee' there was a surcharge of 25p[4] in first class and 15p third class—not a lot compared with the single fares in 1939 from London to Newcastle of £3.93 first class and £2.59 third class; on the 'Coronation' the supplement to Edinburgh was 20p third class—25p in the observation saloon.

In 1939 there was of course the 'Flying Scotsman', which in summer ran non-stop from King's Cross to Waverley in 7 hours—a mere 56.1 mph, but the normal consist was 12 coaches (14 in winter), heavier than that of the streamliners because (except for the restaurant/kitchen cars) the

A view inside the luxurious first class carriage of the Coronation set. Doncaster Works was responsible for construction.

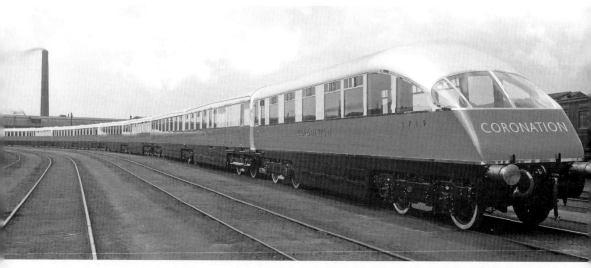

The Coronation set consisted of: third/third brake, third/kitchen third, first/first, kitchen third/third brake and the observation carriage. All except the latter were articulated pairs.

A4 No. 4495 *Golden Fleece* is ready to take the demonstration run of the 'West Riding Limited' out of Leeds Central station on 23 September 1937. *Picture: Yorkshire Post*

stock was not articulated. Equally prestigious and popular for travellers were the two Pullman expresses run on the ECML: the 'Queen of Scots Pullman' (King's Cross–Leeds–Harrogate–Newcastle–Edinburgh–Glasgow), and the 'Yorkshire Pullman' (King's Cross–Leeds, Bradford, Halifax, Harrogate, and Hull)—and on Sundays the 'Harrogate Sunday Pullman'. There comprised trains of heavy Pullman cars, both first and third class. Staffed by a smart conductor and attendants employed by the Pullman Car Company, these luxurious expresses were in effect all restaurant car trains—as were the 'Coronation' and 'West Riding Limited'—with full and ample meals of good food and wine being served at all seats—and travellers had to pay a supplementary fare similar to that on the streamliners. A typical dinner cost 37½p and the supplementary charge for travelling by Pullman was 60p to Edinburgh.

On ordinary trains of the time, first class and third class[5] passengers already had plenty of comfort, the main difference between the classes of accommodation being in the extra space—and the exclusivity—enjoyed by first class: three-a-side seating versus four-a-side in third class. Ordinary fares in 1939 were 1p per mile for first class and 0.66p per mile for third class. Monthly return fares were normally calculated as the single fare plus one-third. A large variety of reduced rate fares were offered, notably cheap day returns (after 09.30) and early morning workmen's returns (before 07.30). Night travel (by specified trains) or Sunday travel, all at single fare, and Season tickets (Monthly at 75 per cent of the cost of six ordinary returns per week). In addition there were various excursion day returns at less than single fare—down to as little as 0.10p per

A4 No. 4498 *Sir Nigel Gresley* travels at speed with the 'Flying Scotsman' service. Built in October 1937 at Doncaster, the locomotive was withdrawn in February 1966 and preserved.

mile, for individuals, members of various clubs, or for organised groups—which if large enough would hire a coach or even a whole train. Reservations could be made for a small charge for not only seats but also even for a private saloon—even an invalid saloon with bed. Rail travel was thus good value for money, and as long as fares were not raised in line or more than wages—which they were not until at least the 1960s, it remained so.

In 1938 an average wage earner could buy 24.5 miles of rail travel (at ordinary fares) for an hour's work. This was unchanged ten years later and by 1958 he could get 42 miles.

Down the ECML in August 1939 there were many fast expresses. Including the Streamliners and Pullmans, Edinburgh had four, Newcastle eight, Leeds and Bradford six, and Hull five weekday daytime services from King's Cross, and on Fridays and Saturdays these were greatly augmented. Daytime services ran through to Scarborough, Bridlington, Filey and Whitby, to Cleethorpes and Skegness *via* Boston, and there were through coaches to King's Lynn and to Cromer. Indeed a feature of the ECML express services was the large number of different destinations served by through portions or coaches on the expresses from King's Cross. There were a number of overnight expresses, most with sleeping cars, especially to Scotland, and these included through coaches to Perth, Inverness and to Lossiemouth as well as to Aberdeen and to Fort William.

At holiday times many relief trains were run, and in summer there were a number of regular Saturdays-only services—although not quite so many as were provided in the 1950s when paid holidays had become universal. In peacetime the ECML north of York also saw several night expresses from London Marylebone to Newcastle, not advertised in public timetables but most running quite regularly. In addition, numerous cheap day excursions were advertised—many

Originally numbered 2511, *Silver King* had been given No. 16 in November 1946 as part of that year's renumbering scheme. The locomotive has been pictured a year later on the up 'Flying Scotsman' south of Doncaster station, near the locomotive shed.

organised by agencies—and were very popular. A number of these, especially on Sundays, were often regularly scheduled, while naturally events such as football matches and horse races led to the running of very large numbers of excursion trains, as did major events such as the coronation. The Special Traffic Notice for a holiday week could run to 150 pages, listing hundreds of special and relief trains.

Needless to say, there were many trains other than expresses run at passenger train speeds on the ECML. There was one 'Motor Car Train'—even in 1939—which ran to Edinburgh—the road vehicles being conveyed in covered vans. Four regular trains were scheduled daily from King's Cross for parcels, newspapers, or mails. There was an evening 'Travelling Post Office' (TPO)—the 'North Eastern Down'—to Newcastle and Edinburgh, and the 'Night Scotsman' also had a TPO van, both exchanging mail bags at speed, and there were one regular and two conditional empty coaching stock trains for Doncaster or York daily (each way).

Local services were extensive in the London area, *i.e.* down the ECML as far as Hitchin, many of them continuing on to Royston and Cambridge, and many local services ran in and out of Grantham, Doncaster, Selby, York, Darlington, Durham, Newcastle, and Edinburgh. In addition, cross-country services impinged on the ECML at Peterborough North, Retford, Doncaster, Selby, York, Northallerton, Newcastle and Edinburgh and country branch trains came on to the ECML at various other places.

Although diluted to a certain extent by stock of pre-grouping origin, the normal coaching stock for the regular expresses and most of the relief trains comprised Gresley's dignified designs with bodywork of varnished teak, elliptical roofs with sloping ends, and buck-eye couplers. The majority of coaches were of compartment stock. Open saloons were however now being employed by the LNER including those with uncomfortable 'bucket' seats and green-and-cream exteriors. Saloon coaches were also employed for restaurant cars, and for the buffet cars—largely pioneered by the LNER. Most of the ECML expresses had restaurant cars, but buffet cars were a feature of the shorter regular services, such as the King's Cross, Garden Cities and Cambridge 'beer' trains, and on cross-country services that impinged on the ECML, as well as on summer seasonal and excursion trains.

As on the other main railways, restaurant cars—first introduced in Britain by the GNR in 1879[6]—were the norm. Breakfast cost 20p, a lunch of three to four courses 22½–25p, afternoon tea 5p, and dinner five course 25p with a choice of good wines.[7] The catering staff worked long hours and pay, at £3 a week for a waiter, was hardly lavish—but there were tips.

On account of the lengthy journeys to Scotland and elsewhere, numerous sleeping car services ran down the ECML in the late 1930s. These ran on five trains from King's Cross to Scotland and one other to Newcastle. One train, the 'Night Scotsman', composed almost entirely of sleeping cars, conveyed passengers from London only to destinations beyond Edinburgh. For those travelling first class the sleeping cars had luxurious single birth compartments, a shower compartment, and electric pressure ventilation and heating; third class cars had four-berth compartments—and no shower section. It cost 37½p to cross the border in a third class sleeper, and a massive £1.05 for a first class one. The sleeping car attendants (one per car or pair of cars) on £3 a week or less had a hard life, sleeping by day and travelling every night. By comparison, a Top Link driver working on the 'Flying Scotsman' would earn £4.60 a week (plus a good mileage allowance) in 1939.

The Passenger's Journey

Let us recollect a London to Edinburgh journey by 'Flying Scotsman' in the summer of 1939—not first class or on the 'Coronation'. We will travel third class, and take a quick look at the whole ECML as it really worked. The third class traveller would probably be a person of adequate means and most likely middle-aged. He would not be a businessman—today's 'executive', for he might otherwise imagine himself to be in too much of a hurry to travel from London to Edinburgh by day, and would go by sleeper overnight, and if reasonably wealthy would journey first class.

It is a weekday, when the morning rush-hour is not quite over as we arrive at King's Cross, in good time for the 10.00am departure.

As at all large stations there were crowds of people of all types, sizes and descriptions. The stations were normally full of the noises of steam engines, of the impersonal and often pompous train announcers broadcasting by Tannoy but little understood, of inspectors' and guards' whistles, of shouts of the impatient, of the wail of children, and of the slamming of doors. King's Cross was quite typical in these respects. Platform 10 was a world in itself—yet with no barrier from the outside world, alike to the ordinary passenger and to railway staff. Almost all the main station appointments were ranged along its side, and above them were the railway offices, both those of the stationmaster and his assistants and also the offices of many of the LNER headquarters departments, including that of the Chief Mechanical Engineer—Sir Nigel Gresley. Along No. 10 were, the buffets, the restaurant and the 'Georgian' tea room, the waiting rooms and ladies' (except for first class, who had a plush new lounge), and down a dingy stairway—the gentlemen's lavatories. Then, there were the booking and enquiry offices; and lost property office (self-service luggage lockers were a post-war development). In 1939 the lost property office employed 17 men and collected about 37,000 articles a year from all over the LNER Southern Area, of which only 20 per cent were claimed back. Attaché cases were abandoned at the rate of 250–300 a month

Above: View southward, towards Peterborough North and London. A Down express is pulling away, headed by Gresley A3 No. 60064 *Tagalie* (built August 1924 as A1 No. 2563 *William Whitelaw*, withdrawn June 1964). Waiting to cross into New England Yard, next to a DMU, is an O2 2-8-0 on a down empties. *Picture: B. W. L. Brooksbank*

Below: Peppercorn A1 Pacific No. 60146 *Peregrine* departs from Doncaster station with a service bound for King's Cross on 27 March 1952. The locomotive was a long-term resident at York shed from June 1950 until July 1963. *Picture: Yorkshire Post*

and outstanding recoveries included: a performing dog on its hind legs, a monkey, a Japanese beheading-sword, a tin of live fish in water, artificial limbs, a belt of American dollar bills, and ten gold dollar pieces.

Our interested—but not 'railway-mad'—passenger, comfortably seated now in the 'Flying Scotsman', would be in one of the new carriages that Gresley had recently had built for this prestigious train, rivalling in opulence the sets used for the streamlined trains. Unlike in modern times and on the airlines, the traveller could expect to be comfortable and the train would be punctual. On the train he would have not only a luxurious seat with more than ample leg-room—even room to stretch out if he were going first class or at a slack time—and a good view out, but he would also be able to get up and stretch and walk the corridors, even to take a draught of fresh air, as well as to smoke unless he had been unlucky enough to find himself in one of the (minority of) 'No Smoking' compartments. He would be importuned by the catering staff to take not only the four main meals (depending on the time of day), but also infinite light refreshments and the opportunity to plaster himself throughout the journey with booze; on the streamliners[8] and Pullmans this would all be brought to him at his seat. A female passenger on the 'Scotsman' could retire to a lounge, and a retiring-room with dressing-tables and a maid in attendance. The prestige trains had double-glazing and pressure ventilation. None of this was provided on the long-distance road coaches that competed even then for the people who could not really afford to go to Scotland by train.

A sense of satisfaction and security engendered in our happy passenger, by being cosily settled in his seat in the train, could be much upset if he happened to read the Company's Bye-Laws and Regulations. Then he would be severely shaken by the fear of doing something wrong in a variety of different ways not least for example if he were a consumptive and had not obtained 'permission in writing of a stationmaster or other officer of the Company, duly authorised in that behalf ', for 'no person suffering from any contagious of infectious disease or disorder shall enter or remain … in or upon the Railway or in any carriage, or to travel on the Railway.' If he (or 'any person having the custody, charge or care' of him), had failed to do this, he was liable not only to be thrown out but was also 'liable to the Company for the cost of disinfecting the Company's premises and any carriage in which such person shall have been…' etc.

The Company also warned about card-sharpers, who (unlawfully) 'played for money or money's worth at any game or pretended game of chance or skill in or upon the railway or any carriage or vehicle thereon'. On the other hand, if he had read these Bye-Laws and Regulations, our passenger might be angry that the Company was under no obligation to provide him with a seat, to run a train to time, or even to run it at all. His only recourse was to abandon his journey plans precipitately and go to the booking office for his money back.

Our passenger in the 'Flying Scotsman' was carried away from King's Cross at 10.00 a.m. on the dot, in luxury. If a foreigner he would wonder when he would ever see the beautiful British countryside, as his train for the first half-hour fought its way out through a succession of no less than nine tunnels to escape from the 'Great Maw'. Once out of London, the discerning tourist was rewarded briefly by a good sample of England's 'great garden', as the train cut through the pleasing Home County of Hertfordshire—a modicum of real charm in the passing scene. After that there followed endless miles of prosperous English farming country with real hedgerows and elm trees still flourishing. This scene dominated the journey for 200 to 300 miles of the ECML. Our foreign traveller especially perhaps, would thrill at the sight of many of the beautiful English village churches, and briefly at the glimpses of Peterborough Cathedral, Selby Abbey, York Minster, and most of all the dramatic appearance of Durham's cathedral and castle as the train slowed over the viaduct before passing through Durham station. Apart from perhaps complaining about the not very exciting English scenery he was seeing for much of the journey, from Darlington to well beyond Newcastle he would no doubt not like the many unsightly colliery waste-tips and the mean housing of the industrial North East.

He may have wondered why the route was called 'East Coast,' for it was not—until he was a little over an hour and a half from Edinburgh, when he at last saw the North Sea. After a glimpse of it at Alnmouth, for a short while the vista over the sea near Beal was however quite romantic, as on Holy Island—one of the most historic sites of English Christianity was visible.

Then, after passing through the famed Borders town of Berwick-upon-Tweed, the train finally ran on the cliffs above the waves near Burnmouth. The best countryside of the journey would then be seen—the edge of the Scottish Borders country, in the last 50 miles or so before Edinburgh, as the train wound through the Lammermuir Hills and came just in sight of the coast once more at Dunbar.

Our tourist on the non-stop 'Flying Scotsman' would have noticed passing through some of Britain's finer towns and cities—and railway centres such as Peterborough, Doncaster, Selby, York, Darlington, and Newcastle. The majority of daytime ECML passengers did not go through from London to Edinburgh, but were bound to and from these intermediate places and those reached from them by connecting routes. All these centres made their distinctive contributions, in terms of traffic and of ambience, to the ECML environment. Let us then imagine our 1939 traveller going, not right through to Edinburgh, but stopping off at one of the important intermediate places on the ECML. What did they impart to the scene?

Peterborough (North station) was where passengers alighted if they were bound for many places in Lincolnshire: Spalding, Boston, Skegness, and Grimsby— even perhaps that famed resort, Cleethorpes, or for places in the Fens served by the former Midland
& Great Northern Joint Line: Wisbech, King's Lynn, even Cromer on the Norfolk coast. At Peterborough, many passengers joined ECML trains to go north from almost anywhere in East Anglia: Cambridgeshire/Isle of Ely, Suffolk and Norfolk. In the 1930s, few passengers so travelling could avoid having to change trains at Peterborough North, and it was not a very pleasant experience. The station was straight out of the mid-nineteenth century—small, devoid of modern amenities and draughty. For the staff it was worse, an operating nightmare on a key position of interchange for both passenger and freight traffic. It must have been a hard task for Control to operate and for the stationmaster.

Grantham station too was an antiquated, uncomfortable station almost unaltered in nearly a hundred years. It was there that passengers for Nottingham, Derby and west thereof, and for Sleaford, Lincoln and other Lincolnshire destinations, had to get out of their comfortable ECML express and bundle into the old ex-GN carriages (some still even six-wheelers) that often formed their slow connecting trains—and there were almost no through coaches to London.

Newark was a quite important stop—but mainly just for Newark, a market town with a range of industrial establishments.

Passenger interchange was essentially nil at Dukeries Junction. There the residuum of the over-ambitious Lancashire, Derbyshire & East Coast Railway crossed the ECML, but there were few trains on that line and hardly any trains stopped at the ECML Low Level station. There were no goods facilities at Dukeries Junction, and the stationmaster must have had a grand time.

At Retford, some ECML passengers might change for stations to Lincoln and Grimsby or to Sheffield (Victoria) on the cross-country ex-GC Manchester–Sheffield–Lincolnshire line. Sheffield was reached more conveniently from St Pancras or from Marylebone, although in pre-Grouping days the GNR had run through expresses to Sheffield *via* Retford.

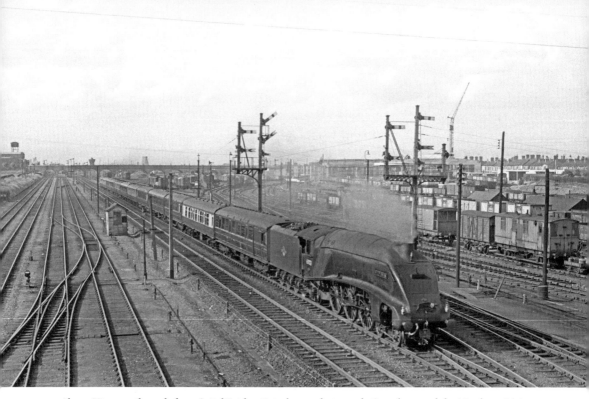

Above: View northwards from Spital Bridge, Peterborough, towards Grantham and the North on 16 August 1958. To the left are the ex-Midland lines to Stamford etc., also the M&GN to Sutton Bridge. Gresley A4 No. 60021 *Wild Swan* is in charge of 'The Norseman'. The engine was erected at Doncaster in February 1938. *Picture: B. W. L. Brooksbank*

Below: Carelessly lacking a headboard is A3 Pacific No. 60053 *Sansovino*, but in fact the service is the up 'Queen of Scots' Pullman. The train has been photographed from Hatchett's Lane level crossing north of Newark Northgate station on 15 June 1957. *Picture: B. W. L. Brooksbank*

In terms of railway operation, Doncaster was a key junction on the ECML. There diverged the main line on to Leeds, Bradford and other towns in the West Riding of Yorkshire, and that to Hull, taking the through trains or coaches from King's Cross and elsewhere off the ECML; it was not normally necessary for passengers to change at Doncaster for these important destinations. Also at Doncaster the ECML intersected with the west–east artery of the former Great Central system, the line from Sheffield to Scunthorpe, Grimsby, and—again—Cleethorpes, but interchange with GC line trains at Doncaster would be principally for local services. In addition, at Doncaster the 'Joint Line' (ex-GN&GE Joint) came in from Lincoln, Sleaford, March and hence from East Anglia generally, but through trains were few in number on that line except on summer Saturdays; otherwise it was more convenient to change at Peterborough, Grantham or Retford. Therefore the majority of ECML expresses for York and beyond did not stop at Doncaster and from the point of view of the ECML passenger Doncaster station was for the people of Doncaster and of the surrounding district. The station was however being quite extensively modernised in 1939—even if incompletely until after the war—and was not as forbidding as many other comparable stations.

With its pivotal position in the South Yorkshire coalfield as the junction of various interconnecting lines, Doncaster was of paramount importance in terms of coal and heavy freight traffic. There the LNER had major Locomotive, Carriage and Wagon Works, employing approximately 3,000 hands. So, while our ordinary passenger disdainfully ignored the busy freight yards and general railway activity, to the professional railwayman, Doncaster meant everything.

Few ECML expresses deigned to call at Selby, the next town of importance down the line, because unless destined locally or for Yorkshire coast resorts such as Bridlington and Filey, ECML passengers would not need to alight there. Selby, like Retford a station of two main platforms and still with its Victorian facilities (including dining and refreshment room), was more an incidental point of intersection of the ECML with a busy west–east line, in this case the ex-North Eastern route from Leeds to Hull and Bridlington.

Soon after Selby came York, considered by many the capital of the North of England, and historically England's second city. York had been the headquarters of the NER until the 1923 Grouping and then that of the relatively autonomous NE Area of the LNER. After Nationalisation it naturally became the headquarters of the North Eastern Region of BR, and finally of the combined ER and NER. The headquarters offices were housed in a large and imposing block, built in 1906 and symbolising the prosperity of the proud North Eastern Railway, and with the station and the Royal Station Hotel befitting the importance of the NER to the city of York. Our foreign tourist travelling down the ECML would certainly have wanted to visit York, and many of our ordinary English travellers would have been going there. In winter months when there were no through services from the London direction to Scarborough, Whitby or other Yorkshire coast resorts, many passengers would be changing at York for these and also for other places in the North and East Ridings. (Before the war, about 2 million passengers a year came to the seaside resorts of the NE Area, mainly on day excursions). On the other hand, York was where passengers coming from many parts of the country and bound for the North East and Scotland joined the ECML.

York was the junction for the main lines from Leeds and from Normanton and thence from Manchester, Liverpool and the Central and Western Divisions of the London Midland & Scottish Railway (LMSR) generally, also for the main line from Sheffield and through there from the Midlands, South Wales, the West Country and Central Southern England. Secondary lines came in to York from Hull and from Harrogate. Although a number of trains from major areas of Britain, from Manchester and Liverpool, from Birmingham, Bristol, and Cardiff, and from Southampton, ran through York on to Newcastle and even Edinburgh, many—being LMSR trains—terminated at York.

Therefore very many passengers changed there. Additionally, there was a corresponding vast flow of freight traffic, and all of this made York the greatest intermediate junction and railway centre of the whole ECML. Together with the very substantial freight traffic down the ECML *via* Doncaster, through York's great freight yards passed traffic to and from most parts of the country. Lastly, at York was one of the principal works for the building of coaching stock, employing nearly 1,500 workers.

Commensurate with its importance, York had a station of magnificent proportions, which had been enlarged as recently as 1938. With 16 platforms on a sweeping curve, most of them under three majestic arches, the station and its sounds had a grandeur typified by the sonorous public address announcements—it being the first British station equipped with 'Tannoy': 'York. This is York Station. Change here for–' Almost all ECML expresses stopped at York, and even if they did not they were slowed to 15 mph to pass through its centre roads. The station was provided with commodious waiting-rooms, dining-rooms, buffets and all other facilities, and a great footbridge across the main lines. Passengers had less reason to complain of dirt and cold than at any other ECML station, and moreover the Royal Station Hotel adjoining was a leading railway hotel. As at other major stations on the former NER, passengers coming to take a train at York were instructed by a splendid map of the NER system featured in ceramic tiles on a wall of the entrance hall. They left the station at York through a glazed portico on to Station Road, busy with local buses and taxis that swept over the River Ouse on Lendal Bridge into the city.

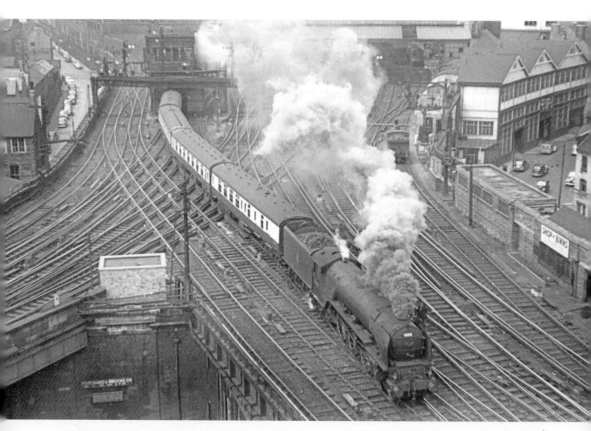

View westward from the Castle Keep over the celebrated, complex crossing of the main lines at the north end of Newcastle Central station. The 'North Briton' is leaving Platform 10 with a fresh A1 Pacific—No. 60150 *Willbrook*. Picture: B. W. L. Brooksbank

After York the next major centre on the ECML was Darlington. Darlington (Bank Top) station, albeit on a smaller scale than York or Newcastle was also commodious and well-appointed. It featured a fine arched span over a great island platform—and a clock- tower, but the approach from the outside world was from a single entrance on Victoria Road or up a ramp from Parkgate, and was not too impressive. Nearly all the ECML expresses stopped there—even the 'Silver Jubilee', for passengers for the important town of Darlington itself and more especially those bound to and from an extensive and populous hinterland that included the great industrial Tees-side conurbation of Stockton/Middlesbrough, also the seaside resorts of Redcar and Saltburn. On the other hand, to some extent passengers on the ECML for Tees-side, West Hartlepool and Sunderland were catered for by trains that diverged at Northallerton and missed Darlington, although some of the trains on this coast line to Newcastle came from Leeds *via* Harrogate and impinged on the ECML only at Northallerton. As well as having a busy service of comfortable local trains to Tees-side, Bank Top was also the terminus of local services to Richmond, to Bishop Auckland, an up the West Durham valleys. Time-worn trains went *via* Barnard Castle right over the Pennines to Penrith and Tebay, in what is now Cumbria and in 1939 was the different world served by the LMSR.

From the railway angle, Darlington was a centre of the first rank, not only by virtue of the passenger traffic outlined above, and of a corresponding flow of freight, but also on account of the presence of major Locomotive and Wagon Works, with over 2,500 workers, rendering Darlington to the NER what Doncaster was to the GNR. Finally, the pioneering Stockton & Darlington Railway of 1825 had given Darlington a head start in the railway business, the passing traveller being reminded of this by the presence of the preserved S&D locomotives, *Locomotion* and *Derwent*, set up on plinths at Bank Top.

Many expresses necessarily stopped next at Durham. The relatively modest station there was sited awkwardly on the side of a hill rather away from the town, and had only Down and Up main platforms and no overall roof. People alighted there for Durham city itself (Durham station issued 132,000 tickets in 1938) but it was a long, steep walk down from the station. It is unlikely they would be changing into one of the rather antiquated local trains that ran to Sunderland from Bishop Auckland, because the service to those places was better from Newcastle or Darlington respectively. If they were bound for the Lanchester valley, up to Consett, they had lost their local service earlier in 1939, but there might have been someone who intended to catch the one early morning train to Waterhouses and he would have to get out at Durham.

Soon after Durham came Newcastle-upon-Tyne. The approaches to Newcastle Central Station from the south, over either the King Edward or the High Level Bridge, were impressive, giving as they did lofty views of the River Tyne and its industry and shipping as well as the skyline of the city. The Central station, with its 15 platforms was large and impressive, but its overall roofs lacked the grandeur of York, and the ambience at Newcastle Central was in keeping with the heavy industry of the city and in which the railways had always played a part. (As at Darlington, the close association of Newcastle with the earliest days of railways was commemorated, by a very early George Stephenson locomotive standing on a plinth on the platform). The station was essentially as built in 1850, but its public facilities were ample and had been recently modernised to a certain extent, and alongside was the prestigious Royal Station Hotel. The city's business district was close by, and Newcastle's yellow-and-white trams took passengers in all directions from the impressive portico of the station in Neville Street.

Newcastle being a large city and county in its own right—the largest intermediate city on the ECML—and having a hinterland with a population approaching a million, the majority of the long-distance trains terminated there. Thus most of the ECML passengers alighted, either for the city itself, or to go on to such places as Sunderland, South Shields or Tynemouth. In addition, Tyneside including Newcastle was a seaport of considerable importance, and trains ran regularly from London to the Tyne Commission Quay at North Shields to connect with passenger ships to Scandinavia. Two other important train services ran from Newcastle, largely independently of the ECML—that to Middlesbrough *via* West Hartlepool and Stockton and that to Carlisle. These lines also catered for more local traffic than did the ECML itself. There was also the oddity of an alternative but very slow service into Scotland, formerly provided by the NBR, which ran *via* Hexham through the depths of Northumberland over to Riccarton Junction on the Waverley route and on to Hawick. Local steam services ran from Newcastle Central to North Wylam, to Leamside *via* Ferryhill, and to Blackhill by two routes.

Rather unusually in the 1930s for a railway company other than the Southern, the LNER ran electric trains from Newcastle Central, with an intensive service of multiple-unit trains. On the north side of the Tyne they were made up of modern articulated stock painted red and cream, and ran on a circular service to Tynemouth *via* Jesmond, Benton and Backworth, back *via* Wallsend (or vice versa), also a less frequent service ran to Tynemouth by the Riverside route. To the south side of the Tyne there was a frequent electric service, using older (refurbished) stock although the line was electrified only in 1938, over the High Level Bridge to South Shields. Our hypothetical ECML traveller, if not a native of the area would have little reason to alight at Newcastle for pleasure, nor was Newcastle Central a great place of interchange, the non-ECML trains there serving primarily the rather close-knit people of the region.

In 1938, 2.72 million passengers bought tickets at Newcastle Central, and the seaside resorts in the district collected 4.11 million tickets—and this was a 'poor year' for the era. That year, Newcastle District also dealt with 1.07 million parcels, 48,000 bicycles and prams, 97,000 items of passengers' luggage in advance, 236,000 milk cans, 1,761 horses, 58,000 (individual) fishes, and 330 tons of poultry and game. In 1958, no less than 14.5 million passengers were carried (excluding those merely changing trains), and Newcastle Central was the busiest provincial station in the country.

As Newcastle was a city of much heavy industry and the centre of a large industrial and mining hinterland, much of the freight as well as the passenger traffic of the ECML southwards was generated in the area, and Newcastle was the repository of many of its locomotives and much of its rolling-stock. All freight traffic across the Tyne, north–south or east–west, which included much coal and other traffic of a local nature, had to pass through Newcastle Central. This, together with the intensive local passenger services, made Central extremely busy—and necessitated renewal of its famous diamond crossings every few years. Northwards from Newcastle down the ECML, traffic—both passenger and freight—was considerably lighter than southwards. Apart from the rich coalfield around Bedlington and Ashington, there were few sources north of Newcastle to generate freight traffic for the ECML and most of the freight was Anglo-Scottish traffic passing through.

The rest of the journey down the ECML—at any rate after Morpeth, was through thinly populated country. Most ECML expresses to Edinburgh then stopped only at Berwick-upon-Tweed. In part they did so in respect of crossing the Border and entering the North British Railway (NBR) system. Berwick itself was not a large place, but was the railhead for a wide and prosperous area of Northumberland and the Borders country. Otherwise, as with the stop made by some expresses at Alnmouth, trains may have stopped partly for the local gentry to be collected by car and taken to some estate in the area, or for passengers to join a branch train to historic Alnwick or Kelso.

So we come to the end of the ECML—as defined in this account. Let us try and imagine how our supposed foreign tourist would have reacted to arriving at Waverley station in Edinburgh—punctually at 5.00 p.m. of course. Discounting his probable compulsion, along with most of the

Passing through Princes Street Gardens, Edinburgh, with the 17.10 express to Aberdeen is A1 No. 60159 *Bonnie Dundee. Picture: B. W. L. Brooksbank*

other passengers at the merest hint of the end of the journey, to collect his coat and his bags and to crush into the vestibule in desperate readiness to get off the train, he might already have had fleeting glimpses of Edinburgh's incomparable skyline. On alighting at Waverley, he would not see the skyline properly until he had laboriously climbed the renowned Waverley steps out of the station to street level. The only civilised way to leave Waverley was by taxi that had come down the steep approach road to the station entrance off Waverley Bridge.[9] Then indeed it will have struck him: the Mound with the Scottish National Gallery, the Scott Monument, the castle, the proud buildings along Princes Street, the majestic North British Hotel with its prominent clock tower, the North Bridge striding across the station complex at a dizzy height, and the trams in their restrained maroon colour in keeping with the dignity of the United Kingdom's alternative capital.

What of Waverley Station itself, the focus of the LNER in Scotland? Waverley was one of the very largest stations in Britain, with 21 platforms the same as London's Waterloo. In spite of being down in the deep natural cleft separating the new from the old town of Edinburgh, and therefore quite well hidden from the city's populace, it was relatively un-sulphurous and clean. The great bulk of the station and all its public and railway offices and facilities were incorporated in a wide island structure, which was flanked by the main through lines with their double-length platforms; in the centre of this was a very fine booking and waiting-hall illuminated through a dome and decorative iron screens. The dignity and splendour of this hall accorded with the ambience of the Scottish capital itself, a city like none other—if our foreign visitor was a Frenchman, he would find Edinburgh in its way more akin to Paris than to London.

The island arrangement worked well, because the great majority of passenger trains originated or terminated at Waverley, and most of the numerous through freight trains went round the city well away on the South Suburban line. From Waverley's many terminal platforms, trains set out from either end of the great station largely independently: they went to the suburbs of Edinburgh, and to destinations

View eastward from The Mound, over Waverley Station to Waverley Bridge and North Bridge. The North British Hotel dominates on the left. *Picture: B. W. L. Brooksbank*

almost all over Scotland—to Glasgow (by two routes) and to the West Highland line, and over the Forth Bridge to Fife, to Perth and Inverness—even Dalnaspidal, and on over the Tay Bridge to Dundee and Aberdeen. The other way they went by the ECML back to Berwick and England or by the Waverley route to the Borders towns, Carlisle and eventually to London (St Pancras) *via* Leeds and Sheffield.

If our ECML traveller was not staying in Edinburgh, he would as likely as not have to change trains at Waverley. A passenger on the 'Flying Scotsman' could stay on the train and continue over the Bridges to principal stations to Dundee and Aberdeen,[10] but it would be a hardy traveller who made the whole trip, Aberdeen not being reached until 10 hours 15 minutes after leaving King's Cross. A number of through travellers would go on by other trains—from Edinburgh to Glasgow (Queen Street), but most people from London and the south to Dundee and Aberdeen used the overnight sleeping car trains. Finally, it must not be forgotten that, as on other trunk routes in the steam age, the ECML had small wayside stations spaced every few miles throughout its length. In 1939 there were 108 stations between Hitchin and Edinburgh (Waverley) but this number had substantially decreased by the end of the twentieth century. However, the wayside stations generally had a very poor service, provided by a few extremely slow stopping trains running over limited stretches of the line. Many had only three or four trains stopping each way per day: life at one of them—at least if also only one or two pick-up goods trains stopped there—was therefore really rather a sinecure, but a poorly paid one. Often their staff occupied their time tending the station flower beds, encouraged by an annual competition with prizes—even after the war. The larger stations, where such efforts would have been justifiable economically, were not normally involved, but on the other hand there were competitions for the Prize Length of permanent way—often won by the men responsible for stretches of the ECML.

Unlike the larger stations, the small wayside ones would be passed almost unseen from an express, but not so the signals. The whole of the ECML main lines was of course worked on the Absolute Block system, much of it protected by track-circuiting at major stations and junctions.

Signals were mostly semaphore, and in general worked manually, as were points at most locations. The GNR's 'somersault' signals, almost unique in the country, were still in use in 1939—a few into the 1950s—in many places down to Doncaster, and large gantries of these rather graceful structures were prominent especially in the London area. In main NE Area centres—notably at York and Newcastle—those great gantries characteristic of the NER, with their multitude of signal and repeater arms were to be seen. The signals on the NB section, with their rather slender lattice posts made of old rails, also had their own character. At King's Cross, between Skelton Junction and Darlington South, and at Edinburgh Waverley, electrical power-signalling with colour lights was installed, and the forests of semaphores had already gone.

Postscript

Some may feel, with some justification, that the ECML did not end at Edinburgh but continued to Aberdeen. Be that as it may, this account goes no further than the Scottish capital. The journey onward was quite enticing: the awesome Forth Bridge and the endless Tay Bridge were crossed, a great deal more of the real east coast could be seen, and there was yet more appeal in the general railway scene. Indeed, the line from Edinburgh to Aberdeen was all so interesting and geographically complex that it merits a separate account on its own. In the age of steam it took over 10 hours to reach Aberdeen from London. It would have been extremely tiring to do the whole journey in the course of one day, and except around the summer solstice it would have been dark long before the end was reached.

The Garden Sidings semaphore signal gantry at the south end of Doncaster station is seen here being removed during the mid-1950s. *Picture: Geoff Warnes*

2

The historical context of the changes on the ECML over the years 1939–1959

The situation of the railways in the late 1930s

By the late 1930s the railways no longer had the near monopoly of inland transport that they enjoyed before the First World War—excluding purely local traffic, inland water transport and coastwise shipping traffic. They were already in severe financial difficulties due to 'unfair' competition from nationwide road transport. Still in private hands, the railways were at a disadvantage compared to road users in having to finance out of revenue not only their rolling stock but also their track, stations and other fixed assets. The private motor car was already relentlessly creaming off especially the 'upper crust' of passenger travel, and in regard to freight the railways were saddled with archaic regulations and systems of ratings imposed on them when they did have a monopoly. Between 1923 and 1938 personal *per capita* income in Britain had increased on average by over a third and the proportion of that spent on travel had risen significantly. However, the railways' share of the market was declining. Total passenger miles by bus and coach, at 19,000 million nationwide in 1938, was almost the same as the rail figure of 20,000 million; tramway and trolley bus usage accounted for an additional 8,100 million passenger miles. Meanwhile, travel by private car was estimated to be already in excess of 25,000 million

As for freight, haulage by road was seriously undermining the railways' pre- eminence. There were about half a million independent commercial vehicles on the road, two-thirds of them 'C' licence lorries and vans carrying a firm's own goods and ton-mileage by road was approaching that carried by the railways. Legislation in 1930 had at least brought some control over private road hauliers, through regulation by licence—at a modest fee—of their vehicles and any common carrier service they provided. On the other hand, maximum railway fares and charges for the carriage of freight were fixed by statute. The statutory rates were aimed to enable the railways to achieve a net 'Standard Revenue', calculated from the railways' revenues before the First World War before road motor transport was an alternative. Naturally, between the wars the railways never came near to achieving such a revenue. Railway charges were open to public scrutiny, and the railway companies were obliged to carry any goods offered to them however unprofitable. They also had to undertake to dispatch goods—no matter how small the consignment—on the day it was received, which resulted in very poor average loading factors. They could not adjust their prices to true costs, which in any case was very difficult to determine. Charges had to be uniform across the country and the scope allowed for downward adjustment to meet the competition was limited. Freight charges set by the railways were traditionally based on the value of the goods and not on the cost of carriage, whereas the road hauliers applied the latter—more realistic—criterion. Unlike those for users of road transport, rail charges had to take into account the interest that had been raised to build the track and stations—and to purchase the land they were built on, while road hauliers

Huntingdon (North) station possessed only one up line and platform until rebuilt in 1976, which was just prior to the electrification of the ECML. A4 No. 25 *Falcon* runs through this bottleneck with an up express on 20 August 1949. *Picture: B. W. L. Brooksbank*

did not have these overheads, except in terms of fuel and vehicle taxes. Besides, their prices were unpublished, and unregulated. They were often quicker,[1] safer and more efficient in their handling and delivery of goods—and they moved goods from door to door without trans-shipment. The road operators were therefore able to cream off the most lucrative business. The only recourse open to the railway companies to counter the competition was to offer 'exceptional' rates—that had to be between 5 per cent and 40 per cent below the standard rates, or (as from 1933) to negotiate 'agreed' rates, *i.e.* flat rates with particular traders—but still less than the standard rate for the commodity, and still settled in open court with other traders able to object and demand identical treatment.

To limit their losses in the area of local passenger services, the railways had themselves invested heavily in bus operations. Instead of running their own bus services, they bought substantial holdings (in most cases 49 per cent) in the major operators, and found their investments profitable. The involvement of the railway companies with bus services led to some coordination of bus and rail services and fares before the Second World War, but these sensible arrangements were not perpetuated after Nationalisation of the railways. The road-haulage industry on the other hand was too fragmented for the railway companies to invest in it like they did in the bus undertakings, other than in one or two larger companies concerned mainly with parcels deliveries. These interests in road transport were handed over to the BTC on Nationalisation, but the process of integration went into reverse before the public control of road haulage was achieved, because the Conservative administration elected in 1951 lost no time in denationalizing road transport.

Definitely the year 1938 was not a good one, and almost all freight revenues were on an accelerating downward trend. In November 1938, Sir Ralph Wedgewood (Chief General Manager of the LNER, until succeeded by C. H. Newton in March 1939) led a movement, jointly with the other railways and sponsored by the Railway Companies' Association, pressing the Government for a 'Square Deal' with respect to road competition and to relieve the railways' obligation to

DARE WE LET THE RAILWAYS DIE?

It is for *you* to decide.

The Railway industry faces a grave crisis.

The prosperity of the Railways vitally affects *you*. It affects you as a trader, as a ratepayer, as a tax-payer, as a purchaser. It affects the housewife, the retailer, the wholesaler. It affects you in peacetime—but what if war should come?

Can any means of transport other than the Railways evacuate in 48 hours London's millions, Birmingham's millions, Liverpool's millions, and millions from other danger zones.

Only the RAILWAYS can cope with the vast quantities of supplies that the nation requires in peace or in war.

Essential in Peace, <u>vital in War</u>, *dare we let the Railways die?*

The danger signal shines red . . . the Railways have asked the Minister of Transport to *clear the lines.** They have asked for the right of way to that efficiency upon which the country depends—upon which *you* depend.

They have asked that the shackles of a century may be removed ; that out-of-date rules applicable to long vanished conditions should go ; *that they should be given the freedom enjoyed by other forms of transport.*

Shall they have this freedom ?

IT IS FOR YOU TO DECIDE.

THE RAILWAYS ASK FOR A SQUARE DEAL—NOW

*ASK FOR A COPY OF "CLEAR THE LINES," FREE AT EVERY RAILWAY STATION IN BRITAIN. IT TELLS YOU HOW THE OUT-OF-DATE RAILWAY RESTRICTIONS AFFECT YOU

ISSUED BY THE RAILWAY COMPANIES' ASSOCIATION

A poster produced by the Railway Companies' Association to draw the attention of the general public to the campaign. The body had been formed in 1867 to promote the interests of the country's railway organisations in Parliament and was active in this role until Nationalisation.

maintain a published ceiling on charges. The hauliers, with a more powerful lobby, countered by asserting that vehicle and fuel taxes were not spent on roads. A compromise had not been achieved in those final months before the war came to alter everything—and very soon after the war a public demand for Nationalisation of the railways. In the first half of 1939 the downward trend in passenger receipts was accelerating, although freight receipts were improving rapidly by the outbreak of the war. Rearmament was no doubt the reason for this change and of course as soon as the war started the profitability of the railways was transformed.

Wartime (1939–1945)

The Second World War brought tremendous changes to the railway scene,[2] as it did to every other aspect of life. The changes on the railways were basically of four kinds: Government control; major reductions in the frequency, speed and comfort of passenger services; a substantial increase in freight traffic; and lastly, damage—acute due to air-raids, and chronic due to reduction of standards of maintenance.

Based on their system of control of the railways during the First World War, in the years between the rise of Nazi Germany and the outbreak of the Second World War, the Government had drawn up plans for similar direction in the event of another major war. When the Germans invaded Poland on 1 September 1939 the plans were activated. The railways were taken over by the Ministry of (War) Transport,[3] and they remained under Government control until the end of 1947, the eve of Nationalisation. In the ministry responsibility for railway matters was assigned to two divisions, Traffic and Maintenance, the heads of which were accountable to the Railway Control Officer. He provided the link with the Railway Executive Committee (REC). The REC, consisting of the chief executives of the big four railways and the London Passenger Transport Board (LPTB), with

G. Cole Deacon of the Railway Companies' Association as secretary, was constituted in September 1938 and was in being as an advisory body from that date until the outbreak of war.

Early in 1939, detailed instructions were drawn up in secret and circulated to general managers, for the 'control of the railways in the event of armed conflict', and these included the appointment of liaison officers and long lists of addresses of officers responsible for all the military and other government agencies with whom the railways would have to cooperate. Meanwhile plans were drawn up well before the outbreak of hostilities to cope with the immediate demands. These included evacuation of children and hospital patients—from London in particular, and of treasures, gold and key Government and business departments, also the removal of naval ammunition from coastal depots[4] and of perishables from the docks to inland cold stores. Upon the outbreak of war, sixteen consultative committees were set up to deal with different aspects of railway matters and report to the main REC. The most important, and one which sat almost daily, was the Operating Superintendents' Committee, chaired by the LNER's V. M. Barrington-Ward. Naturally, a major aspect of the REC's work in preparation for the war was concerned with Air Raid Precautions (ARP).

The assumption of control of the railways by the Minister of Transport entailed the negotiation by the Government of satisfactory financial arrangements with the companies, and therefore of their costs. In effect, the railways were 'hired'—for the duration of the war and for one year after its end. It was agreed that all revenues should be pooled, and a scheme was devised for the sharing of revenues and their taxation. A guaranteed net revenue of £43.5 million per year was to be distributed between the five principal bodies, in the proportions of 34 per cent to the LMSR, 23 per cent to the LNER, 16 per cent each to the GWR and SR, and 11 per cent to the LPTB; half of any further profits above the £4.5 million up to £56 million could be taken (in the same proportions) by the railways, the other half and any profits above £56 million being retained by the Exchequer. The arrangement was designed to give the railways some reward for their efforts and therefore encourage them to be efficient. It soon transpired that the railways were being called to take on more than enough traffic and to work to maximum capacity, while the companies were open to criticism that they were 'profiteering from the war' because their competitors—chiefly road transport undertakings—were artificially handicapped by wartime restrictions. The need for people to travel and for goods to be transported was as great as ever and would quickly become greater, and the resources of the railways became a major limiting factor in the prosecution of the war. Therefore the Government changed its mind and forced a more stringent financial agreement on the companies in January 1941, whereby the Exchequer now kept all net revenues above the annual £43.5 million, although it did set aside a special trust fund of £10 million a year for the railways to draw on after the war to pay for arrears of maintenance. Meanwhile the railway companies agreed not to charge the cost of war damage and extra maintenance against revenue.

The REC also had to take on the determination of pay levels with the unions. Just before the war broke out, the railway companies had been in extensive discourse over pay and conditions with the railwaymen's Unions;[5] the National Union of Railwaymen (NUR), the Association of Locomotive Engineers and Firemen (ASLEF) and the Railway Clerks' Association (RCA), and in November 1939 the Railway Staffs National Tribunal secured the men an increase in wages broadly of 5 per cent. This in turn forced the Railway Rates Tribunal to agree to the companies' request for increases in fares and charges. However, the Government was very anxious to avoid the railways—or anyone else—passing on their wartime costs to the consumer and thereby fuelling inflation. For this reason they allowed only one limited increase in railway charges—in 1940, 10 per cent in July extended to 16.7 per cent in December. Further wage increases were conceded to the staff throughout the war, and thus the railways had to foot the bill for these increases in costs. At the same time the Government negotiated reduced rates for their own enormous freight traffic.[6] Even so, in the event the profits made by the railways during the war were very large. Net operating revenues advanced from £39.9 million in the last pre-war year to a peak of £105.6 million in 1943, prices having risen in the period by a mere 26 per cent. The outbreak of war placed the railways right away in the position of being able rapidly to increase their net revenues, because almost at a stroke their major competitor, private road transport, was stifled by the imposition of stringent restriction on the use of oil and later of rubber as well.

As a result of the unified Government control of the railways, it was possible to alter radically the routing of traffic—especially freight—away from that benefiting individual companies to routes that used the network most efficiently. Many streams of traffic were rearranged. For example, much traffic on the overloaded West Coast Main Line (WCML) was diverted to the ECML and the former GC main line. Special attention was paid to the increased traffic exchanged between the LMSR and LNER on the one hand and the GWR and SR on the other, especially by diverting it away from the overburdened exchange points in the London area. We shall see later how wartime necessities changed the traffic on the ECML. In any case, the demands of war enforced the coordination of all modes of inland transport in order to make the best possible use of limited resources, such as had never before been attained in peacetime. Besides, in order to cope with the greatly increased freight traffic and the burgeoning needs of the Armed Forces in regard to special traffic in troops and military supplies, systems of operation by working timetable were frequently superseded by *ad hoc* control.

Wartime passenger traffic

The peacetime passenger services were pared to the minimum considered necessary for essential purposes. Private motoring almost had to cease, yet more people than ever in peacetime, including the millions of servicemen on duty and on leave, needed to travel—and to travel further; the demand was for more carrying capacity. The basic wartime timetable, established from December 1939, represented a coaching train-mileage of only 70 per cent of the pre-war figure, and in light of the numbers of passengers travelling and the full loads conveyed the coaching stock was used much more 'efficiently'. Excursion trains and published seaside holiday trains were abolished, but the REC did allow the railways to provide relief trains to published services quite liberally during the first two years of the war—although they were not advertised in advance. Later on, the demand for rolling-stock and crews for extra freight and military traffic was so great that the running of unadvertised reliefs was rigorously curtailed, and almost all restaurant cars (and most sleeping-cars) were withdrawn.

In spite of the wartime discouragements and discomforts, passenger journeys fell only from 1,237 million in the last pre-war year to 989 million in 1940. After that they grew progressively to 1,335 million in 1943, and after a crescendo of 121 million per month in the summer of 1944, reached a peak of 1,377 million in 1945 (11 per cent above pre-war). In terms of passenger miles the rise was dramatic: from 19,000 million pre-war (1938) to 32,300 million in 1943, and eventually to a climax of 35,248 million (186 per cent of pre-war) in 1945. About half of the wartime journeys were by servicemen on duty or on leave, they (and many others) travelling free or at various concessionary rates. In July 1942, the number of servicemen travelling on free warrants was 2 million while 6 million servicemen and dependents travelled at concessionary rates and these numbers increased by 50 per cent between 1942 and 1943.

After that, to avoid overwhelming the capacity of the trains completely, the issue of free warrants for servicemen and civil defence personnel had to be curtailed, as did the widespread distribution

A4 No. 5 *Sir Charles Newton* stands at the head of the 'Flying Scotsman' service at Edinburgh Waverley during June 1947. The locomotive had been built at Doncaster, as No. 4901 *Capercaillie* and with a double chimney, in June 1938. At this time the engine was allocated to Gateshead and would remain there until October 1963. After brief spells at St Margarets and Aberdeen *Sir Charles Newton* was withdrawn in March 1964.

of concessionary fares. By 1943 the overall average distance a person travelled had risen to 25.4 miles from 15.9 miles immediately pre-war, an increase of 60 per cent;[7] it rose further to as much as 26.9 miles in 1945, and was still 23.9 miles in 1946 and fell little thereafter. People—particularly servicemen, whose average journey on warrant was 150 miles—were making far more long-distance journeys during the war than in peacetime. The figures for 1945 were so high because on top of the service travel enormous numbers of people went on holiday that summer. Trains were then provided for them, but the 1944 peak occurred during the *Overlord* period of restricted services and the overcrowding was unbelievable. Besides, it must be understood that the statistics for passenger journeys were derived largely from ticket sales, and owing to 'fare-dodging' during the war and after it, the true number of passenger journeys may have been a great deal higher.

It was by no means only servicemen who had to travel up and down the country because of the war. Dispersal of families, businesses and Government departments,[8] and the widespread movement of non-military workers such as the Land Army, Irish immigrants, repair gangs, construction and munitions workers, and many other categories living away from home, entailed countless civilians travelling around for justifiable personal reasons. Except for the tiny minority who were allowed petrol, they had to go by train—or locally perhaps by bus. By the middle of the war petrol was allowed only for those who really needed it with the result that car numbers fell from the August 1939 figure of 2.03 million to 0.72 million in 1943, but they were already back to 1.49 million in August 1945. Although long-distance coach services were virtually abolished, bus numbers remained little changed (at about 90,000), and like the trains tended to be overcrowded, as they filled the needs of most people for local transport—for work or recreation.

The authorities tried very hard to discourage non-essential travel with 'Is Your Journey Really Necessary?' and other such exhortations widely proclaimed—and in February 1942 *The People* newspaper invited its readers to contribute ideas on ways to 'ration' travel for the war effort. Many of the readers' suggestions were much more unpleasant than the Orders and Restrictions that the Government did in fact pose. These were bad enough: no seat reservation—except for first class passengers on Government business on some of the busiest routes (such as the ECML); fewer—and eventually no, restaurant cars; much fewer sleeping cars—and reservation of first class berths for those on Government business, and no towels, soap, rugs or pillows in them; no train heating except in the dead of winter; no heating in local station waiting-rooms—unless passengers were stranded in cold weather; and so on.

All excursion fares were abolished, including (from 1942) cheap day returns. Still, it was comparatively cheap to travel by train. After having been unchanged for years and increased just by 5 per cent in 1937, the only increment in the war was in July 1940 when ordinary fares went up by 16.7 per cent to 0.66p/mile (third class), and this was hardly noticed. Indeed, any discouragement of non-essential travel during the war was on the whole unsuccessful—certainly with one of the present authors.[9] A threatened system of travel permits was never implemented, not even one that would have applied only to certain designated routes—which included the ECML in particular. Travel for purposes of 'holiday, pleasure or recreation' was banned to the 'restricted' east and south coast resorts during the 1940–42 period when a German invasion was a possibility. Again from mid-1943 to August 1944 when it was so vital to keep the Germans guessing about

Providing you

TRAVEL ONLY WHEN YOU MUST

It doesn't matter how you say

IS *your journey really necessary?*

*

is **YOUR** *journey really necessary?*

*

is your **JOURNEY** *really necessary?*

*

is your journey **REALLY** *necessary?*

*

is your journey really **NECESSARY?**

*

RAILWAY EXECUTIVE COMMITTEE

A poster produced during the war by the Railway Executive Committee asking passengers to think twice about using the overstretched railway network. The *Daily Express* cartoonist Carl Giles also produced a characteristic alternative for the Committee.

the Allied preparations for *Overlord*, a strip 10 miles inland from the Humber round to Penzance, the Bristol Channel and the Firths of Forth and Clyde was made into Regulated Areas,[10] and for the four months April to July 1944 they were Restricted Areas. Nor was the ultimate brutality— total abolition of first class—imposed, except on London Suburban services from October 1941. With the services ordering their officers—but to the financial embarrassment of many a junior officer—to travel first class, this was hardly a viable option anyway.

Trains of unprecedented length were run, most restaurant cars were used as ordinary passenger carriages, and in compartment stock the arm rests were screwed back to allow more people to squeeze in. In 1943–44 when very few reliefs could be run, the demand for travel was so great—18-coach trains on the ECML with seats for 500–600 were regularly conveying 1,200 (even up to 2,000) passengers—that often hundreds of people were left stranded because it was physically impossible for them to board the trains. There were even instances where passengers had to be turned off trains because so many had jammed themselves in that coaches sank on their springs and their running-boards were fouling platform edges.

With long-distance trains often overcrowded, a long journey, especially the seemingly interminable journeys in the darkness or the black-out and with the delays caused by the awful weather of the first and second winters of the war, became an exhausting and depressing necessity. Without doubt, rail travel in wartime could be quite an ordeal. People and their baggage—and that of servicemen tended to be singularly bulky—jammed the corridors and vestibules and made a visit to the lavatory a major undertaking. On the rare train that had a restaurant car, gaining access was impossible, and conditions resembled those of mid-Victorian times, with hordes of passengers—especially lively and vociferous young servicemen—storming out of the train to the refreshment rooms at principal intermediate stops. Passenger train schedules were much slower than in peacetime, with longer station stops, a speed limit of 60 mph under normal conditions and—at first—drastic slowing during air-raid alerts. Timekeeping was also very poor, for a number of reasons.

At the beginning of the war lighting restrictions for passengers were draconian—just a blue bulb. People could not stand that, and they were soon replaced either by shaded white lights or by full lighting with heavy blinds ferociously kept drawn down. Night-time journeys then became tolerable—and a lot safer. Travel after dark was made claustrophobic—even dangerous—by the minimal lighting allowed in carriages (extinguished during alerts) and on stations, and confusion was confounded by the idiotic removal of station name boards (in August 1940). The pressures of war and the shortage of labour quickly led to stations, that had been well kept, becoming dirty and eventually decrepit, and their dinginess was accentuated by the necessity for the blacking-out of all roof glazing. Moreover, the shortages that continued after the war resulted in the stations staying that way for many years.

Military specials

The special trains began even before the actual declaration of war on 3 September 1939. There was a certain degree of military mobilisation before the outbreak, and then in the few days before that date the long-planned programme of evacuation of children from London and other large cities was carried out, in expectation of devastating air-raids as soon as the war began—but which did not occur for nearly another year. As the Forces were mobilised, industry was brought quickly to a high pitch of activity, and Allied Forces (especially from Canada and then the USA) were brought in to make Britain eventually 'one enormous armed camp', a steadily increasing number of troop specials and special freight trains of military equipment greatly overfilled the gaps in traffic left by the reduction in normal peacetime services.

The military traffic itself comprised special troop, and—after D-Day—ambulance and prisoner-of-war—trains on the one hand, and special trains of military equipment, ammunition, petrol and stores on the other. In addition, numerous non-military specials were run on Government account, such as evacuation specials, trains to bring workers to London to repair flying-bomb damage—and to take rubble out to build airfields, and Ministry of Food, for fish and meat to and from Scotland.

A large bureaucratic system, the Movement Controls, was rapidly evolved during the war for the organisation of military traffic. At the War Office, there was the Directorate of Movements under the Deputy Quartermaster-General, with under him separate directors of personnel and of freight movements.[11] Among the branches headed by each of these senior officers were Q(M)4 and Q(M)5, respectively responsible for movement of personnel and stores within the UK and to and from the ports. At the sharp end were the Railway Traffic Officers (RTOs) with their assistants, established at the principal railway centres up and down the country. Working in liaison with the Railway District Operating Superintendents, the RTO was responsible for the actual execution of the movements planned 'higher up'—by Movement Control at the War Office or at the HQs of the relevant Army Command or District.[12] This was for movement of relatively large bodies of troops in coach-loads or complete train-loads and of their stores, but the RTO's office also had to deal with countless journeys by individual servicemen or of small groups. The RTO had other jobs as well, such as liaising with the military police on the station in their role of checking for men who were 'AWOL'[13] or misbehaving in other ways. The RAF and the Navy had corresponding Movement Control organisations, at the Admiralty and the Air Ministry (or Navy division or RAF Command Group). When the US Army arrived from 1942, at first they sent liaison officers to work at British Army Movement Control Districts, but in July 1942 USA Transportation Corps, (ETOUSA)[14] established their own Movement Control organisation, modelled on the British and often sharing its offices.

There were mass movements of troops from the very first days of September 1939,[15] when the British Expeditionary Force was being sent to France. An indication of the scale of these operations is the fact that the movement of the personnel of just one Army division would require 45 trains. During the war the railways ran on behalf of the Government no fewer than 258,624 special passenger trains, and 279,935 special freight trains; the peak year was 1944, with 82,205 and 96,157 trains respectively. Much of the mass movement of troops and supplies for operations was to and from the principal ports, especially on the Bristol Channel, the Mersey, and above all the Clyde—where at Glasgow a new station solely devoted to troop movements was built at King George V Dock, and at Faslane on Gareloch a completely new port was constructed.[16] Then in 1945 almost as many troop specials as ever were needed for the men coming home on leave from abroad and later for demobilisation.

Prior planning of special trains was naturally done as much in advance as possible and in great detail, although arrangements often had to be flexible, especially in relation to the traffic connected with the uncertain sailing and arrival dates of ships in incoming convoys that were delayed or re-routed. Sometimes, as in the military evacuation from France in 1940 ('Dynamo' and 'Aerial'), plans had to be improvised at very short notice and in those circumstances train orders were made by telephone and probably no permanent records were ever made.

As the war progressed and the requirement for military special trains grew inescapably, a standard schedule of paths between main military depots and the ports was evolved, although each train had to be scheduled in advance and the staff informed by means of Special Traffic Notices (STNs). The ports were divided into seven groups: North-West England, South Wales, South Coast,

London Docks (including Tilbury), East Coast, North-East England, and Scotland. Each train was allocated a unique code, sometimes seen chalked on the first wagon, having four elements: date of departure, source, departure time, and destination. The despatches under this plan were normally scheduled at six-hour intervals, chosen to conform to a pattern of acceptance at the destination, and the schedules were based on trains travelling at an average speed of 15 mph. There was also a more long-standing coding system for train identification, which was displayed in a headboard on the locomotive and incorporated a designation of the originating command and the date of the month. The 'paperwork' relating to all these military special trains would make fascinating reading, but seems not to have survived. Perhaps this was just as well considering that over half a million special trains were run for military and other purposes during the war.

Wartime freight traffic

During the last two years or so of peace, rearmament had already been producing an increase in merchandise and minerals traffic, while the resulting resurgence of industry necessitated an expansion in the output and movement of coal. Right from the outbreak of the war freight traffic on the railways began growing much more rapidly. One year into the war the tonnage of freight being carried by the railways was 13 per cent above that of the last three years of peace, while the average length of haul was up by no less than 33.1 per cent, and thus the really major increase was in ton-mileage. Mainly because of greater carryings of coal the figures tended to be highest in the autumn and winter months, when on the other hand severe weather, long hours of darkness and staff sickness combined to make operations all the more difficult.

The growth in freight traffic during the war was massive. Net-ton miles rose from 16,700 million (5,190 million merchandise, 3,182 million minerals, 8,300 million coal) in the last pre- war year to a peak in 1943 of 24,400 million (9,660 million merchandise—86 per cent above pre-war, 5,360 million minerals, 9,340 million coal). In 1944 the net ton-miles were almost the same as in 1943; the traffic density persisted at only a lightly lesser level in the first half of 1945, 10,700 million ton-miles being recorded in the first six months of that year.

The difficulty the railways had to tackle from the outbreak of war—one they were already becoming aware of during the period or rearmament beforehand—was that of inadequate capacity to carry greatly increased freight class traffic, often by unusual routes or on lines and to destinations having relatively light traffic in peacetime. The limiting factors were: line capacity, wagon supply, availability of locomotives, and number of trained operating staff. Apart from the increased output of industry for war purposes, other factors that underlay the augmentation of railway freight traffic there were the severe restriction of motor transport, the decline in the transport of freight—and especially of coal—by coastal shipping (due mainly to higher charges and greater delays of coastwise shipping under dangerous wartime conditions), the transfer of much import and export traffic from east to west coast ports, and lastly the growth of traffic in military supplies.

Tremendous congestion occurred at times of severe winter weather, and at places particularly affected by the war. Usually it was relieved by clearing yards on Sundays—and even on Christmas Day. On a number of occasions partial or even total embargoes (restriction orders) had to be put on acceptances of traffic for a few days until the congestion had been relieved; indeed, on major routes such as the ECML, embargoes of some sort were in force for most of the time. Congestion was most frequent and severe at bottlenecks, such as the exits from South Wales, the ECML through Northallerton, through Carlisle, and at points of exchange between the LMSR or LNER and the GWR (and SR), such as Bordesley, Banbury, Reading and in the London area. This was because in the free market circumstances of peacetime, facilities at the exchange points had not been designed for the transfer of more than the essential minimum of traffic between the companies. Furthermore, it had been normal for wagons to be handed over to the receiving company at these junctions not marshalled according to destination, leaving the marshalling to be done later. The great increase of exchange traffic in the war however called for the running of through pre-marshalled trains over these junctions, and the overall control exercised by the REC enabled through trains of this kind to be arranged.

The delays and congestion caused early in the war by working in the black-out—especially in shunting-yards, by gross speed restrictions imposed during alerts, severe winter weather and by the Blitz, played havoc with schedules and rosters forcing widespread adoption of the control of freight trains on an *ad hoc* basis. This was of long-term benefit in bringing about more efficient operation by central traffic control. The strict limitations of the supply of oil and rubber prevented extensive use of road transport to relieve the railways. Nevertheless, in October 1943 the Ministry of War Transport were forced in desperation to relax a little the restrictions on the use of lorries. In the peak year of 1944, 64 per cent of the freight moved was carried by rail, 20 per cent by road (mainly on short hauls), 10 per cent by coaster (mainly on hauls of over 200 miles) and 5 per cent by canal.

The Inter-Company Rolling-Stock Control (ICRSC) was established pursuant to a Committee of Enquiry in March 1941, and undertook the gargantuan task of the day-to-day organisation of the supply of empty wagons of the right type in the right numbers at the right place. (Until that date, the LNER had its own All-Line Freight Rolling Stock Control Office, at York). All private-owner wagons (and containers) had been requisitioned on the outbreak of the war, adding 589,000 to the total pool and bringing the wagon stock to over 1.2 million. These measures improved wagon utilisation and very few new wagons needed to be built during the war—although by the end an inordinate number of the requisitioned wagons were unusable. The IRSC played a key role in organizing the pooling and distribution of special wagons, and it also kept an indent on nearly 0.5 million wagon-sheets and over 0.25 million wagon-ropes, which with a great shortage of covered wagons were vital for the protection and securing of manufactured goods from the weather and from pilferage. Every station and yard throughout the country sent daily records of its stock position to their headquarters offices, which passed summaries on to the ICRSC office. The task was achieved largely by the railways' internal telephone and telegraph system, employing a comprehensive set of code-words and phrases.

In other similar ways the REC through its sub-committees was able to expedite the flow of freight traffic by a number of measures. They arranged re-routing away from the worst bottlenecks—if they could. They cut marshalling delays by great extension of the block-load system, and by adopting the system of 'nominated loading', in which the dispatch of goods from particular consignors was undertaken only on certain specified days and to specified destinations. They abolished wagon number-taking at all inter-company exchange points, and they imposed much heavier demurrage charges—although not on Government depots and factories which (apart from collieries) were by far the worst offenders in delaying the turn-round of wagons. The centralised control of trains by telephone already in operation on parts of the railway system was expanded, and as well as the installation of new control centres and emergency telephone networks, special telephone links were set up to allow daily conferences to be held between the four Chief Operating Superintendents simultaneously sitting at their respective headquarters. Later, in August 1942 the LNER—the most decentralised group—on its part established its own Central Traffic Office (at Marylebone), to provide an all-line operating organisation responsible for controlling movements of traffic and the distribution of locomotive power between its three areas. Such centralised control was essential when under wartime conditions the flows of traffic were also more varied and unpredictable.

On the outbreak of war, a serious shortage quickly developed of available coaster capacity, due (at the beginning and end of the war) to the requirement to ship coal to European countries previously importing German coal, to German mine-laying and bombing in the North Sea, and to the requisition of coasters for military operations. The coastwise transport of coal from the North-East to London and other ports in the South-East at one time fell by a third, two-thirds of the coal consumed by public utilities in this part of the country—about 10.5 million tons a year in London—being carried by sea in peacetime. There was therefore a vital need to divert to rail the coal shipments from Northumberland and Durham to the south. The fall in exports was more than compensated by the increased home consumption for war industry. Coal that had normally left the country through ports in the North-East and South Wales was now dispatched inland, and for much longer distances than in peacetime, a change that affected the LNER's ECML notably.

Coal was absolutely vital, and the crisis that arose in January 1940 led the Government departments concerned not only to introduce convoys of coastal shipping, but also to institute what were called 'convoy' coal trains, the output of single collieries being routed right through without intermediate marshalling to single destinations or major consumers. These were run not only to London and the South-East and South-West but also to Lancashire, for there the growth of war industries had increased the consumption of coal well above the amount that could be mined locally. Paths from the North-East for 200 of these trains per week were arranged, although usually not more than 170 actually ran each week, and 5 million tons per year came south in convoy trains—although in the mid-war years four or five times as much came by sea. Naturally, the iron ore traffic—which increased by 150 per cent in ton-mileage during the war—was also run in block trains, as were several other bulk commodities.

Throughout the war, mishaps which caused traffic disruption became more and more frequent, on account of the working difficulties, the extra burden of traffic, and later the arrears of maintenance. There were numerous minor collisions and derailments due to wartime causes, the more extraordinary being barrage-balloons coming down and fouling lines or signal wires, or even in once instance when a locomotive ran into a parachute. Direct enemy action disrupted traffic at times, but rarely for more than a day or two. What is perhaps less well known was the frequency with which Allied—and occasionally enemy—aircraft crashed on or very near railways. These amounted to about 200—a remarkable figure until it is understood that many thousands of aircraft—only a small fraction being those of the enemy—crashed somewhere in Britain during the conflict. More serious railway accidents—not attributable to enemy actions—seem to have been no more common than in peacetime.

In the winters of the war the most disruptive factor was severe weather. Even in the absence of air raids, exceptionally bad weather coupled with the very large increase in freight traffic added to other wartime difficulties, and many temporary embargoes had to be imposed. Quite often total blocks were placed on certain sections of the system, affecting all freight traffic except perishables, certain essential traffics (collectively known as 'RECEX') and that denoted as 'Government Priority'. Trains had to be stored wherever there was spare track until they could be forwarded—usually on Sundays,[17] and it became almost routine for hundreds of trains to be held up every day in this way without motive power.

Dislocation of railway operations was probably greatest during the earlier part of the war, especially in 1940 and 1941. In spite of the absence of air raids, in January 1940 the worst winter weather of the century—snow, ice, and fog—coupled with the new difficulties of working under wartime conditions, caused a reduction of up to a half in freight movement. This brought about a serious shortfall in the delivery of coal to London and the south, and for over a month this reached crisis proportions.

During the winter of the Blitz (September 1940 to May 1941) the disruption was not so much a consequence of air raid damage, not inconsiderable as this was, but was due more to the drastic speed restrictions imposed during the frequent air raid warnings and to interruptions and diversions caused by unexploded bombs.[18] The throughput of freight traffic in the London area was diminished by 30–50 per cent early in the Blitz, owing to drastic lighting restrictions during the prolonged alerts making yard shunting extremely difficult, coupled with the enforced slowing of trains to 15 mph. The problem was relieved to a considerable extent by changing night shifts to double day shifts and by running trains in daylight hours as much as possible. In the autumn of 1940 the problems of the transport of vital coal to London and the south were so grave that the War Cabinet set up an all-powerful coal committee, headed by the Lord President (Sir John Anderson) to coordinate all aspects of the movement of coal. They devised all measures they could—some extremely unconventional—to ensure that public utilities and factories were kept going and the population did not freeze.

Air raid damage in the London area—especially on the SR, was seriously holding up the movement and discharge of coal, and many collieries had to curtail production on account of shortages of empty wagons. In November 1940 the average number of loaded coal wagons for the SR held up on the LNER on any one day was 2,000–3,500 on the GN Section and 500–700 on the GC Section, 1,500–3,000 for the south *via* Banbury, and 1,000–1,500 at London depots; figures for the LMSR traffic through London were similar. The measures pursued by the Coal Committee included the use of diversionary rail routes, the slapping of heavy demurrage charges on coal consumers to speed up the turn-round of wagons, and the provision of special dumps of coal near the collieries and on the fringes of the London area.

The diversion of London's seaborne coal to rail was all the more inconvenient because of the facilities at the major gas works and power stations on the Thames were geared to discharge from vessels on the river and not from rail wagons. This problem was circumvented to some extent by running coal trains to wharves on the Essex bank—much augmenting the traffic of coal from Ferme Park Yard to riverside destinations on the Tilbury line of the LMSR, to be tipped into barges for delivery upstream. Fortunately the enemy did not continue with major air raids over Britain after May 1941, except for the V-weapon offensive—over London and the south-east—of June 1944 to March 1945, and the coal crisis of the 1940–41 winter did not recur. Yet, in the winter of 1943–44, serious shortfalls in deliveries of coal to London and the south were threatened as a result of the extra burden put upon the railways by the removal of coasters for conversion for D-Day operations coming on top of unprecedented intensity of other traffic.

The clearance of import traffic from the west coast ports—notably those on the Clyde—was a constant headache, partly as a consequence of the diversion of shipping from east coast ports. Routes most frequently affected were those that converged on Carlisle, and the GWR main lines out of South Wales. To an extent because of saturation of the WCML through Carlisle forced traffic on to the ECML but also because of the convoy coal trains, congestion on the NER section of the ECML also came to threaten at times to bring inland transport in Britain to a halt.

As the war went on, new problems arose, with the progressive arming of the Forces—not least the vast programme of airfield construction and then the supply of fuel and armaments to the Air Force squadrons, the export of large amounts of raw materials, military equipment and supplies to Russia, and the commitment to ever greater military activities overseas. There was a relentless expansion in the needs of the war industry and of the armed services for all forms of transport continuing into 1942—and all this to some extent before the build-up of the United States Army and its Air Force into Britain from May 1942 under the *Bolero* plan. By late 1942 the pressure of traffic forced some relaxation of the lighting restrictions in marshalling yards and at about this time an easement of the normal limits on freight train lengths.

Earlier in the war the critical factor had been the physical capacity of the railways to carry more traffic. That problem was addressed systematically by the REC in a March 1941 plan for spending £5 million in the next year—and a great deal more after that, to enhance traffic flow over principal routes including the ECML, and to provide extra facilities for marshalling freight and servicing locomotives. In the event, between 1941 and 1944, £11.5 million of public money was spent on additional running lines, loops—even bridges—on the bottleneck and overloaded sections of the system and effectively almost throughout the country. After most of this construction was completed, line capacity in the last two years of the war was then no longer a principal limitation to the railways' ability to respond to the increasing demands.

By mid-1941 the rate of growth in total freight traffic on the railways overall was running at about 5 per cent per year, but during 1942 and 1943 the burdens on the railway system grew even more, due to the accumulation of several factors. Already during the last ten weeks of 1942—without difficulties due to the weather, except for fog at times—traffic congestion attributable to *Bolero* forced both the LMSR and the LNER to put further embargoes on the acceptance of Anglo-Scottish freight traffic. Most of the mass influx of the men of the US Army from America also entailed the running of an equivalent number of train-loads of equipment—including armoured fighting vehicles (AFV)s—and supplies,[19] which were usually dispatched on slower convoys in advance of the men. A measure of the impact on the railways is exemplified by the arrival in late August and early September 1942 of five US armoured divisions, each bringing 390 light and medium tanks, 200 heavy tanks following in December 1942 to February 1943. Under *Bolero*, 30,000 cased vehicles were shipped over to Britain, and a number of assembly depots were constructed to which these large cases had to be transported by rail on specially adapted wagons. By June 1944 there were 1.54 million US Servicemen in Britain, and by April 1944 they alone were chartering 228 special trains of stores per day.

In the autumn of 1943, repeated and wider restriction orders had to be imposed affecting acceptance of the less immediately vital traffic on all the railways except the SR. The railways were threatening to break under the strain, as they were now handling well over 900,000 loaded wagons a week. The necessity for embargoes at this time arose from the combination of enormous war demands, episodes of fog, and also a widespread epidemic of influenza. The major limiting factors by then were the number and availability of locomotives, of operating staff—especially footplate men—and of skilled workshop fitters.

The shortage of locomotives was eventually eased somewhat by the temporary use of British and American military freight engines. Until these were available new construction of heavy freight locomotives, hampered by the commitment of the companies' workshops to the production of military hardware, was inadequate for the railways' needs. Furthermore, an inordinate proportion of existing locomotive stock was immobilised because of arrears of maintenance. Breakdowns were becoming increasingly frequent, and between November 1942 and March 1943 an average of 1,000 to 1,500 trains per week were being cancelled and 10,000 delayed owing to non-availability of locomotives.

The labour shortage became most acute towards the end of 1943 when it was aggravated by up to 10 per cent of staff being off sick at any one time. Servicemen with railway experience were released for footplate and other duties, and also prisoners-of-war were brought in to do labouring work. The crisis continued into the first month of 1944, when men were needed more than ever for the extra traffic for the military build-up to *Overlord*.[20] Poor and dirty working conditions, including the necessity for night and weekend shift work, along with rates of pay that compared unfavourably with those in war factories, led to slow rates of recruitment of boys leaving school. Some alleviation of the shortage had been achieved in mid-1942 by the complete reservation from military service of all railway 'conciliation' grades,[21] and in early 1944 by concerted recruitment and redirection from less essential vacancies. (However, youths under 18 were 'non-directable' and could only be persuaded, not forced, to join the railways). Inevitably, with so many inexperienced and relatively unskilled men coming on to the railways, standards of work declined, and overworked and poorly maintained engines deteriorated. Still, the long and irregular hours worked by footplate men and guards must undoubtedly have been off-putting.

To plan the preparations for *Overlord* in 1944, a special official committee on Inland Transport was set up by the War Cabinet, and this met weekly from February until about September. It recognised at the outset that the railways were already carrying 46 per cent more freight ton-miles than they were before the war and 70 per cent more passenger miles. In the peak month of September 1943, 940,000 loaded wagons were forwarded per week and although wagon supply was critical there simply were not enough staff or locomotives to operate any more trains than were already running. The earlier impediment—limited line capacity—had by then been mastered, although further new works would be undertaken for *Bolero*, and with the timely help of the new military freight locomotives just enough motive power could be mustered. The most serious shortage was that of labour. The Ministry of Labour was in the event able, from March 1944, to divert the railways enough men from industry, recognising that any likely disruption of industrial production would be far less harmful to the success of *Overlord* than would a failure of the railways to deliver men and supplies on schedule to the embarkation ports. Nevertheless, not only did the *Overlord* operation itself require 38–40,000 tons of freight to be moved per day in 1944 from February until several weeks after D-Day in June, but many of the small ships used for coastwise transport would be requisitioned from May for up to four months to deliver supplies to the Normandy beach-heads and therefore the traffic they carried had to be moved in other ways. Road transport was carrying about the same tonnage as the coasters, and could be more than doubled—mainly for short-haul work. In addition, in order to free ports in the south of England for the *Overlord* operations, their import traffic would have to be diverted to more northerly ports, thereby leading to longer hauls by rail. As well, heavy movements of troop trains, particularly southwards from the Clyde and Mersey, would further delay freight traffic.

For all these reasons it was necessary to make cuts in normal (wartime) carriage of both passengers and freight, because during the build up to D-Day and for some time afterwards no further traffic could be sustained. A 'Transport Balance Sheet' was drawn up in February 1944 and kept updated. The balance sheet, together with the projected needs for 'Operational Traffic' showed that in order to be able to carry the extra 1.25 million tons per month of military and munitions traffic (plus an increase of nearly as much coal) planned for about six months from March 1944, roughly equivalent reductions had to be made in the offerings of other traffic. Already measures had been taken by the Government to limit the need for transport, as by the zoning schemes such as adopted by the Ministry of Food, but now actual cuts in industrial production had to be planned to relieve the railways' freight burdens; from May 1944 they had as well to make considerable reductions in long-distance passenger services. Sufficient locomotives and crews then became available for the build-up programme to be carried through largely as planned.[22] In the month or two before D-Day, although most lines were worked to the limit, the greatest burden fell on the routes to the south coast ports and to London and the other Thames ports, even though traffic not related to *Overlord* through all these ports was dramatically curtailed. On certain routes, the public services were taken off altogether at times—and, for security reasons, without notice.[23]

The movement of men and supplies to the south, to sustain the immense military operations in north-west Europe, slackened to a certain extent after September 1944 but continued still at a high level until Victory in Europe in May 1945, special freight trains falling only from 32,200 in June—September 1944 to 25,600 in January–March 1945. In the four months June–September 1944 no less than 866,200 loaded wagons were dispatched from War Department depots and 404,670 from US Army depots, figures respectively up 173 per cent on the same period in 1943.[24]

After VE-Day, while the troop specials—now increasingly in the 'homeward' direction— continued to be numerous for some months, the military freight traffic tailed off quite rapidly. Throughout the winter of 1944–45, the amount of freight that had to be moved declined only slightly compared to the previous winter, whereas there was still a shortage of coasters, now needed for shipment of coal for the armies and the liberated populations in Europe. This meant that more coal had to be moved by rail, and the railways did once again become congested to the extent of having to impose frequent embargoes on freight. Labour continued to be in short supply and the railways could no longer depend on a supply of directed men, although Italian prisoners-of-war were employed extensively. At the same time there was much staff sickness, punctuated by spells of severe weather. There was again a dearth of locomotive power, because the military freight engines had gone to the Continent and inordinate numbers of locomotives were stopped for repair. A mounting backlog of maintenance also exacerbated the chronic scarcity of wagons. Even in March–May 1945 total ton mileage was still only 5 per cent less than the very high level of the year before, and after the end of the war in Europe a lot of the traffic in military supplies was substituted by that for the relief of the people of the liberated nations.

The return of peacetime and the run-up to Nationalisation
The end of the war in Europe on 8 May 1945 (VE-Day), followed by the end of the war with Japan on 15 August (VJ-Day), marked occasions of unimaginable relief and release for every adult person. Soon after VE-Day, the civilian population of Britain, exhausted to the limit by nearly six long years of war, having suffered sometimes real danger, losses (or the fear thereof) of loved ones, hard work, long hours—including in addition night duties such as fire-watching and ARP work, and above all the tedium and drabness of everyday life. They all seemed to have one idea: to go away, preferably to the seaside, 'for a break'. Restrictions on travel to the seaside had been lifted by September 1944, but only after VE-Day were people provided with the extra trains. Of course they had to be trains, for severe petrol rationing was still cutting private car and long-distance coach travel to the irreducible minimum. The result was again—as had occurred in 1944—queues of half a mile long at London termini on Saturdays in the summer of 1945, and the *ad hoc* provision of train formations to clear the never-ending stream of would-be passengers. Yet there were still occasions—even after the war was over, when not enough trains could be provided and passengers were left behind.

As we have seen, the continuation of great movements of civilians and servicemen during the last months of the war in the first half of 1945 combined with the rush for holidays to produce an all-time peak of passenger-journeys that year on the railways as a whole. After that—in spite of petrol rationing, there was a gradual falling off, all-line passenger miles declining by 35 per cent between 1945 and 1947. Meanwhile, fares were increased in July 1946 to 33 per cent above pre-war and then in October 1947 to 55 per cent above—increases still substantially less than inflation,

Above: Ex-WD 2-8-0 No. 90432 clanks southward past York Racecourse platform with a rake of LNER 20-ton hopper wagons on 25 April 1950. This locomotive was taken on loan by the company in December 1943 until September 1944 and later returned in November 1945.

Below: Doncaster depot as seen from the north end of the yard. Two locomotives on the left are ex-works, these are: C12 4-4-2T No. 67391 and A4 Pacific no. 60010 *Dominion of Canada* (with bell). The date is 10 April 1949 and both had evidently just received a general overhaul. *Both Pictures: B. W. L. Brooksbank*

which was 55.6 per cent above pre-war in 1946, 73.4 per cent in 1947. Freight rates were increased in July 1946 to 25 per cent above 1937 rates, and finally to 55 per cent above in October 1947: subsequent increases were allowed, to 81 per cent above 1937 rates in May 1950 and to 99 per cent above in April 1951, which brought them up eventually in line with inflation—temporarily, freight traffic remained well above the pre-war level and therefore in the early post-war period the railways' receipts from both passengers and freight remained buoyant.

Nevertheless, the net earnings of the railways as a whole fell from £62.5 million in 1945 to £32.5 million in 1946 and minus £16.2 million in 1947, because costs had risen since before the war on average by about 80 per cent while until July 1946 the Government had frozen charges. The most unsatisfactory statistics on the eve of Nationalisation related to overdue repairs. The remarkable achievements of the railway companies during the war left them with large profits on operating revenue, even if much of the extra gains had to be paid to the Exchequer under the wartime financial agreements. The railways had been disinvesting capital already before the war, and now their burdens were redoubled by huge arrears of replacement, compounded by excessive wear and tear during the war on rolling stock, track and other equipment. The money set aside in the wartime Arrears of Maintenance Trust Fund was quite inadequate, because prices had risen sharply while railway charges remained frozen. The Government—even a Labour administration—decreed that resources had to be restricted to those current pre-war, *i.e.* no extra was allocated to catch up on arrears, let alone modernisation, by the first year of Nationalisation arrears of maintenance amounted to no less than £179 million.[25] More particularly there were shortages of materials, and labour post-war was both lacking in numbers and in quality.

During the war the railways lost only 637 passenger vehicles by enemy action, but over 12,436 were damaged, while about 1,000 coaches and vans had been converted for use in ambulance trains. There had been 3,375 wagons destroyed (including 636 requisitioned wagons) and 20,242 (including 4,062 requisitioned) were damaged.[26] For a number of reasons, repair and replacement was much delayed, and at December 1947—well over two years after the end of the war—the proportion of the coaching stock under or awaiting repair was three times what it had been in December 1938, and the proportion of wagons 7.5 times the 1938 figure.[27] Most critically, although only seven had been destroyed and 450 damaged in the conflict, more than a third more locomotives (7.8 per cent of the stock) than in December 1938 were at this time under or awaiting repair at Works. Locomotives were breaking down about once in every 50,000 train-miles (almost twice as frequently as before the war), and as well the quality of coal was much poorer and failures to make adequate steam were commonplace. Furthermore, no more mileage of track was being re-laid than in 1938, so the wartime arrears were not yet being overcome and severe speed restrictions had to be imposed on most routes until they were. These conditions were to persist for several more years, and they were as bad on the LNER—the operators of the ECML—as on the other railways.

The first five years or so after the war, both before and after Nationalisation on 1 January 1948, were grossly abnormal in many ways, and although the management strove to restore the railway system and services to their pre-war condition this was unrealistic. The nation was economically almost destitute as a result of the war and could only regain wealth by curbing imports—notably oil—and by concentrating all new investment on plant needed to manufacture goods for export. Thus shortages and rationing were at first even more severe than in the war. Motor fuel was rationed and its supply to owners of private road vehicles was curtailed, to a diminishing extent, until 1953. Traffic on the railways remained at a high level, but once road hauliers were released from Government control (from August 1946); merchandise traffic began again to be lost to road.

Raven B16/1 Class 4-6-0 No. 61445 powers past York Racecourse platform and heads southward with an express freight on 24 April 1950. *Picture: B. W. L. Brooksbank*

The problem however was not now that—as before the war—road transport was cheaper and often gave a better quality of service, but that due to their run-down state the railways were incapable of carrying all the traffic on offer. The first post-war winters put a great strain on the railways, and they were forced to resort to further restrictions on freight movements, their problems being aggravated by labour troubles, including dock workers' strikes in October 1945. In addition, in 1947 the terrible weather and the consequent coal shortage forced temporary cuts in passenger train services. It also gave rise to a short-lived scheme for converting locomotives to burn crude oil—not in fact pursued very far by the LNER. The Ministry of Transport had to take special measures at those times to pass over freight to road haulage. These were still in force in the winter of 1947–48, when the weather turned out to be quite mild and the railways could have coped; as a result traffic became lost to road permanently. Despite the railways' shortcomings—temporary or inherent, with the steadily increasing industrial activity and a rise in real incomes the level of their traffic was in fact maintained through most of the 1950s. Net ton-miles of freight on British Railways (BR) in 1948 was 21,500 million, reaching a peak in 1951 of 22,900 million (40 per cent higher than in 1938) and remaining well above 20,000 million until 1957, after that the decline began. The proportion of total national ton-mileage carried by road rose from 37 per cent in 1952 to 50.5 per cent in 1959, while the railways' share, which had been 41 per cent in 1938 and 52 per cent in 1946, fell in the 1950s from 43 per cent to 32 per cent. (The rest was by coastal shipping, and this—about 6,900 million ton-miles—changed little).

The freight ton-mile figures were in part kept buoyant by the coal traffic. There was a fall of at least 25 per cent in national coal output during the war from the 1938 figure of 231 million tons. In the 1948–53 period it was still a little below pre-war, now far less coal was being exported and instead it was being carried on longer hauls, the average journey of a wagon of coal being

28 per cent longer than in 1938. Because they were needed to transport most of the coal to the generating stations, the railways also came to benefit from the post-war increase in coal consumed for electricity and gas generation. Household consumption of coal fell between 1938 and 1946 substantially, but during the same period electricity consumption more than doubled.

The Transport Act 1947, the Railway Executive Period (1948–52) and the Transport Act 1953

The benefits of efficiency gained by a planned distribution of traffic between rail and road, which had been attained by strict central control during the war, encouraged the idea of state ownership and control of all public transport. It was perhaps fortunate that the political swing to socialism at the end of the war led to the election of a Labour Government committed to public ownership of the railways, for it is unlikely that it would have been possible for private capital to restore the run-down railway system. Nevertheless, the valuation placed on the railway undertakings was probably too high. As a result, the Nationalised British Railways were saddled with greater central charges on capital than might otherwise have been the case, and this burden was a root cause of their subsequent decline. Expectations for the nominally 'unified' transport system that the Transport Act 1947 envisaged were not in the event fulfilled. The extent to which the shift to the private car and to road transport would so rapidly undermine the railways' profitability was not appreciated.

In fact, the 'Roads Lobby' (especially the British Road Federation) was already very powerful and managed to have even the Socialist 1947 Act modified in the critical matter of 'C' licence' lorries: instead of being restricted to 40-mile journeys as was originally intended, there was no mileage restriction enacted. As a consequence, these lorries carrying their owners' own goods, which already numbered 0.365 million or 60 per cent of the national fleet of road goods vehicles, rapidly multiplied. Their use took away most of the gain in general merchandise traffic resulting from a steadily growing manufacturing output which might otherwise have been secured by the railways. The 1947 Act however did Nationalise most of the road haulage industry, but this was highly profitable and at the time helped to 'balance the books' for the BTC as a whole, although the non-railway operations of the BTC were unable to wipe off more than a fraction of the losses that BR accumulated.

The 1947 Transport Act established the British Transport Commission (BTC), subservient to the Minister of Transport, a statutory public corporation for the control of 'all' national transport, *i.e.* all except private cars and 'C' licence vans and lorries. The philosophy behind the Act had been that State control with a public (*i.e.* State) obligation to provide transport services to all—whether or not they were profitable—was necessary both to provide the most efficient transport system and to avoid abuses of monopoly and 'wasteful competition' between modes of transport. The aims of integrating the rail and road spheres of public transport embraced in the Act could not be achieved unless the true economic costs of both public and private transport—not to mention the environmental costs, such as the slaughter of over 5,000 people a year on the roads, were accepted by the consumer. They were not, nor indeed were they really known to the BTC. The Transport Act still required the BTC to cover all its costs, including central charges and depreciation, 'taking one year with another', and with the Government-controlled Transport Tribunal forbidding fare increases. Consequently from the outset it would appear that the BTC were obsessed with cost-cutting as opposed to enhancing efficiency by modernisation. At the same time, throughout the 1950s—and also the 1960s—an inflated bureaucracy created desk jobs that cost far more than was saved by closing branch lines, the number of administrative staff employed per mile of railway operated by the BTC in 1958 growing to twice the pre-Nationalisation figure.

Yet the latent pressure to shift to road transport was always present, and once the nation was able to afford unlimited imports of oil, while restoration of some national wealth brought the return of a Conservative administration in 1951, the floodgates were opened. At that time (1951) BR were carrying 20,600 million passenger miles and 22,900 million ton-miles of freight—almost their highest output ever—and were making a working profit that was very nearly enough to cover central charges on capital as well. The new Government briefly thought of making private road transport pay a levy to support the railways, but soon discarded the idea. Indeed—without even serious consultation with the BTC, the Nationalised transport system was radically reformed in the 1953 Transport Act. Little more than lip service had been paid anyway to integration of rail and road transport, for example running local bus services to connect with trains, or the widespread introduction of containerisation of freight much disliked by the unions—as witness what happened over the docks. Any possibility of achieving an integrated transport system under state planning was now lost by the denationalisation of the road haulage industry, and by a general philosophy of allowing private industry and private and sectional interests to prevail. 'Integration' was substituted by 'competition' and by decentralisation with abolition of the Railway Executive; it was not possible to denationalise the railways because on their own they were not financially viable.

While it is undoubtedly true that modernisation of the railways was unduly delayed until the late 1950s and the 1960s there were two major factors outside the control of the Railway Executive which worked against the financial viability of the railways. Firstly, the 1947 Act did not abolish the 'common carrier' duties of the railways referred to earlier. This was supposed to occur after the 1953 Act, but it took several years to implement and in the meantime the BTC was not able to begin to achieve a balance of charges in the face of relentlessly increasing costs—especially wages, and of the restrictions imposed by the Government on the allocation of both finance and materials needed for modernisation. The funds provided were not even sufficient for catching up on the arrears of maintenance, and the only new works of any magnitude undertaken before the mid-1950s were the completion of projects funded and begun before the war.

The problems of British Railways and their causes

Already in 1950, estimates could highlight the vastly greater fixed costs of the railways, and also the hidden subsidy of road services, underlying the carrying of passengers respectively by train and by bus. In terms of passenger miles, costs of long-distance coaches were marginally higher than main-line express trains, but branch-line rail costs were over ten times those of country buses. Much of the problem with local passenger trains was that they often carried only a handful of passengers—less than a single-decker bus load. On the freight side, British Railways at that time were not doing so badly: it cost them £1.34 per net ton-mile to carry merchandise and £0.65 to move coal, but long-distance road costs still ranged from £0.81 to £1.17 per net ton-mile, and such advantage as the road haulier had was to a great extent due to his much better load-factors. But still, rail freight traffic entailed a great deal of empty wagon mileage, long-distance road hauliers usually securing a load in each direction, while they could pick and choose their traffic and were not obliged to run to a fixed schedule.

During the first five years or so of Nationalisation, the BTC was not only starved of materials—especially steel until it was decontrolled in 1953, to re-equip and modernise the railways but also of finance. It was unable to maintain the level of investment with which it began in 1948, when it was allocated 4.4 per cent of total UK capital investment, for in 1951 this fraction was down to 3.3 per cent.[28] Between 1948 and 1953 the capital value of BR remained static, while that of all UK industry and trade increased by 21 per cent in real terms. Capital equipment costs rose by 35 to 55 per cent during those five years, and average labour costs went up by 28 per cent while 'productivity' rose by less than 10 per cent. While the prices of materials and labour were constantly rising, the BTC was delayed for nearly a year by the deliberations of the Transport Tribunal before it was able to raise fares and charges in 1952 and even so was not allowed to match charges with costs.

At Nationalisation on 1 January 1948, British Railways took over 19,639 route miles of railway (52,253 track miles), 20,148 locomotives (83.8 per cent of the number in stock at Grouping in 1923), all but 110 being steam. It had also 411 steam locomotives loaned from the Ministry of Supply—and soon to be taken into BR stock, 2,049 rail-motor vehicles (all electric except for three steam and four diesel railcars), 40,257 passenger vehicles and 1,223,700 freight wagons. Between 1948 and 1952 the BTC was provided with funds sufficient just to relay 9,475 miles of track (1,895 miles per year), and up to 1953 to build a mere 2,060 new locomotives, 9,900 coaches and 209,300 wagons. Otherwise, superannuated rolling-stock had to be repaired and put back in service. Corrected to 1948 prices, capital expenditure on the railways was held to £30–£42.5 million per year (£5.0–10.0 million on ways and structures) until 1952, although it then rose gradually to £98 million (£40 million on ways and structures) by 1959 as the Modernisation Plan got under way.

The effects of the shortages of materials and funds was only too obvious in the shabbiness of the stations and the sloth of the trains. Growing staff shortages in the early days of Nationalisation were filled by imported—and later by immigrant—labour, until gradually mechanisation and modernisation of operations such as permanent way work—and eventually acceptance by the Unions of radically lower staffing levels, allowed substantial reductions in the labour force.

A train out of Edinburgh Waverley, possibly bound for Dunfermline or Kirkcaldy, is headed by Robinson/Gresley D11/2 4-4-0 No. 62677 *Edie Ochiltree* on 13 August 1948—the day after the ECML became blocked due to torrential rain. *Picture: B. W. L. Brooksbank*

When in 1952 investment on the railways was only £40 million per year (just £11.6 million on ways and structures), investment on road transport by contrast was already over £300 million per year (£100 million on private cars). Even in 1959, when the railway Modernisation Plan was well underway railway investment had risen only to a paltry £168 million (£62 million on ways and structures), while investment on road transport had risen to nearly £800 million of which £420 million was on private cars—and the motorway-building programme was only just beginning.

At the same time, the wide adoption of paid holidays as the norm after the war, the reduction in the working week with the gradual abandonment of Saturday morning working—and of shift working except in a few industries, led to an increase in leisure time. A growth in real personal wealth and in the proportion of *per capita* income spent on travel combined with other social factors to maintain constant the aggregate of passenger miles by rail, namely 21,000 million in 1948 and 22,300 million in 1959 and varying by less than 10 per cent in the interim. This was so even though the proportion of all their travel expenditure that consumers spent on all public transport fell from 67.7 per cent in 1950 to 35.95 per cent in 1960.

The transport revolution of the 1950s and its consequences for British Railways
Although in the 1953 Act many of the old restraints on railway charging were removed, the BTC still had to settle their maximum rates through a 'Quango', the Transport Tribunal. In the event the very prolonged process was extended for a further year by ministerial intervention. The Conservative minister (Harold Watkinson) introduced in 1956 'deficit financing' by allowing substantial—but temporary—borrowing by the BTC to cover its losses, in exchange for the agreement by the Commission as an 'anti- inflationary measure' to postpone increases in charges already sanctioned, even though this ran counter to the Commission's obligation to make a profit. At the same time the Government allowed the price of coal to rise at double the rate of inflation between 1956 and 1962. Therefore both bureaucracy and politics hampered the BTC's attempts to match charges with costs, and they were still obliged to maintain un-remunerative services without Government subsidy. Repeated delays in the process of increasing charges after the concession of wage claims were believed to account in large measure for BR's deficits up to 1955. The delays were such that it was not until July 1957 that a new charges scheme came into operation and the railways were free at last to charge rates that could attract the type of traffic they were best able to carry and discourage what they could not. Maximum charges were then still fixed, but at least they no longer had to be published. Meanwhile, rail freight ton-mileage fell between 1951–53 and 1960–61 by a quarter—most of the fall being after 1955. The market share fell from 45 per cent to 29 per cent, although the volume of freight carried remained above pre-war levels until 1962. Even the railways' traditional bulk traffics in coal and minerals were drifting away to the roads. Large privately-owned lorries were allowed on the roads after the 1953 Transport Act, and anyway licensing regulations and road traffic laws were flagrantly breached, and the shift to road accelerated when the many emergency arrangements for road haulage made during the Rail Strike of 1955 became permanent.

Within the limitations of their scarcity of funds, the Commission and the Executive did try to take steps in the early years of BR to improve the profitability of the railway freight sector. Emphasis was placed on using more containers to get round the inherent advantage of the lorry in providing door-to-door transit; on building wagons with automatic brakes and running more braked freight trains at higher speeds and with minimal intermediate marshalling; on constructing wagons of 21—24.5-ton capacity for coal and minerals—depending however on facilities for their handling being provided at collieries, power stations etc.; on providing special wagons for powders and liquids; and on rationalising domestic coal distribution by building coal concentration depots.[29] Really substantial progress in freight movement had to wait until the 1960s with the advent of diesel (or electric) haulage, as well as a consistent policy on the vacuum versus air-brake systems, by which time it was too late to recover much traffic lost to the roads.

Ordinary fares in October 1947 were 1.02p/mile third class (0.68p/mile monthly return) but were reduced to 0.73p/mile when monthly returns were abolished in 1952, rising to 0.78p/mile in June 1955. In 1959 ordinary fares were set at 0.83–0.94p/mile (depending on distance), an increase of only 34–38 per cent since January 1948. These rates were lower than in 1947, although there were now no monthly returns—only day returns; in real terms passenger fares were half what they had been in 1938. However, while average rail fares had gone up by 130 per cent since 1938, average bus fares went up by only 64 per cent. Meanwhile, railway costs had risen much faster than their changes: it was calculated that whereas in 1949 passenger traffic contributed £30 million to track and other 'indirect' costs, by 1958 it contributed nothing to them.

Freight rates, in 1947 some 55 per cent above pre-war, were raised subsequently in several stages so that by 1959 they were 144 per cent above pre-war—roughly the same degree as average passenger fares. On the other hand, the consumer price index was by then 171 per cent above the figure for 1938. In Western Europe rail freight rates were generally much higher than in Britain, and more realistically set. It was calculated that at the end of the 1950s for £1 the railways of Britain produced an average of 60 ton-miles, but public road hauliers attained only 37 ton-miles. (The productivity of 'C' licence vehicles was about half that). Although the advantage of the railways

View northward to Welwyn South tunnel at Welwyn North station on 2 June 1951. A Class H freight is headed by ex-WD 2-8-0 No. 90287. *Picture: B. W. L. Brooksbank*

was to some extent due to the large tonnage of coal and minerals they conveyed at relatively low rates, it was evident that firms—and, even more, private individuals, were prepared to pay a lot more for road transport because of its 'other advantages'.

The railways made a working surplus until 1955, but central charges were so high that the BTC suffered a deficit as a whole in every year after Nationalisation except in 1951–53, and even this disappeared if the hidden subsidy of the wartime Arrears of Maintenance Fund was not counted as 'revenue'. The deficit reached the £100 million mark by the end of the 1950s—and was to rise still further, partly because of the interest charges on the further borrowing necessary. The trend for rail charges to lag behind costs continued into the early 1960s to represent a substantial decrease in real terms compared to pre-war, and the BR deficit widened further. From 1958 onwards BR lost money in both passenger and freight sectors even with respect to direct costs; only the parcels sector made a profit. The average wagon-load of merchandise was merely a little over four tons, and even though two-thirds of the merchandise was still being loaded at private sidings, it is not hard to see the cost advantage of a lorry load of 10 tons—with probably little empty mileage. It was estimated that 30 per cent of railway freight costs related to provision and repair of wagons and another 39 per cent to marshalling *en route* and shunting and haulage at the terminal. These costs of railway merchandise traffic were being carried on the back of the much more profitable coal and minerals traffic, but with industrial recession in 1958 and a decline in heavy industry thereafter profits in these other sectors could no longer cover losses on merchandise traffic.

The outstanding problems that BR was suffering in the post-war period concerned labour costs. There was a chronic shortage of adequately skilled labour, because of the expectations aroused by the 'Welfare State', together with the rather high wages and generally better working conditions in private industry. As the result of a number of wage increases that had been granted, wage costs had become—for BR and for all industries, a relatively greater proportion of total costs. Under strong railway unions, labour costs had risen inexorably, while over-manning continued to be rife. By the end of 1959, average earnings for railway work were 77 per cent above even those in 1948, whereas retail prices had risen by only 51 per cent. The total railway labour force in 1954 had fallen by only 8 per cent (to 577,000) and was to decline only to 519,000 by January 1960, still 80 per cent of the total in 1948, yet 'productivity' was estimated to have risen by only 17 per cent. Along with the many other failures of the state-owned monolith to improve efficiency, such as by bringing in diesel multiple units on branches or abolishing manual signalling and manned level crossings, the overstaffing and antiquated work practices were fundamental causes of BR's afflictions.

The 1955 Modernisation Plan and its reappraisal: the decline of British Railways in the later 1950s

The British Transport Commission (BTC), bereft from 1953 of the Railway Executive—and taking over and expanding its premises at 222 Marylebone Road in London, was reconstituted as an interim organisation in 1953, before being reorganised in January 1955 to take on more directly the responsibility for the railways. In practice this work was undertaken for the next year or so by several committees. The new BTC, headed by General Sir Brian Robertson, was an elaborate set-up of military style under a 'General Staff', and in effect a substantial bureaucratic enlargement—under a Conservative Government—swelling the BTC's administrative costs by more than was saved later by branch line closures. The reorganisation and decentralisation of the control of BR resulting from the 1953 Act further delayed the preparation of plans for modernisation, which had already been put off for far too long for the reasons alluded to above. The attitude of

A quite dirty A4, No. 60008 *Dwight D. Eisenhower* allocated to King's Cross, travels past Hitchin Yard signal box with an express, which is perhaps the early morning up West Riding Limited, on 2 November 1957. *Picture: B. W. L. Brooksbank*

Government—and the people—can be contrasted with that on the European Continent, where the post-war governments, traditionally more directly involved with their railways than was the case in Britain, placed a much higher priority on the restoration of their war-ravaged railways than on the motor vehicle and the roads.

The BTC's stated objective in the Modernisation Plan was 'to exploit the great natural advantages of railways as bulk transporters of passengers and goods and to revolutionise the character of the services provided for both, not only by the full utilisation of modern equipment but also by purposeful concentration on those functions which the railways can be made to perform more efficiently than other forms of transport.' The plan was costed at £1,240 million (soon raised to £1,660 million) over 15 years. However, this was still a small investment compared with the £600 million a year already being spent on roads in Britain, or with the £200 million per year being spent by the Federal railways (of comparable extent) in West Germany. More especially, the true value of this apparently large Government handout for modernisation was much less than it seemed because half the sum would have had to be spent anyway just to cover arrears of maintenance and keep the railways going. The costing of major modernisation of the railways, such as of electrification, was made on a different basis from that applied to the costing of motorway construction, in which the time saved by drivers and hauliers switching to the motorways was set against the costs.

Although earlier Conservative Ministers of Transport, under the influence of the powerful 'Road Lobby', had been pressing the BTC to close un-remunerative branch-lines, at this stage rationalisation by the closure of lines and stations was not a major objective as it was calculated to save no more than £3 million. The extent of the modernised railway system was still envisaged as essentially unchanged, and much greater savings were expected to be achieved from the new commercial freedom being negotiated. The planners imagined that the railways would break-even financially by 1961–62, but the forecasts they made in 1954 when drawing up the plan proved too optimistic; this was especially so in the freight sector, as we have seen. Shackles on charging policies were only relieved when the Area Boards were set up under the 1962 Transport Act with much more devolved executive authority. The Government did seem to feel more positive towards the railways than it had been earlier in the 1950s, and introduced consecutive Railway Finance Acts of 1957 and 1959 empowering the BTC to borrow £1,200 million for the plan and also up to £400 million to cover revenue deficits,—but in doing so burdened BR with even greater interest charges.

By 1958, annual deficits were growing, even though the widespread introduction of diesel multiple-units (DMUs) on secondary and branch-line services was radically cutting their operating costs (63 per cent on average) and usually much improving passenger revenue (34 per cent on average). It seems that a great opportunity was missed of attracting many more passengers because when the DMUs were belatedly brought in there was at first no radical increase in the frequency, speed or convenience to passengers of many of these services. In the late evenings, on Sundays and at other leisure times they remained abysmal, and people continued to find it more convenient—and ultimately essential—to use their private cars.

Other benefits of modernisation were slow to reveal themselves, and it seemed after all that BR could only be got 'out of the red' by cost-cutting. As a result the planned rates of scrapping of steam locomotives and of the introduction of main-line diesels were accelerated. Indeed, a

BR Class 9F 2-10-0 No. 92039 (built December 1954, withdrawn October 1965) is pictured on 16 March 1957 at the north end of Hitchin station with an Up Class F semi-fitted freight. *Picture: B. W. L. Brooksbank*

great deal of money was wasted by a too rapid acceptance of inadequately tested diesels of types that were unreliable, having been built mainly by relatively inexperienced private contractors. Besides, with its high initial cost and mechanical complexity, the true economic advantage of the main-line diesel over the equivalent modern steam locomotive was far from overwhelming. Electric motive power was the outstanding winner, but that was economically justifiable only on routes of high traffic density.

The paralysis caused by the two-week ASLEF strike in mid-1955 had accelerated the drift of freight to the roads—notably the traffic in essential perishables such as fish. The new charging system when it finally began to operate in mid-1957 seemed to have come too late to reverse the downward trends in freight revenue. Net ton-miles rail-borne in 1959 of 17,700 million were the lowest since the war in spite of significant reductions in charges (in real terms), and road vehicles were carrying as many ton-miles—and five times the tonnage—as were the railways.

The freight transport market became dominated by the costs of the firms carrying their own goods in 'C' licence vehicles, on roads for which the vehicle and fuel taxes they paid were orders of magnitude less than the cost of building and maintaining the roads to the standard needed for heavy lorries. This contention may be debateable because it depends upon the way these costs are calculated, but there is no doubt that the tax burden carried by the operation of heavy lorries is not commensurate with the damage they cause to the roads and motorways, let alone wider environmental harm.[30] In terms of such wider considerations the real cost of building new roads is probably double that ascribed at the time by the Ministry of Transport. Thus, it was impossible for BR to reduce its charges to compete, when it had to pay for its fixed assets, including track and signalling and ultimately for the land on which they were built—that together nonetheless made the railways infinitely safer than the roads. Apart from this, a blind eye was usually cast on constant flouting of speed limits on lorries, on their overloading and inadequate maintenance, and on excessive hours worked by their—often non-unionised—drivers.

In the later 1950s the loss of freight from the railways was also an inevitable result of the relative decline of coal-mining and of the iron and steel industries in Britain. The 1952 Clean Air Act had already caused the disappearance of much of the traffic in domestic and industrial coal, and the average length of haul of coal was diminishing as more and more large electricity-generating stations were being built near the principal coalfields. Conversely, recent industrial growth in Britain had been largely in the higher-value manufactured products—including motor cars, for which road transport was usually more appropriate. Meanwhile, the efficiency of rail freight transport was improving only marginally.

In reaction to the mounting and accelerating deficits of BR, together with doubts about the ability of the Modernisation Plan to restore its viability, a Parliamentary Select Committee on Nationalised Industries was examining the BTC and the fortunes of BR in depth (it reported in 1960), while in the meantime the new—and still Conservative—Government was also rather secretly examining the problem with its own Special Advisory Group (headed by Sir Ivan Stedeford). The outcome of the two studies was a lot more new legislation embodied in the 1962 Transport Act—introduced however by a Labour Government.

The Stedeford Committee went a long way towards identifying the sources of BR's losses. These were not yet, at that time, on the freight side, which was as a whole profitable, but on passenger operations—notably the stopping-trains although not particularly at that time the 'commuter' services. It was these parts of the passenger services that were candidates for subsidy. None was forthcoming, and instead in the light of the Modernisation Plan the Government wrote off some £500 million of the accumulated debt and another £700 million of the debt was 'suspended' until the railways should begin to make a profit again, while powers were given for grants of up to £450 million during the ensuing five years.

It has been argued by Henshaw and others that there was a conspiracy by the Ministry of Transport, to run down the railways deliberately. In that Ministry, under the all-powerful influence of the motor and oil industries and their satellites, along with the motorway construction interests, the careers of most senior civil servants depended on furthering road transport. The case made by Henshaw to interpret the crushing of railways in Britain by an all-pervading Roads Lobby with enormous political power is a compelling one, but it needs to be understood in the context of the desire of every man to have his private transport and of the deep influence of democratic forces in Britain. The idea of a conspiracy is based mainly on the thesis that branch lines could have been made profitable, by quite modest cost-cutting and an expenditure on modernisation of equipment that was miniscule compared with the cost of new roads. It is asserted that the BTC went out of its way to cut services until they were useless anyway and then distorted the statistics to make it appear that the lines were losing more money than they really were. In particular there was a deliberate disregard of the contributory revenue produced by the branch (and secondary) lines towards the viability of the system as a whole. Indeed, it is axiomatic that the profitability of a transport network must break down if its branches are severed. However, it seems that in many cases the losses on remote branch lines and at wayside stations would have persisted whichever way the calculations were made or whatever working economies were possible. The question of direct subsidy is another matter, but at least in the 1950s—if not after Marples and Beeching—the BTC and the Regions do not seem to have been whole-hearted in their apparent determination to cut services, and the Government was prepared to provide road bus services as an alternative— albeit this was not usually a viable one. (The first major closure, that of the M&GN Joint system in March 1959, had come about following a hardening of the attitude of the Government, under a new Minister of Transport (Harold Watkinson) already unsympathetic to the idea of any 'social obligation' of the railways).

What was perhaps more sinister was the failure of the Government to publish the Stedeford Report, and their focusing down on the financial problems of the country branch-lines—in which in terms of the overall deficits of the BTC were relatively minor; cynics would say that this was in order to force people to buy cars. In any case, the fundamental problem was the universal shift towards private transport, coupled with the political impossibility of making people pay, by adequately targeted taxation or by road pricing, the economic (and environmental) costs of their private transport. Besides these factors, there had been very great technological improvements in the performance, efficiency and comfort of road vehicles of all kinds, and concomitant reductions in the real costs of road transport. At the same time, while the cost to the BTC of diesel fuel was falling, relentlessly rising were the costs of coal—up 18 per cent between 1956 and 1960—of materials, and above all—especially after the Guillebaud Report on the Comparability of Railwaymen's Wages—of Labour.

Certainly under Marples a more aggressively commercial philosophy prevailed.[31] Marples radically cut the investment in railway modernisation, and he brought a 'new broom' in the person of Dr Richard Beeching to head the BR Board from January 1963, replacing the 'pro-rail' Sir Brian Robertson.[32] Beeching had been a member of the Stedeford Advisory Group, and his famous report, *The Reshaping of British Railways* was published in March 1963. Although strictly coming after the end of this chronicle, the findings deserve to be recalled in light of their revelation of the situation as it existed at the close of the 1950s, where BR's share of national passenger traffic (passenger miles) was still one-sixth and of freight (ton-miles) one third.

Above: Gresley V2 Class No. 60852 was erected at Darlington Works, as No. 4822, in March 1939 and was in service until September 1963. Apart from a few weeks spent at Copley Hill in early 1946, the engine was allocated to Doncaster. Here, No. 60852 works a Class C freight through Newark on 15 June 1957. *Picture: B. W. L. Brooksbank*

Below: Heaton-allocated Gresley A3 Class Pacific No. 60092 *Fairway* is with an unidentified train at Grantham station on 2 May 1955. *Picture: Bill Reed*

Just over seven miles north of Newark, Crow Park station (pictured here on 18 July 1956) was opened by the GNR on 1 November 1882. Services were withdrawn completely on 6 October 1958. *Picture: R. Stephenson/ B. W. L. Brooksbank Collection*

Beeching reported that total railway traffic in 1961 was losing marginally even on direct costs, with stopping-passenger services and wagon-load (and sundries) freight losing heavily. The small gains on operating fast and semi-fast passenger services, on parcels and mails, and on coal and minerals, were not bringing about a positive margin overall. Even the coal traffic—so suited to rail—was a lot less profitable than it should have been, mainly because terminal facilities were geared to the traditional 10—or 12- ton wagons.

The railway network had been shortened since 1951 by a mere 2,000 miles, and it was still nearly 17,500 route miles. Half of this mileage carried 4 per cent of the passenger- miles and 5 per cent of freight ton-miles. Sixty percent of the goods stations handled less than 100 tons per week and accounted for only 9 per cent of the tonnage. The average wagon load (including coal and minerals) was a mere 9.3 tons, and—unsurprisingly—half of the tonnage was carried less than 50 miles. There was evidently still much scope for further incursion of the lorry into the business, but that transfer of freight to road had already gone far was evidenced by the fact that most of the siding-to-siding traffic was being moved through only a small proportion of all the sidings available.

What Beeching achieved and the revolution brought about by the reshaping of British Railways is another tale, not to be recounted here. It is enough to remind people that in spite of rationalisation and modernisation, and in spite of direct Government grants for un-remunerative services after the 1968 Transport Act, BR's working surplus remained relentlessly negative. The real savings in costs achieved by the massive closures of the 1960s, which were only expected to save less than a third of BR's current deficit, were matched by a fall in revenues due in part to the closures themselves. This was because Beeching's criteria of profitability were set way above the levels that would be set by far less biased accountants today.

Great Ponton station pictured from the south end on 28 May 1956—16 months before closure. The station was a short distance north of Stoke Summit, which was the highest point on the ECML between London and York. *Picture: R. Stephenson/B. W. L. Brooksbank Collection.*

A very detailed analysis that Beeching made of most aspects of railway traffic and operations, mainly of data collected in April 1961, showed how grossly inefficient was the handling not only of freight sundries traffic but also of wagon-load traffic. The chief factors contributing to their unprofitability were fairly obvious: labour-intensive transhipment between rail and road delivery services at terminals, transhipment *en route* of sundries between wagons, wagon marshalling, and the slow transit speed of un-braked freight trains. As is well known, Beeching not only recommended the closure of most of the small loss-making services, stations and depots, but also the revivifying of railway freight traffic by the introduction of 'Liner Trains'. These would employ road–rail containers to avoid transhipment, and move rapidly between major centres in dedicated trains of continuously-braked wagons with minimal intermediate marshalling. But the Government of the day resolved instead on the building of a nationwide network of motorways, and the Liner Train idea never came to fruition to any substantial extent.

By the end of 1959, considerable strides had been made since January 1955 with modernisation. Long-welded track had been laid on 185 miles of main line, 630 miles had been re-signalled and 443 route-miles were now fitted with the automatic warning system (AWS). A total of 1,490 diesel locomotives (including 421 for main-line work) were in service and 4,386 steam locomotives had been displaced by these and by 3,192 DMU and 2,012 electric (EMU) vehicles brought into use; 4,231 new coaches had replaced 10,815 old ones. Nearly one-third of the wagon fleet now had power-brakes, but it had been decided to fit the less efficient vacuum-brake—at immense expense. Plans to fit mineral wagons with these brakes (and automatic couplers) were frustrated by inadequacy of handling facilities, as was the building of wagons of larger capacity. The embedded idea that wagon-load—let alone sundries—traffic by rail could be made profitable in the face of a heavily subsidised road transport industry was long in dying—beyond the period of this narrative. Therefore the great sums that were spent on new mechanised marshalling yards for this traffic were largely wasted.[33] Another scheme of the period that came too late, and indeed hardly got off the ground before it was abandoned—in favour of motorways, was the improvement of the Cambridge–Oxford–Reading–Redhill–Tonbridge ring as a freight route to bypass London.

A measure of the situation on BR as the 1950s drew to a close is afforded by the following facts. In 1958 the BTC's freight traffic receipts were £370 million while private ('C' licence) transport was spending over £1,000 million a year on moving their own goods by road. Passengers on BR and London Transport rail services were contributing £162 million while buses drew in £109 million, but private car owners were spending £1,100 million on their 4.5 million cars and 1.5 million motor-cycles. In 1958, BR was moving 19,400 million ton-miles of freight while 22,800 million were being moved on the roads. Public transport was conveying 70,700 million passenger-miles (25,000 million by rail), while private cars were carrying 50,000 million. Expenditure on new railway vehicles was £116 million in 1958, but private individuals spent £130 million on goods vehicles and £500 million on cars—and this does not include enormous costs incurred by firms on the purchase and maintenance of 'company cars'.

The brief history just recounted of British Railways during its first 12 years until the end of 1959 is intended to provide an overview of the circumstances under which the ECML had to be operated. Having previously been all part of the LNER, the ECML after Nationalisation came administratively into three separate Regions of the new BR and these differed somewhat in character. Nevertheless, for operating purposes it was natural to maintain the ECML much as it had been. Train services changed hardly at all for many years after Nationalisation, and the links between the Eastern Region and the rather small North Eastern Region were so close that the two Regions were merged into a single Eastern Region in January 1967.

3

Passenger services on the ECML in Summer 1939 and in the war and changes thereafter until the end of the 1950s

Summer 1939

The basic pattern of ECML express services was one of quite fast trains between King's Cross and Leeds, Bradford and other West Yorkshire destinations, Hull and the Yorkshire Coast resorts, Darlington and Newcastle, and on to Edinburgh, Glasgow, Perth, Dundee and Aberdeen. Subsidiary express services ran to Boston, Grimsby and Cleethorpes. The services to Glasgow, Perth and Aberdeen were in competition with those of the LMSR—which was quicker only to Glasgow. The West Yorkshire services were also quicker by a considerable margin than those of the LMSR from St Pancras, while the services to Newcastle and other East Coast destinations had no competition—other than from the embryonic Air services. The principal expresses down the ECML and to intermediate destinations on it were therefore providing an essential service for travellers from London and the south-east to parts of England where some 15–20 per cent of the population lived and at least a third of the population of Scotland. At York the ECML tapped almost all the traffic to the north-east and about half of that to Scotland from most of the rest of England and from much of Wales.

Passenger services provided by the LNER along the ECML in the last months of peace before the outbreak of the Second World War in September 1939 were comparable with those run by the LMSR on its corresponding trunk routes. Secondary and branch services that fed the ECML were also analogous and they were typical of the era, one during which competition from the motor bus and to a certain extent the motor car in country districts was already serious. Branch services were being rendered unprofitable to the extent that such substantial cuts in services had been made in the 1930s, in comparison with their standard prior to the First World War that their inadequacy was driving away custom and a vicious circle was being set up.

Road competition in the 1930s was hardly yet serious as far as long distance expresses were concerned. These remained profitable, and on the ECML as elsewhere they were arranged in the first place for the business community and received widespread support from it. No businessman or official expected to be able to travel up to London for a day's appointments and get back home the same day from more than about 100 miles, or for a day's meetings from about 200 miles from the capital. This meant that sleeping car services from more than about 200 miles, for example Newcastle at 269 miles, were very popular for these purposes. Although luxury trains were provided in the form of the 'Yorkshire Pullman' and the 'Queen of Scots Pullman', there was a market for high speed daytime services. Indeed by the mid-1930s travel by Air,[1] albeit unreliable and expensive, was becoming a genuine alternative for the Newcastle or Edinburgh business 'executive'. It is said that the 'Flying Hamburger' in Germany spurred Gresley and the LNER to introduce the 'Silver Jubilee', and later the 'Coronation' and 'West Riding Limited' high-speed trains—the Streamliners.

A4 Pacific No. 4489 *Dominion of Canada* has sped through Rossington station while on a preliminary run with the 'Coronation' set in mid-1937. *Picture: Yorkshire Post*

As matters turned out, while the early evening Down 'Silver Jubilee' was a great success, the Up train was less so, the departure times of none of the three high-speed trains in the Up direction really being enough in the morning to allow much time in London for business; anyway the Up 'Coronation' left Edinburgh at 16.30. Their operation over a line with largely nineteenth-century signalling was a problem: they could not come to a halt in one block section, and so two sections had be kept clear ahead, *i.e.* double-block working.

The schedules of the ECML expresses in the late 1930s, even apart from those of the high-speed trains, were far from leisurely. The LNER had 23 daily runs, totalling 2,896 miles, timed at 60 mph or over in summer 1939. This was very much the same total as attained by the GWR, and although less than the total of the (larger) LMS, their fastest run was 65 mph, whereas the LNER had six runs at over 67 mph, and three at over 70 mph. Loadings were normally at least 14 coaches (or about 450 tare tons), and the policy was not to resort to piloting other than in emergencies except to a limited extent in the NE and Scottish Areas—albeit on a route with no really severe gradients. Heavy trains—and important ones such as the 'Flying Scotsman'—were regularly piloted in the Up direction from Edinburgh, because of Cockburnspath Bank.

In 1939 the principal motive power for the express services on the ECML was provided by the 100 or so Gresley Pacifics (Classes A1, A3 and A4). The Class C1 Ivatt Large Atlantics were still playing some part at the southern end, while the Raven Class C7 Atlantics and the Gresley D49 4-4-0s were employed to a limited extent along the northern part. The new Gresley Class V2 2-6-2s were also beginning to share in this work, presaging their comprehensive use alongside the Pacifics during and after the war. Suffice it to say that in the late 1930s the express passenger locomotives on the ECML were as capable—in some ways unequalled—in the handling of the quite exacting schedules and loads as were the equivalent modern locomotives of the other three Groups.

What is immediately striking to the present day observer is not only the comparative snail's pace of the express trains in steam days, but also their relative infrequence. This was only partly compensated by the existence of many branch-line services, which are no longer available. On the other hand, compared to recent times, the number and variety of summer Saturday extras and through workings were much greater. Conversely, the Sunday services were memorable for their sparseness and slowness on the main line, and their absence from many of the branches. This was a reflection of the quasi-religious proscription of Sunday work or travel in the Victorian era, leading later to the Trade Unions negotiating higher pay for Sunday work

In 1939 there were still a large number of branch services feeding to the ECML—many in a terminal stage of dissolution. Several of these were withdrawn at the beginning of the war—to be quickly reinstated in most cases, but some for the duration and two permanently, 15 were taken off in the first ten years afterwards. Likewise in 1939 there were still exiguous services of slow trains calling at the many wayside stations on the ECML itself, the survival of many of which after the war was brief.

However, we are not setting out to compare the ECML of steam days with the electrified route of later years, but rather to recollect the facilities for rail travel in the late 1930s and to compare the railway scene then with that in the war and in the early post-war years.

The 1939 train schedule lists seem remarkable today in some other ways. There was the variety of different destinations served, by dividing and combining sets of coaches *en route*. From King's Cross some 'unusual' destinations, such as Cromer and Horncastle (and on Sundays, Gainsborough), were served, and—by sleeping car only—Nairn, Lossiemouth and North Berwick. Indeed a feature of the main line services down the ECML from King's Cross was the number of destinations reached by the portions of any one train—amounting to three or even more, most often separated at Doncaster but also at Wakefield Westgate, York, Edinburgh and elsewhere. Then there were some strange and most complex cross-country through services. Perhaps the most remarkable of these was the so-called 'Aberdeen–Penzance' service. At 24 hours this was by far the longest regular service in Britain—but it was only available from Aberdeen in the southbound direction, as was the sleeping car attached from Swindon on to Penzance. In the northbound direction the train ran from St Erith to Glasgow—and no sleeping car. Still, the LNER was running on it one of its novel new buffet/restaurant cars each way between Newcastle and Swindon, returning next day from Swindon to York. So, some crazy passenger had the chance of making in the same seat such unlikely journeys as from Laurencekirk to Marazion, or from Lostwithiel to Polmont.

Another strange pre-war service on the ECML was the Swansea (High Street)–Newcastle restaurant car express from the GWR to the LNER, in that it ran from Gloucester *via* Cheltenham South, Andoversford and Chipping Norton to Banbury—even conveying a restaurant car over this Cotswold backwater, part of which was closed as long ago as 1951. Thus one could travel in the same coach from Bourton- on-the Water to (say) Northallerton—and back. Even odder were the through coaches from Southampton (Terminus for Docks) to Glasgow (Queen Street)—also Scarborough on Saturdays only. These started out on a stopping train up the bucolic Didcot, Newbury & Southampton line, so it was possible for someone to climb into a carriage at Churn in the remote and isolated Berkshire Downs and not get out until he reached Lenzie Junction—for example. But the return journey could not be undertaken without a large number of changes, including crossing London, and anyway the southbound through coaches from Glasgow terminated at Basingstoke and conveyed Southampton passengers only if they were catching a Cross-Channel boat. In any case, anybody misguided enough to try to travel from Glasgow to Southampton by this service would be subjected to a wait in the train of nearly an hour at York on the way; it was quicker to go *via* London.

The through services using the ECML in parts on summer Saturdays embraced a further extensive variety of through coaches and routes. Many of these extra trains were third class only and had no restaurant (or refreshment) car, particularly after the war.

There were regular publicised Boat Trains on the ECML, notably the expresses from King's Cross to Newcastle Tyne Commission Quay—the 'Norseman'. These trains ran in connection with the steamship services of the B & N Line to Stavanger and Bergen, those of the Fred Olsen Line to Oslo and of Swedish Lloyd to Gothenburg. The several continental services from Hull on the other hand were provided with Boat Trains as needed, rather as the SR serviced the Channel crossings. (Parenthetically, it should be recalled that in summer 1939 a journey could be made from London to Newcastle, Dundee or Aberdeen by perhaps a more relaxing mode even than the ECML—on regular twice-weekly services by sea).

Travellers could also, for £20, go for a week on the 'Land-Cruise' train, the 'Northern Belle'. This first class only luxury train offered trips in June (two in 1939) from King's Cross to the North of England and Scotland. Customers lived on the train, with the best shower-bath sleepers, hairdressing saloon and even a 'wardrobe van', and of course the choicest food and wine. The varied itinerary included daytime coach and steamer trips, as well as covering such lines as the West Highland to Mallaig. (For the 'mountainous' stretches the train was divided into two parts, on account of the weight of the sleeping cars). For humbler folk, there were the camping coaches, located at wayside stations near the sea or in the Dales; some of these were moveable and set off from York on a week's tour of beauty spots. The LNER even offered 'self-catering apartments' in closed stations, e.g. Castle Howard, Akeld and Kirknewton.

The regular express services on the ECML were supplemented in peacetime by a host of special trains for public use, the timings of which were not given in the normal timetables but were provided in handbills and on posters. In addition to these—mostly run on summer Saturdays only, the railways ran a large number of relief trains at times of heavy traffic—especially at Christmas and Easter—for passengers paying standard fares, as extra parts of regular trains to usual destinations. A few were regular from the operating point of view—designated 'Q' for 'when required' in the Working Timetables (WTT). The majority of reliefs were arranged at relatively short notice, and their details were set out only in Special Traffic Notices (STNs) provided for the staff.

Another category of (public) special trains were the excursions, for passengers to be conveyed at greatly reduced fares, singly or as parties, the last often in chartered whole trains. The excursions could be period, day, half-day or evening excursions, or there were also overnight trains at cheap fares, such as the specials from London to Newcastle and Scotland. The excursion trains comprised firstly quite regular trains, often on Sundays, to major 'normal' destinations, but also to seaside resorts. Many more of these trains were scheduled in 1939 than after the war. The most numerous excursion trains were those that ran—again especially on Sundays—to seaside resorts, beauty spots, or to popular venues like Belle Vue Zoo at Manchester. The takings on these depended very much on the weather, but the NE Region of BR—with public spirit—displayed the weather forecast on blackboards at stations such as York and Newcastle. Then, there were the numerous excursions run to take the crowds to major events: to soccer and rugby football matches culminating in the Cup Finals in London; to horse-race meetings—Newmarket, Doncaster, York, Thirsk, Catterick, Sedgefield, Stockton, Gosforth Park (Newcastle), producing much traffic of this kind for the ECML. Finally, there were special trains, often chartered, for a variety of other events and occasions, from the eclipse of the sun to the Coronation. Lastly, 1939 even before the war broke out, the railways were called upon to provide a number of military specials; naturally, these were not advertised at all.

Many of the excursions and other special trains ran from unfamiliar stations—even in some cases originating at places such as collieries or factories where there was no normal passenger station. There were a great number of combinations of routes taken by special traffic on the railway network, many of which were followed throughout the year by freight trains. Their use served to widen the experience of train crews, and came to be especially useful in the war, when strange routes and destinations naturally figured very much in the case of military specials. In regard to the ECML, the various routes to Scarborough serve to exemplify the complexities. From the north, trains could either run from Pilmoor *via* Gilling (with double reversal at Malton), or *via* York (with one reversal). From the west the usual route was *via* Leeds and York, but trains from places such as Blackpool or Burnley might come over the Pennines to Skipton and reach York *via* Ilkley and Harrogate. From the south, apart from taking the direct route from York *via* Malton, many trains ran *via* Bridlington, following the routes of trains that terminated there. They came principally through Selby, Selby in turn being reached from Doncaster or from Gascoigne Wood Junction on the line from Leeds. Trains from the Sheffield direction reached Gascoigne Wood Junction by the loop off the Swinton & Knottingley Joint line at Milford Junction—and the S&K led at Dearne Junction from the GC system, either from the west *via* Wath or from the south *via* Mexborough; again, at Burton Salmon on the S&K, trains came from West Yorkshire *via* Lofthouse and Castleford or off the L&Y *via* Wakefield and Normanton.

Even when recognising that before the war only a small minority had their own cars, the regular passenger services provided by the railway companies—here exemplified by the LNER's ECML, for either short—or long-distance, journeys seem very inadequate by the standards of mobility we have come to expect in recent decades. The long-distance trains may have been as comfortable as today at least—and of course infinitely safer than travelling by road, but how sparse were the services! On Sundays, the sole day when most people were free to travel any distance, they were quite insufficient. In the 1950s they were scarcely any different, British Railways signally failing to confront the advance of private transport by providing services—even on the electrified lines of the south-east, that would encourage people to use the train for their leisure-time needs; rather, they give up and withdrew most of such services. Seen the other way round, the cessation on most lines of local services after about 9.00 in the evening—even on Saturdays, and their total absence on Sundays, reflects the way of life of the working man and his family which existed in the 1930s and still to a great extent prevailed in the 1950s. Perhaps it was the eventual ready availability of the private car, then of free motorways, which so radically altered that way of life.

If we take Doncaster as an example on the ECML of a major working man's town, the last stopping trains—alike in 1939 and 1955—on any of the six lines radiating from the station left well before the pubs or the cinemas closed—even on Saturdays; it was much the same at York, Darlington, Newcastle or Edinburgh. We know that bus services were very little better, and the conclusion once again is that people were much less mobile than they are today. Fundamentally, they could not afford much more mobility in those days, and they had to stay at home—before the war without even television, or go to the local pub or cinema.

The Second World War

The August 1939 timetable was adhered to until 10 September. Thus a final summer Saturday service remained on 2 and 9 September—for holiday-makers and others to get home, except that many trains from London and other large cities were cancelled during the period 1 to 4 September for the Evacuation trains. A major feature of the timetable plans for the outbreak of the war, affecting the ECML as much as any other line, was the programme of evacuation of children from

London and other major industrial cities, planned many months in advance. It was put into effect on 1 September and completed during the ensuing three days, very extensive cancellation even of freight services being required to furnish the crews and locomotives needed. (The REC must also be admired for the detailed and quite explicit plans and instructions that they drew up, from May 1940, for the action to be taken by railway staff, including immobilisation of locomotives, demolitions and the evacuation of non-essential civilians—'In the Event of a German Invasion'.

From London a staggering 1,577 Evacuation specials were run, of which about 120 ran down the ECML, albeit mainly for relatively short distances—no further than Peterborough and Spalding. Because it was feared that main-line termini might be bombed, a lot of the children were entrained at suburban stations (Bowes Park or New Barnet for the ECML), to which they were taken by bus from the nearest Tube station. In addition, in the first ten days of the war a similar number of LNER special trains took evacuees from Tyneside, Sunderland and Tees-side—again mainly not for any distance along the ECML, also from Leeds and Hull. Overall the ECML was heavily involved in these great operations.[2] In July 1940, when a German invasion seemed imminent, and again in 1941, the evacuation of children was actually put into effect from the north-east industrial area and from certain coastal towns in East Anglia and Kent. Later, in July–August 1944 during the V-1 offensive, 1,400 officially sponsored special trains were run from London to evacuate children and also hospital patients, while many more special trains were put on during this period by the District officers, to carry away the large numbers of 'self-evacuees'—people who on their own wanted to get away from the Flying Bomb menace; and a certain number of these evacuation trains ran down the ECML. Special trains were run on Sundays for relatives to visit the evacuees, travelling at concessionary fares, but nearly all the evacuees had drifted back to the big cities by the end of the war, and for their return only a mere 115 trains were needed for the whole of London.

In the emergency timetables first brought into operation on 11 September 1939, the services on the ECML and the other main lines all over the country were savagely cut by half and decelerated. The train frequencies approximated to those of a Sunday service—and at an average speed of 45 mph. Indeed in the ECML emergency timetable of 2 October the Sunday service was now for once the same as on weekdays—an excellent principle that was normal practice on the Continent but has never prevailed in Britain. Just one day and one night train were provided to Edinburgh (9 hours 45 minutes), two day and two night trains to Newcastle, one day train to Leeds and York (combined to Doncaster), and one overnight train to Aberdeen (14 hours).

All reduced-fare facilities were withdrawn at first, as were seat reservations and restaurant cars—and ECML 'expresses' reverted briefly to the practice of mid- Victorian times of making stops of about 20 minutes at Peterborough or Grantham for people to rush out and get some food.[3] Peacetime through services to coastal resorts were almost completely eliminated, and these remained served only by a residuum of connecting trains. Swingeing reductions were also made in local and branch line services. The dire air raids, gas attacks and the rest that were expected did not happen. It was realised almost immediately that the cuts had been rather overdone, and as early as 16 October on the LNER many trains and restaurant cars were reinstated, while the limit for average speeds was set at a more acceptable 50 mph. On 14 December a more adequate train service in terms of both frequency and speed was re-introduced. However, sleeping car accommodation was severely restricted and from 1942 drastic cuts were again made in provision of restaurant cars.

With the introduction of the great programme of 'convoy' coal trains on the ECML in February 1940, severe cuts in express services had to be made again. Then, for much of the war, services on the ECML settled to the following pattern. On Mondays to Saturdays (and including overnight trains) there were seven services to the West Riding, one to Hull, one to Cleethorpes, nine to

View southward from the level-crossing at Ranskill station on 27 May 1956. The addition of the ROF (Explosives) factory in the war necessitated the provision of the shelter for workers on the right. *Picture: R. Stephenson/ B. W. L. Brooksbank*

Newcastle, five to Edinburgh, and one to Aberdeen. Many of the trains made more intermediate stops than in peacetime, and there were fewer through coaches. In the NE Area, this sparse service of main-line expresses was supplemented only by a morning service from Darlington to Edinburgh, one each from York to Glasgow (Queen Street) and to Edinburgh, and also expresses from Leeds to Newcastle *via* York, from York to Newcastle (two), and from Liverpool to Newcastle *via* Leeds, Harrogate and Ripon. In summer of 1943 and after representations to the REC from C. H. Newton, some improvements of passenger services were allowed for a while, with the re-introduction of a midday service each way between King's Cross and Edinburgh, and of relief night trains on the route. This was possible after completion of the widening of the line between York and Thirsk, while less block coal traffic was being run on the ECML after partial revival of North Sea coastal shipping. Also the drafting in of many WD and USA locomotives eased matters.

In mid-1944 services were cut again. The scant remaining restaurant cars were taken off, to release stock, crew and paths for the huge extra burden of military traffic associated with *Overlord*, the Allied invasion of Europe. Between 22 May and 31 July 1944, the period of this 'stand to' programme, from King's Cross there was only one through Leeds/Bradford train (passengers otherwise had to change at Doncaster), two to Newcastle and three to Edinburgh.[4] The worst of the cuts were restored by October 1944, and then the services were improved gradually as the war in Europe came to an end. Thus the new timetable in June 1945, after VE-Day on 8 May, showed a tentative beginning of a revival from the stringencies of the war.

Wartime on the ECML saw the birth in 1940–41 of four new regular cross-country services, primarily for the benefit of servicemen on leave. Three ran from Colchester, to York, to Leeds and to Edinburgh (overnight); the York train ran *via* the GN&GE Joint, the other two *via* Peterborough. The fourth train was the celebrated 'Ashford Belle', introduced in September 1940—but until December 1940 only for servicemen, and publicly advertised very soon after. Envisaged as a means for soldiers on leave from their camps in the south-east to avoid trekking through Blitz-torn London, the train followed routes also intensively used by wartime special trains, including the former GC main line. It took a nominal 12 hours—up to two hours more during the Blitz—with two reversals and four changes of locomotives, to reach Newcastle from Ashford (Kent) *via* Redhill, Reading, Banbury, Sheffield and York. Sometimes it was found necessary to run reliefs from North Camp northwards, but the 'Ashford Belle' was withdrawn in the May 1944 cuts. It was replaced in September 1944 by a train—not in the public timetable but freely available—from Southampton to Newcastle by the same route (from Reading West Junction). Coaching stock was provided by both the LNER and SR, and there was a buffet car—with NAAFI prices,[5] also a travelling RTO.[6]

The contrast in wartime with the frequency and speed of trains in peacetime on the ECML was stark, and looking back it seems incredible that on the whole—but not quite always—this meagre service sufficed, carrying as it did quite as many passengers as in peacetime. The decelerations are exemplified by the almost nine hours the 'Flying Scotsman' took during the war to reach Edinburgh from London, or the best time of nearly six hours of an express to Newcastle. To allow more passengers to be conveyed, the restaurant car facilities were radically reduced, especially after May 1942 when also sleeping car bookings were controlled in order to ensure that priority was given to people on urgent Government business.

Local services for getting people to and from work had to be maintained much as in peacetime. They were even greatly increased where workers needed to be conveyed to and from war factories, notably the 44 Royal Ordnance Factories (ROF) that worked round the clock in three shifts and seven days in the week, and for some of which special new lines and stations were built. The ROFs had to be served by fleets of trains to convey thousands of workers from large centres of population often some distance away. Relatively few ROFs were in the eastern part of the country, but the ECML was concerned directly with the Engineering ROF at Birtley in Co. Durham and the Explosives ROF at Ranskill in Nottinghamshire, slightly indirectly with the Filling ROFs at Thorp Arch and at Aycliffe and the Engineering ROFs at Spennymoor and at Maltby, not to mention with a number of other large wartime Depots.[7] At Thorp Arch, opened in May 1941 and where 18,000 people were employed, a ring line with stations at Walton, Roman Road, Ranges, and River was built off the Church Fenton–Wetherby line. The normal services on the lines through Harrogate and on the Leeds–Hull line through Selby were radically cut in 1942, partly to make more paths available for ECML freight bypassing York, but also partly to allow enough trains to serve Thorp Arch ROF, some of which also came from York. (Thorp Arch ROF resumed production early in the 1950s, so some of the munitions workers' trains continued to run until the end of 1958). For Aycliffe ROF, stations were built at Simpasture and Demon's Bridge on the Shildon–Tees-side line. Thus some of the 25 or so trains daily to Aycliffe ROF impinged on the ECML at Ferryhill—and the public service between Spennymoor and Bishop Auckland was withdrawn permanently from December 1939 and that between Ferryhill and Leamside in July 1941. A big aircraft factory (used for breaking up damaged aircraft) was built beside the Darlington–Eaglescliffe line at Urlay Nook, where a new halt was constructed to serve it. Ranskill ROF, built just to the east of the ECML south of the station, was served by a number of trains from the Leeds direction through Doncaster, some of which picked up workers at Bentley (a stop not on the public timetable), from Gainsborough *via* Retford and from Mansfield *via* Tuxford. Down south, the vital De Havilland Aircraft factory acquired its own (unadvertised) halt, at Lemsford Road on the Hatfield–St Albans branch.

Cuts in local services were made mainly at off peak times, especially late in the evening. In the London area, services were radically altered after April 1940, when the Northern Line 'Tube' extensions were opened, and after October 1940 when the through trains from Moorgate and from Broad Street ceased on account of Blitz damage.[8] On the Cambridge line virtually all trains now called at all stations. Certain services feeding to the ECML were suspended in September 1939 altogether, if for only two or three months: Moorgate–King's Cross, Broad Street-Finsbury Park, Hatfield—St Albans, Finchley Central—Edgware, Hertford North–Langley Junction (not restored until 1962).

In the first half of the war, relief trains were put on freely at weekends and other peak times. Indeed some trains such as the 'Flying Scotsman' had a relief almost daily—but they were mostly not advertised except on blackboards at the stations. For example, no less than 200 extras were run down the ECML from King's Cross over the Christmas 1939 period, and 37 trains were still run on Maundy Thursday in 1940. Some holiday trains were run that summer and camping coaches were still available, but there was no Bank Holiday in August 1940. By 1942 the demand for locomotives and crews of the inexorably burgeoning freight and military traffic forced the REC to impose severe controls and this kind of provision became out of the question even if a few relief trains were put on at the last minute at times of the heaviest pressure such as Christmas.

There was indeed grievous overcrowding, the ECML expresses being among the most severely affected. Statistics on tickets[9] issued and collected at particular stations show that passenger traffic fell off a little in 1939 compared to 1938—and no wonder when recalling those stringent cuts in services in September/October 1939 and the appalling delays before the speed restrictions were eased, but then it grew enormously. In the peak month of 1942 (August) passenger receipts nationwide were 23 per cent above those of August 1941, and at Easter 1943 the LNER reported that passengers from its London termini were 41 per cent above those at Easter 1942. The establishment of a standard RAF Bomber station was 2,500 persons, so it can be imagined how many RAF and USAAF personnel used the ECML trains on postings and leave, and how the resulting movement of countless thousands of airmen greatly added to the overcrowding of the ECML passenger trains. At Grantham, a fairly typical ECML station but with an inordinate number of airfields in the vicinity, passenger journeys increased by 55 per cent between 1941 and 1942 and by the peak year of 1945 were 158 per cent above the 1938 figure.

The withdrawal of cheap day fares in October 1942 probably led to some easing of the civilian pressure, and a redistribution of the stops made by the exiguous service of the ECML expresses relieved the overcrowding a little, but it was more than compensated by the persistent growth in numbers of Service passengers. Already by the middle of the war the majority of the passengers on long-distance trains—and 80 per cent of those travelling over 200 miles—had come to be servicemen, and this was so as much on the ECML as anywhere. For example, on the ordinary Friday of 23 January 1942, when five relief trains were put on from King's Cross down at least to Doncaster, 65–90 per cent of the passengers were servicemen. In fact, when from mid-April 1944 service leave was drastically curtailed until D-Day there was a decline compared with a year before of 22 per cent in LNER passenger receipts, but this lasted for only two to three months and then the numbers continued to increase well into 1945.

The feeding of the great numbers of servicemen making long rail journeys presented special difficulties, and in the winter of the Blitz the LNER ran one of its buffet cars exclusively for them on the 13.00 King's Cross–Edinburgh, staffed by the WVS,[10] but the experiment resulted in even worse blockage of corridors and was not perpetuated. Instead, at stations such as York, Darlington and Newcastle large semi-removable refreshment stalls were set up on the main platforms to supplement the station buffets and the small trolleys that were wheeled around. Apart from the extra refreshment facilities provided by the railway, the Salvation Army, WVS and other voluntary organisations built hostels for servicemen—where bed & breakfast cost just 7.5p:—at King's Cross, York (former Parcels depot) and Edinburgh Waverley stations, as well as 24-hour canteens there and at Grantham, [11] Retford,[12] Doncaster, Darlington, and Newcastle.

King's Cross, at least as much as any other main-line London terminus, was vital for essential (civilian and military) purposes in the war. Innumerable soldiers and sailors passed through, but on account of the large number of Bomber Command airfields served by the ECML, King's Cross also became poignantly for many air crew the last they ever saw of London before they flew to their death on missions over Europe. Countless thousands of airmen thronged Peterborough, Grantham and York stations.[13] Wayside stations handled unprecedented numbers of them, even expresses stopping at the little station of Heck for Snaith and Burn Airfields. Large numbers of US Army airmen also used the terminus, coming up to London from their bomber bases in the East Midlands and from some of those in East Anglia, and as well (during 1944) men of the IXth US Troop Carrier Command from their bases near Grantham and Newark.

Although many unadvertised reliefs were run at busy times, the LNER's chief response to the burgeoning passenger traffic was not so much to duplicate timetabled trains as to double their length, the result being trains of 20 or more coaches.[14] Such gargantuan trains were far too long for the platforms at King's Cross, where 14 coaches was the maximum capacity and so they had to be divided. Thus Down trains were loaded at two platforms, joined up and then drawn out through the tunnels up the 1-in-107, without a pilot and without more than a brief shove from the tank engine that had brought in the empty stock. Likewise, Up expresses coming into King's Cross—often already late and out of course, had to be divided by a pilot engine on arrival and placed in two platforms; in the process many impatient passengers in the rear half of the train would have climbed down on to the ballast. It was of course very difficult for these enormous trains to run to time, not least because they had to 'draw up' at most intermediate stops, often twice or even sometimes three times, but Gresley's magnificent big engines were usually proficient. On the other hand, failures were not infrequent, especially later in the war and in the first few years after it, because of maintenance issues and poor coal, and these failures caused havoc to the free flow of traffic—even occasionally to serious accidents.

The problem of 'time lost to locomotive' became progressively more serious, and from May 1943 a strict limit of 18 coaches was set for ECML expresses, by which time almost all restaurant cars were being used as seating vehicles. Despite schedules being extended, punctuality was abysmal. This was especially so when air raids began in 1940. From August 1940, the lateness of Down ECML expresses at Newcastle jumped from about 20 to 60 minutes late—or even in November 1940 to 90 minutes, with a similar degree of deterioration for all Up expresses into King's Cross. More specifically, in July 1940 the 'Flying Scotsman' was achieving on average almost a punctual arrival in Edinburgh, but this average fell to 45–55 minutes in September–October 1940, and continued to average about 20 minutes late even after the Blitz and for much of the rest of the war. The 17.25 King's Cross to Newcastle deteriorated from an average of about 15 minutes late at Newcastle to averages approaching two hours late in November 1940. In the Up direction, things were even worse and the 13.05 from Edinburgh (allowed nine hours) found itself arriving almost every night at King's Cross in an air raid; its average lateness plummeted from 10 minutes in August 1940 to three hours in some weeks of September and October. The problem in the autumn of 1940 was not so much air raid damage as such but the draconian speed restriction of 15 mph during an alert—even in daylight. Even when the speed restrictions during alerts were relaxed—and after the

Blitz alerts themselves became much less frequent, punctuality still left a great deal to be desired. The average lateness of principal expresses was about 20 minutes during the summer and fell to an hour or more in the winter. There were many reasons for this, but the basic problems were congestion (near overloading of line capacity), increasingly frequent locomotive breakdowns and poor steaming, and recurring traffic mishaps. Compounding these were the over-long, over-crowded trains—and the inordinate numbers of parcels to be handled—prolonging station times, and in winter the usual problems with fog and frozen points. All this bore very heavily on the overworked staff, and there was a greater prevalence of staff sickness—especially in late 1943.

The part played by the LNER—and its ECML—in conveying special military traffic was tremendous. In fact throughout the war the LNER was involved with no less than 127,000 trains on Government account, passenger (mainly troop) trains and freight trains each accounting for about half of this total. In 1944 alone it ran 41,500 (or 114 a day) of these specials; in the first six months of 1945 the figure was 20,000, falling to 14,000 in the second six months. If it is assumed that two-thirds of these LNER trains used the ECML in whole or in part, we have for the ECML all-war figures of about 42,000 passenger and 42,000 freight trains—an average of 19 trains a day in each category. Such an estimate corresponds with the number in 1944 (26 per day, of the two categories combined) reported to have run in the NE Area, because the great majority of these latter presumably ran on the ECML. As early as April 1940 many of the 202 train-loads of the Expeditionary Force to Norway which sailed from Leith or Glasgow must have passed along the ECML.[15] Then, in the great improvised operations, *Dynamo* and *Aerial*, for distributing the defeated armies brought back from France in June 1940, the LNER played a major part in bringing numerous train-loads of troops up to camps in the north, down the ECML at least from York. It provided 47 out of the total of 186 trains collected for the Dunkirk evacuation, in which a total of 572 train-loads were conveyed from south coast ports during the nine days of the Operation *Dynamo* and another 226 in Operation *Aerial*.

The great majority of the airfields of Bomber Command and many of other Commands of the RAF, subsequently of the Eighth and Ninth US Army Air Forces, were located in territory that constituted the 'catchment area' of the ECML and thus produced immense traffic to the line in personnel and in military supplies. Indeed, in June 1944, over 60 airfields of Bomber Command Nos. 1, 3, 4, 5, 6 and 8 Groups, plus seven of the USAAF 1st Bombardment Division, were more or less directly served off the ECML. In addition, airfields of the RAF and USAAF catering for fighter, troop-carrying, Army co-operation, coastal, maintenance etc. Groups accounted for half as many again of airfields providing traffic on the ECML. As well, there were a number of major Army establishments served by the ECML, such as the vast Army garrison complex at Catterick and in the wide spaces of Lincolnshire, Yorkshire (for the Tank Corps, especially in East Yorkshire), and Northumberland. From these camps tens of thousands of troops were conveyed to other parts of the country and to embarkation ports in the south and in Scotland.

For Operation *Torch*—the invasion of North-West Africa in November 1942, 440 troop specials and 680 special trains of supplies were needed. They ran mainly to Merseyside and Clyde ports—and about half from entraining areas connected with the ECML, between late October and early December 1942, most being run between 7 and 12 and between 21 and 26 November. For *Bolero* and then *Overlord*, the LNER was called upon to cope with an average of eight troop trains and four supplies trains per day from Scotland to the south and east of England throughout 1943 and much of 1944. As well as with the troops being brought in through Glasgow but also with those entering at Liverpool, the LNER assisted the LMSR to a considerable extent. Many of the US Forces that came in through the Clyde, and later through Hull or Immingham, were also carried on the ECML.

The assembly of the field force for *Overlord* began on 26 March 1944, and in five weeks 796 troop specials were run from the ports (mainly west coast),[16] and in April 1944 nearly 200 train-loads of troops were dispatched from Scotland alone to the south, and in the same period internal movements of British Army units[17] between Scottish and Northern Command and South-East Command required 241 special trains. Nearly half of these probably came by the ECML at least as far as York, although in the NE Area troop trains were often routed *via* Leamside, Ripon and Church Fenton. South of York a great many specials were routed up the former GC main line, reached either *via* Mexborough West Junction or *via* Tuxford, the latter junction in turn offering alternative routing including the ex-LD&EC line through Langwith Junction. Eastbound trains were brought from Liverpool over the Cheshire Lines system, joined at Hunts Cross West by means of the loop from the LMSR at Allerton Junction, then *via* Godley Junction on to the LNER proper (GC section). After going over Woodhead to Sheffield Victoria, these trains would either go northwards *via* York, or—more often—south up the GC main line, or *via* Retford on to the ECML; in some cases to the eastern counties *via* Nottingham Victoria and the Allington Junction–Barkston East Junction cut-off, Sleaford and Spalding (for the M&GN) and March, or *via* Peterborough East.

By the end of 1944, each day an average of 3,000 British servicemen alone were coming home on leave, and from 5 January 1945 a regular BLA (British Liberation Army) leave train—originating at Dover—was run down the ECML, initially with often highly-polished Pacifics carrying a name-board. Then from about April 1945, the Dieppe–Newhaven cross-channel service having recommenced in January, this train ran from Newhaven *via* Kensington—and it also sometimes carried a Nazi flag at the rear. Two regular leave trains were put on from Parkeston Quay, one to Glasgow (with buffet car) *via* Peterborough and the ECML and the other to Manchester *via* Peterborough East and Rugby; there was also one from Southampton, *via* the GC line to York and on to Newcastle *via* Stockton. After the end of the war in Europe, from October 1945 leave trains were run from Hull[18] to King's Cross in connection with a boat from Cuxhaven. None of these trains appeared in the public timetables. At the same time, numerous specials to Hull were conveying German servicemen released from British prisoner-of-war camps.

As early as October 1941, the Government selected Dispersal Centres throughout the length of Britain, and began to draw up plans for demobilisation of servicemen but of course it was only after VE-Day that they began to be implemented. In general the men were expected to make their way home from the dispersal centres by ordinary train services, but in June 1945 it was found necessary to institute a daily (including Sundays) special overnight train from Euston to York (via Northampton), balanced by a return working and complemented by a train from Taunton to Edinburgh (and reverse) which connected with the first train at York. Indeed, on the LNER Southern Area passenger journeys in the 12 weeks ending 12 October 1945 were 8.0 per cent higher than in the same period in 1944. That summer there was also the rush to the seaside, and as early as June 1945 the military camp at Filey was partially handed over to Billy Butlin, to restart his famed Holiday Camp, for which the LNER built a brand new branch and station in May 1947.

Main line passenger services after the war until the end of the 1950s

The great ECML trains of the LNER were gradually restored between 1946 and 1950 to some of their pre-war glory and certainly to peacetime frequency. Cheap fares that had been abolished in the war were reintroduced for party travel in August 1946, but not for individuals until late 1947 or early 1948. The holiday crowds in 1945 were dealt with by numerous reliefs—mainly unadvertised. Some of these appeared in the timetable as 'Saturdays Only', but in practice ran in the summer virtually every day; others were put on as required, often at the last minute. Both track

Peppercorn A1 Pacific No. 60118 *Archibald Sturrock* passes Holbeck (High Level) station while heading out of Leeds towards Harrogate with the Yorkshire Pullman service on 2 August 1952. *Picture: Yorkshire Post*

and locomotive repairs were, as already noted, in a poor state after six years of war. A large backlog of track relaying had accumulated, and this necessitated the continuation of a 75 mph overall speed limit, which in March 1947 was curtailed to 60 mph because of water-logging of the formation. Meanwhile the incidence of locomotive failures due to mechanical problems had risen to double the pre-war level. The proportion of locomotives under or awaiting repairs mounted steadily, having many causes which on the LNER included design weaknesses in Gresley locomotives built with high standards of maintenance in mind. Another constant cause of trouble just after the war was 'lack of steam due to inferior coal'; over British Railways as a whole the incidence of serious delays due to 'bad steaming' being three times in 1947 the level it had been in 1939. This led to gross delays and frequent requirements to 'stop for assistant engine'. Thus Christmas—always a difficult time—was chaotic at King's Cross in 1946, with trains leaving one or two hours late for reasons by no means wholly due to the weather. In the four weeks ending 25 January 1947, 49 per cent of ECML expresses were more than 45 minutes late, but worse was to come with the Fuel Crisis caused by the frightful weather early in 1947. Along with a shortage of locomotives owing to so many being under or in need of repair, radical cuts had to be made between February and June in passenger services; even the Summer timetable had 10 per cent less passenger train-miles than in 1946—and the railways were prohibited from running any more reliefs. Passenger journeys originating on the LNER Southern Area actually fell by 16 per cent in 1947 compared to 1946, but at least the punctuality of the principal expresses improved—modestly from an average lateness of 40 minutes to 26 minutes.

No. 60139 *Sea Eagle* is seen at speed on a four-track stretch of the ECML with the Tees-Tyne Pullman. The date is between April 1957 and April 1959 as a King's Cross shed code is visible.

Loads on the ECML remained heavy in the early post-war years, some trains again including portions for three destinations as well as individual through coaches, although both loads and destinations varied somewhat with the seasons. Some but not all of the variety of subsidiary destinations served before the war by the LNER came back on the notices under BR. Thus by 1955 were added: Lincoln, Ripon, Halifax, Scarborough, Saltburn, Fort William (by sleeping car), and Newcastle Tyne Commission Quay, also on summer Saturdays Skegness, Bridlington, and Filey Holiday Camp.

As before the war, scores of reliefs were run at exceptionally busy times such as Christmas, Easter and Whitsun, on summer Saturdays[19] and on special occasions such as the Cup Final and other major football events, the St Leger, the Grand National and other race meetings. Many excursions were also run for the Festival of Britain in 1951 and for the Coronation in 1953. In the pre-motorway days of the 1950s, major football events could require the running of phenomenal numbers of specials for the fans. To give one example: for the Cup Semi-Finals on 26 March 1955 no less than 52 excursions were run from the Newcastle/Sunderland area to Birmingham. Reliefs and excursions would bring to King's Cross locomotives from depots otherwise rarely seen in the terminus—although some were common enough on fast freight, fish trains, etc.: Sheds such as March, Retford, Ardsley, Bradford, Colwick, Darnall, Lincoln, Neville Hill, Darlington, Hull Dairycoates, or Botanic Gardens. In the 1940s, when these non- ECML sheds had old GN, GC and NE types on their books, the variety of locomotives was wide, but by the 1950s the specials rarely brought anything more extraordinary than a B16, otherwise the usual B1 or perhaps a K2 or K3.

Thompson A2/3 Pacific No. 60512 *Steady Aim* enters the west end of Newcastle Central with the 'Queen of Scots' service during 1948. The imposing signal gantry was operated by No. 3 Box which is in the background.

It was common for conditions to become quite chaotic at King's Cross at times of pressure, and the *Railway Observer* relates how at Christmas 1950—'Scenes [at King's Cross] of such confusion and congestion were witnessed as never before been known in the history of the East Coast Route'. The writer went on to describe the congestion of 24 engines queuing to get into Top Shed, and to list a number of late departures of well over an hour. It was little better at Christmas 1954 for example, when there were three derailments and ten engine failures. Again, at Christmas 1957 services were totally disorganised, this time by severe fog as well as exceptionally heavy traffic on account of the return of a modicum of petrol rationing. Innumerable reliefs were run, and 21 extra diagrams were operated from King's Cross on 21 December and on 22 December no less than 27; Down expresses—and some Outer Suburban trains—were delayed for over an hour, and Up expresses for over two hours. At Newcastle they had fog as well, also a derailment on the High Level Bridge which blocked all its lines for over an hour at the busiest time.

The summer timetable of 1945 showed little overt change—after all the war was not yet over in the Far East. It was the winter timetable that year which first announced the reintroduction of several more through expresses. Also, with the introduction of regular sailings from the Tyne to Norway in January 1946, the Boat Trains to Tyne Commission Quay from King's Cross ran once again. The London–Edinburgh time of the 'Flying Scotsman' (on which the restaurant car was restored) was cut by 50 minutes to 8 hours 5 minutes; commensurate reductions were made in the scheduled times of many other expresses. Nevertheless, another four years elapsed before any substantial accelerations were possible, although apart from the constraints in 1947 already mentioned—the frequency of scheduled trains down the ECML was increased successively each summer, but especially in 1949. With summer Saturday through trains to the seaside gradually reintroduced on a scale eventually exceeding those of 1939, and abundant reliefs run at peak times, the passenger services down the ECML became perhaps more interesting than the freight.

The 'Flying Scotsman', the 'Aberdonian' and the 'Night Scotsman' had never lost their names throughout the war, and other named trains soon reappeared after it. The 'Yorkshire Pullman' was reinstated in winter 1946 (via Leeds), when through King's Cross–Leeds locomotive workings

No. 60017 *Silver Fox* was one of the first four A4 Class Pacifics built at Doncaster in the latter half of 1935. The engine has stopped at Grantham with an Up express during July 1956. *Picture: Bill Reed*

were restored. Summer 1948 saw the first post-war King's Cross–Edinburgh non-stop schedule (by the 'Flying Scotsman' in 7 hours 50 minutes) and the reappearance of the 'Queen of Scots' Pullman to Glasgow Queen Street *via* Leeds and Harrogate. In winter 1948 a new 'Tees-Tyne' Pullman was introduced and the 'West Riding' came back—albeit not as a streamlined train, for none of the pre-war luxury trains ever came back. In summer 1949, the 'Flying Scotsman' became no longer the non-stop and instead a new non-stop — the 'Capitals Limited'—was put on, allowed 8 hours: the 'White Rose', non-stop King's Cross to Wakefield, was also instituted that summer. In winter 1949, the 12.20 King's Cross–Newcastle was named 'The Northumbrian', and the 08.48 Leeds City–Glasgow *via* York the 'North Briton'. The summer timetable of 1950 reintroduced the 'Scarborough Flyer', the name the 'Norseman' for the thrice-weekly boat express from King's Cross to Tyne Commission Quay, and the 'Tynesider' for the 23.30 King's Cross–Newcastle sleeping car express. On Sunday 15 July 1950, a special was run from King's Cross to York and back (outward by the 'Towns' route *via* Boston, Lincoln and Knottingley), hauled by rebuilt Pacific 60113 *Great Northern*, to celebrate the centenary of the opening of the GNR main line.[20]

For winter 1950, there were further modest accelerations: the 'Flying Scotsman' now took 7 hours 45 minutes for its journey—with stops at Grantham and Newcastle, but high-speed expresses from King's Cross there certainly were not—not yet, a speed trial in May 1946 having shown that a great deal of work on the track had to be done before pre-war high-speed schedules could be contemplated. Thus 90 mph was prohibited anywhere until 1951. The first post-war 60 mph booking (of the 'North Briton' between Darlington and York) was effected in 1949, but it was several years before mile-a-minute schedules became common again on the ECML. Innovations in 1950 included the beginnings of the standardisation of departure times from King's Cross, and of the turn-round there of Up expresses without leaving their platforms of arrival—although it

'The Northumbrian' leaves Grantham for London behind Peppercorn A1 No. 60157 *Great Eastern* on a murky day in September 1957. *Picture: Bill Reed*

was 1956 before the practice was adopted extensively. Changing engines of London expresses at Peterborough, Grantham, Doncaster, or York was phased out after the war. Many locomotive rosters through from London to York and Newcastle were brought back from May 1946, but the main change in this regard came in summer 1950. However, this was not for long: on account of poor timekeeping on long-distance through runs, the rather poor mechanical condition of the Pacifics and V2s and inferior standards of maintenance, forced a complete rearrangement of rosters in 1951, to give locomotives and crews relatively short runs. Nearly all trains were again re-engined and re-manned at Peterborough or Grantham. Meanwhile, in the 1948–51 period there were many London–Newcastle (and Edinburgh) through locomotive rosters—the Edinburgh engines being from Haymarket Shed and not confined only to the non-stops. Accordingly, there were a considerable number of lodging-turns for the footplate men—albeit unpopular, especially with Tyneside men. The Haymarket A4s, along with Pacifics and V2s from Gateshead, Heaton, York and Copley Hill as well as from Doncaster, Grantham and New England, now came up to London regularly. The two new series of Pacifics—(6 ft 2 in A2s and 6 ft 8 in A1s)—became prominent in this period on the ECML, the former being unpopular on expresses and therefore employed more often on fast freight. In addition, from March 1950 through working was restored of Immingham engines to King's Cross, but now they were almost always B1s and not the GN Atlantics or the variety of GC 4-6-0s seen before the war.[21]

The diagrams on which the ECML Pacifics (helped by the V2s) were operated have been documented elsewhere so often and so fully that it would be superfluous to repeat them here. Noteworthy nonetheless were the alterations in 1951, for at that time there was an influx of the new A1 Pacifics and a considerable rearrangement of allocations, including the return of A3s to the GC main line. In spite of the changes in diagrams, a very considerable degree of long-distance

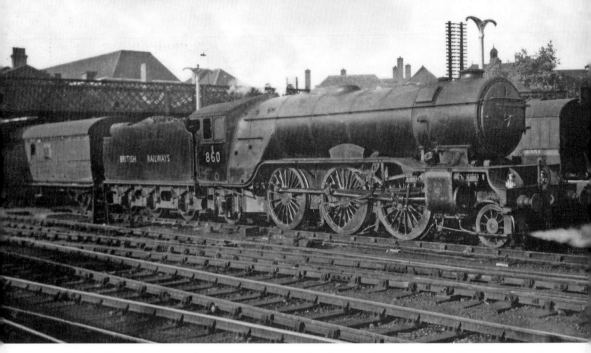

V2 Class No. E860 *Durham School* was one of twenty-five class members to receive the 'E' prefix shortly after Nationalisation, being so altered in February. The engine is seen at Doncaster in July and would become No. 60860 by November.

light-engine working became necessary, and this continued for many years; the sight of a Pacific running light at speed down the southern half of the ECML became a daily—if slightly odd—experience.

At all events, the Gresley Pacifics of both the non-streamlined (now all Class A3) and streamlined (A4) classes, the Thompson and Peppercorn Pacifics and the indomitable V2 2-6-2s, had many more years of hard work and remained the staple motive power of the fast trains on the ECML throughout the 1940s and 1950s.

Summer 1951 saw the introduction of another named express, the 'Heart of Midlothian', an afternoon London–Edinburgh train. There were also some minor accelerations, and six runs (totalling 265 miles) were scheduled at over 60 mph. In summer 1952 the crack 'Capitals Limited' was accelerated to reach Edinburgh in 7 hours 6 minutes. That summer a daily through service was introduced: Newcastle–Swansea. This important cross-country service had not run since before the war, except briefly in winter 1946 and subsequently as a summer Saturdays only service, and unlike pre-war, running *via* Oxford and Swindon. From 1951 the through coaches were routed *via* Birmingham and Gloucester; by summer 1957 it had developed into a complete Newcastle–Cardiff train, the two sets of coaching stock being shared between the NE and Western Regions.

In October 1952 the centenary of King's Cross Station was celebrated with an exhibition including locomotives, then in the winter 1952 timetable the first faint sign of real accelerations on the ECML was shown by the introduction of a new King's Cross–Leeds express, leaving London at 08.00 and taking 168 minutes (with one stop) to cover the 156 miles to Doncaster–seeming at that time quite an achievement.

In April 1953 the pre-war overnight reliefs from Marylebone to Newcastle were reinstated and ran to Edinburgh, running throughout the summer season. They ran down the former GC main line but avoiding Sheffield Victoria by the Darnall loop, thence to York and onwards. Called

Above: This scene was captured at Barnby level crossing, Balderton, just south of Newark. V2 No. 60812 is seen rushing south with an express in the late 1950s. The engine was constructed (as No. 4783) at Darlington in September 1939 and was withdrawn during March 1963. *Picture: Malcolm Crawley*

Below: Peppercorn A1 No. 60145 *Saint Mungo* takes the 'Flying Scotsman' on the Up Fast through Otterington station during 1953. Opened in March 1841 by the Great North of England Railway, so becoming part of the NER main line, Otterington was closed completely in 1964, but some of the buildings still remain. *Picture: Yorkshire Post*

'Starlight Specials', they proved very popular for a few years. The 'Starlight' return fare to Edinburgh was only £3.50 in 1955 and £4.25 in 1958, compared with the ordinary return fare (third class) in 1955 of £5.73; many of the trains conveyed a cafeteria car, but they had no sleeping cars. Summer 1953 saw some really substantial accelerations. In particular the 'non-stop'—the former 'Capitals Limited', now renamed 'The Elizabethan' in honour of the Queen's Coronation—was speeded up to reach Edinburgh in 6 hours 45minutes, but it ran in the summer only and it kept to its former non-stop schedule every summer until 1961. Also from June 1953 the new morning express to Leeds and Bradford now had to run from Hitchin to Doncaster at 65.8 mph, while the Up 'Tees-Tyne' Pullman was scheduled non-stop from Darlington at 62.3 mph. The Coronation itself on 2 June 1953 naturally brought a number of reliefs and excursions up to King's Cross. The most noteworthy excursions were overnight runs of the 'Tees-Tyne' Pullman from Newcastle and the 'Yorkshire Pullman' from Leeds and Bradford.[22] The ECML line speed limit having been relaxed to 90 mph, in the summer 1953 timetable there were 15 mile-a-minute runs, totalling 1,883 miles and no less than 89 per cent of the total for the whole country. The winter 1953 timetable was heralded by the running in late September of the two preserved GN Atlantics (No. 990 *Henry Oakley* and No. 251) on outer-suburban trains, before hauling twice the 'Plant Centenarian' specials to Doncaster and Leeds. The 'Bradford Flyer'—now also with a Newcastle portion, was speeded up further, to cover Hitchin to Retford start-to-start at 66.7 mph.

Summer 1954 brought some further accelerations, notably of the 'Elizabethan' to 6 hours 30 minutes, and a few additions to the ECML timetable. The daily aggregate of mile-a-minute runs was now 22 (2,098 miles), although other Regions were doing better and this distance represented only 48 per cent of the national total. The winter timetable of 1954 brought little further change, but the summer timetable of 1955—delayed because of the ASLEF Strike—showed some more welcome accelerations on the ECML. For example, the London–Edinburgh time of the 'Flying Scotsman' was cut to 7 hours, and near 60 mph averages for the hard Newcastle–Edinburgh stretch was attained by several trains, while on the York–Darlington 'speedway' as many as 14 trains were scheduled at over a mile-a-minute.

A portentous development that summer was the 'Car Sleeper Limited', BR's belated response to the 'love affair with the motor car.' A service was put on from King's Cross to Perth on Wednesday and Sunday nights, and these bypassed Edinburgh Waverley, the locomotives being changed at Niddrie West. It was very popular, and in summer 1956 it ran every night. The motor vehicles were end-loaded into covered vans which had a total capacity for 20 cars, and passengers travelled either in third class sleepers or in open saloons. The charge was set at £15 for car plus driver and £4.50 for each additional passenger. The popularity of the service soon necessitated the running of several motor-car vans on each train, and further car sleeper trains were introduced in the following summer. One ran (Wednesdays and Saturdays only) Newcastle *via* York, Sheffield and the GC line to Northolt Junction, thence *via* Greenford and Kensington on to the SR to Dover, connecting with a car ferry. Another ran (Mondays only) Newcastle–Exeter St Davids *via* Birmingham and Bristol, and a third (Sundays only) York–Inverness. In summer 1957 several more car sleeper sets were in operation on the ECML, the services of 1956 being augmented by three services a week, Marylebone–Perth. The facilities were further expanded in summer 1958, with a King's Cross–Perth service now running every night (Fridays excepted).

Perhaps the most 'ominous' innovation of summer 1954 was the first operation on BR of a passenger service by diesel multiple-units (DMUs). Indirectly associated with the ECML, this radical change involved the local trains between Bradford Exchange, Leeds Central and Harrogate. It was followed by the introduction in 1955 of DMUs (based at Lincoln and Norwich) on East Anglian and

Lincolnshire services, thus bringing them to Grantham and later to Peterborough, the transformation being largely completed in 1956. In winter 1955 the Newcastle–Middlesbrough service went over to DMUs, maintained at the modernised and adapted South Gosforth electric train depot.

As 1955 was the last year before the Modernisation Plan began to come into effect, before the extensive introduction of DMUs on local services, and perhaps a peak year for summer Saturday travel, it can be taken as an 'index' year' of this early period of BR. Moreover, the demand for rail passenger travel in 1955 was still healthy, as is exemplified by the passenger counts (including season ticket journeys) for July 1955 at King's Cross (241,000), Finsbury Park (53,000), Hatfield (27,000) and Hitchin (46,000). In summer 1956 a considerable expansion of the long-distance services was attained by extension of the regular-interval principal, with quick turn-round at King's Cross. Loads were restricted to 12 bogies and reservations suspended on Saturdays. This was very useful on summer Saturdays, when there were expresses every hour between 08.40 and 15.40 to Newcastle and every half hour to West Yorkshire, but if anything went wrong chaos could result in the cramped and awkward confines of King's Cross.

In winter 1956 a new King's Cross–Edinburgh express—the 'Talisman'—was introduced, leaving London at 16.00 hours and taking only 6 hours 40 minutes. Then, in the summer timetable of 1957, another Edinburgh express was put on, leaving King's Cross at 07. 45 and named the 'Morning Talisman', the 16.00 departure now being called the 'Afternoon Talisman'; both ran non-stop to Newcastle, as did three more expresses. The 'Afternoon Talisman' was a successor in a way to the pre-war 'Coronation', but took 40 minutes longer to reach Edinburgh.

In winter 1957 the 'Morning Talisman' was renamed the 'Fair Maid' and extended to Perth—as was also the 'Heart of Midlothian', the latter being routed by the former LMS line *via* Larbert and Stirling. (These extensions to Perth were however cancelled a year later, and the 'Morning Talisman' got its name back again). The 'Flying Scotsman' was further accelerated, its King's Cross–Edinburgh time being cut by 37 minutes to 6 hours 58 minutes. The 'Aberdonian' was much altered, to leave King's Cross at 22.15 instead of 19.00, and was 50 minutes faster throughout, having no public stops before Inverkeithing. The new 19.45 from King's Cross now had through carriages for Elgin; the 'Night Scotsman'—all first class sleeping cars and no seating accommodation at all, was 2 hours 24 minutes quicker to Edinburgh. Many other expresses were speeded up by omitting former stops, while more through King's Cross–Hull trains were put on, running independently of those to West Yorkshire and making intermediate stops missed by the others. Finally, the through Lincolnshire services were much improved. At the end of 1957, the number of mile-a-minute runs over the York–Darlington 'speedway' had risen steeply to 24—the fastest being 66.2 mph. It should be noted that all these improvements antedated the introduction of main-line diesel locomotives on the ECML by at least a year.

In summer 1958 there were some further accelerations of ECML expresses and the addition of more night expresses. The number of regular 60 mph runs had now risen to 35 (2,436 miles, 25 per cent of the national total). The accelerations were still not attributable to the introduction of main-line diesels, although the new 2,000 hp Type-4 (Class 40) diesel-electric No. D200 first ran trials on the ECML in March 1958, and one of these locomotives first worked the 'Flying Scotsman'—as far as Newcastle, on 21 June 1958. Regular diagrams for the diesels began in July 1958, on the 'White Rose' as far as Doncaster, and on the new 'Heart of Midlothian' as far as Peterborough. In September 1958, a fourth Pullman service was brought to the ECML, the 'Master Cutler' Pullman. Using a name previously given to a Sheffield express from Marylebone, this train ran up from Sheffield Victoria early in the morning—and back in the evening—quite quickly (58.7 mph with one stop (at Retford), and employing a Type 4 diesel from the outset.

English Electric Type 4 (later Class 40) No. D208 is working an express passenger service at Grantham on 12 September 1958. The locomotive was only a few weeks old and was one of five trialled on the ECML. *Picture: Bill Reed*

The winter 1958 timetable also saw the introduction of yet another fast 'business' train, the 'Tees-Thames Link' (06.48 Middlesbrough to Doncaster), operated by a DMU set and connecting at Doncaster with a locomotive-hauled non-stop express to King's Cross—but the service did not run in the opposite direction. At last in the winter 1958 timetable five very intensive Class 40 diesel diagrams were introduced between King's Cross and Newcastle and/or Sheffield, each of about 4,500 miles per week, Pacific diagrams being cut drastically as a consequence. The ER celebrated its introduction of the new diesels on to the ECML with an exhibition, held on 14–15 September 1958 in Noel Park goods yard on the Palace Gates branch, displaying the latest main-line diesel locomotives and the DMUs alongside modern and not-so-modern steam locomotives associated with the GN Line.

The reliability of the diesels left a lot to be desired, and substitution by a steam locomotive was a very common occurrence. In spite of the operation now of a sizeable proportion of ECML expresses by diesel power, neither the summer nor the winter 1959 timetables (beginning in November) yet showed any dramatic changes, although another new named express was introduced—the 'Tees-Thames', which was a necessary development of the previous year's 'Tees-Thames Link' into a through express, 07.05 Saltburn to King's Cross returning at 14.00.

Major accelerations were not possible until the diesels were both numerous and more reliable. The original BR Mark I standard coaches gave a poor ride at more than about 60 mph and were not improving BR's faded public image—until later when the Commonwealth bogie was introduced. At the end of 1959, when Gateshead was acquiring a considerable stud of Type 4s, they were allocated regular diagrams, most of which took them in the Edinburgh direction. No mass movements of ECML Pacifics had yet taken place: the A3s previously on the former GC section had been returned to the GN lines and King's Cross had gained nine (and lost one by withdrawal), New England two, Grantham four, and Gateshead five, while Doncaster had lost four, Copley Hill three, and Heaton

A Derby lightweight two-car DMU has worked a local service into Grantham station during July 1956. *Picture: Bill Reed*

A4 No. 60017 *Silver Fox* on the level ground north of York with 'The Elizabethan'. Apart from four months at Peterborough New England shed before being condemned for scrap in October 1963, the engine was allocated to King's Cross from new. *Picture: Yorkshire Post*

three. A1s had been moved, in that Doncaster had gained twelve (ten from Grantham and one each from Ardsley and Copley Hill); lastly, one A2 had moved from Grantham to New England.

During the late 1950s, the 'swan-song of steam' was sung by the running of a number of steam-hauled enthusiasts' specials on the ECML. Speed restrictions were relaxed where it was safe, and Gresley's Pacifics were 'given their head'. Notably, on 23 May 1959, No. 60007 *Sir Nigel Gresley* on the Stephenson Locomotive Society's 'Golden Jubilee Special' achieved an official post-war record for steam of 112 mph—descending Stoke Bank of course.

4

Restaurant, Pullman and sleeping car facilities, Post Office services, Royal trains, and hotels on the ECML, 1939–1959

Restaurant cars and buffet cars

In 1939 restaurant car meals were provided on the great majority of ECML expresses. On Mondays to Fridays about 15 regular departures from King's Cross had restaurant cars. They also ran on many of the Saturday extras and the relatively infrequent Sunday services. Although a number of trains, notably the Cambridge and the Cleethorpes expresses from King's Cross and the 08.45 to Doncaster, had buffet cars instead; meal facilities were proffered also on the principal ECML expresses not emanating from London. The catering vehicles plied mainly between the major ECML centres, with the staff—of six men—often undertaking the double journey (e.g. to and from Leeds) in one working day, but the vehicles also worked through to Ripon and to Scarborough. On the Newcastle and Edinburgh runs the staff lodged overnight, as they did often on long-distance excursions when they slept in hammocks on the train. Buffet cars were definitely considered 'modish', and they were especially favoured by those who liked to drink at all times of the day, for—like the restaurant cars—they were unaffected by licensing laws.

Catering vehicles were built to last, and on the ECML before the war there were still a number of pre-Grouping sets running, although the majority were Gresley LNER vehicles. They had to be solidly built—especially the kitchen cars, for not only was much heavy equipment carried but the staff needed a steady vehicle in which to cook, serve and wash up, also there was a large store for 'bonded goods' which needed to be secure from pilfering in sidings. The Gresley cars included his articulated triplets in which the kitchen car was attached permanently to restaurant saloons at each end, one for first class the other for third class. Then there was also the unique quintuplet, which had ordinary compartment seating vehicles permanently attached at each end of a triplet catering set. This normally ran on the 10.15 King's Cross–Leeds and 17.30 return, and was probably more nuisance than it was worth because a defect in any one part effectively put five whole vehicles out of action. During the war the set was stored at Nottingham, and in 1950 was returned to the Leeds run, but only for two years after which it was broken up. On the ECML in the 1930s a kitchen car had to have the equipment and food for up to 500 meals. Thus having a restaurant on each side of the kitchen facilitated the waiters' work by 'swing service', as also did their practice of 'silver service'—serving passengers from dishes rather than trying to carry bowls of soup on a swaying train.

Unlike on most other railways where oil–gas was employed for cooking, Gresley's kitchen cars were all-electric. The all-electric kitchens needed to be supported by a system of charging the batteries from electrical supplies to allow some cooking to be done while the kitchen car was not on the move. However, the batteries could not carry the whole load, and therefore not only did charging facilities have to be available at the main carriage yards (such as Holloway, Hornsey, Heaton and Craigentinny), but also a range of mains electrical points had to be provided at some

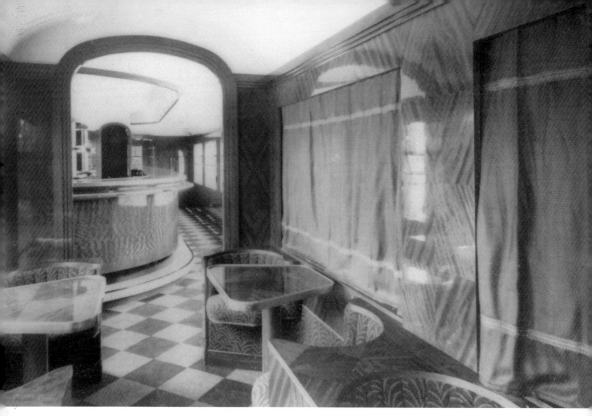

A view of the interior of the buffet lounge car built at Doncaster in 1948 for the 'Flying Scotsman' set. This type of carriage had been introduced to the service ten years earlier.

principal ECML stations. To prevent the cooks embarrassed by unplanned cooling of hot-plates and ovens while they were in the middle of preparing dozens of meals, men rushed to plug in the kitchen to the mains when the train stopped then unplug it before the guard blew his whistle. Therefore the more modern electric kitchen cars running on the ECML in the 1930s were fitted as well with anthracite stoves to keep the ovens and hot-plates going. The anthracite/electric kitchen car was perpetuated in the new stock built for the ECML services directly after the war. It was only under the BR regime that electricity and anthracite for cooking were eventually abandoned and the standard fuel for kitchen cars became propane gas. In the meantime on the celebrated Aberdeen–Penzance service, in 1939 a new type of vehicle had been introduced—a car with both a restaurant and a buffet section served from an integral kitchen. The sets ran between Newcastle and Swindon, yet still somehow managed to run on electricity only; after the war they too were converted to use propane gas.

The LNER had indeed been the foremost of the big four in the development of buffet cars, and it had some 70 in service just before the war. Some 25 of these had been open thirds, one end having been covered by the installation of a small kitchen and service counter, leaving seating for about 24 passengers in a 2-to-1 arrangement with tables. The rest were purpose-built cars to the same basic design, either typical Gresley in varnished teak or with plywood panels in green and cream for incorporation into the tourist train sets. The first buffet car trains were used for the King's Cross–Cambridge fast service introduced in 1932, but by 1939 the majority of the buffet cars were employed in the NE Area, mainly on the services from Newcastle to Middlesbrough and to Carlisle.

During the war there were no changes in catering stock, except a large reduction in the number in use. For a month or so after the outbreak of war, restaurant cars were taken off entirely. But they were soon restored, and in 1940–41 there were still about ten regular restaurant services from

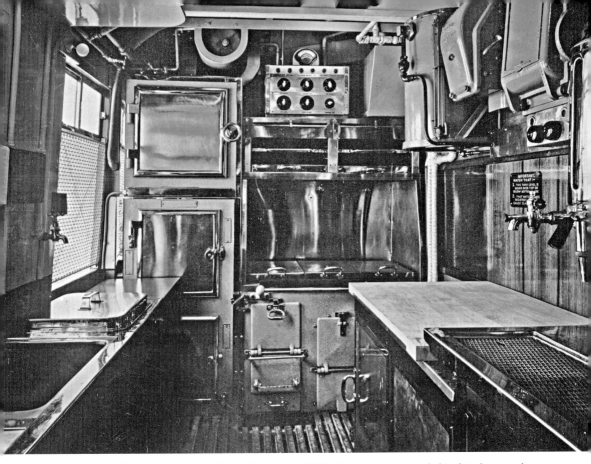

The introduction of an anthracite range for cooking in the LNER's kitchen cars is recorded in this photograph taken on 12 July 1938.

King's Cross, and many other ECML trains had buffet cars—some for servicemen only. In March 1941, the LNER was still running daily 36 restaurant cars and 21 buffet cars on the ECML—and on the midday King's Cross–Edinburgh service one of each. Like so much else in wartime, there was now a 'standard' restaurant car lunch and dinner (each at 12.5p) and tea (at 5p)—even the service charge was regulated (at 1.5p). In 1942 the services were cut down again to three, to two in 1943[1] and to none at all in summer 1944. Thereafter there were none until winter 1945, when the 'Flying Scotsman' alone acquired a restaurant car and one Newcastle service a buffet car.

Generally, the number of restaurant services—if not their quality—were back to pre-war levels by 1948, although the Cambridge line services did not return until late in that year, and many buffet car services that had run from Newcastle to Middlesbrough and to Carlisle before the war (surviving until 1941) came back only very briefly in the late 1940s although one or two were perpetuated in the 1950s on the Carlisle trains. Likewise, the buffet car services between Leeds and Scarborough had a very transitory post-war revival. After the war Thompson-built two buffet lounge cars, which were employed on the ECML non-stops. Later in 1958, many of the standard buffet cars were rebuilt as restaurant buffet cars to the design of those introduced in 1939 mentioned above. During the 1950s therefore buffet cars came to be employed on a number of ECML services, including King's Cross to Edinburgh, Grantham, Peterborough and Cleethorpes as well as to Cambridge, also Newcastle to Liverpool, York and Colchester.

In the 1950s snacks were more in vogue, supplied often in new buffet pantry cars, and full meal services were definitely a lot less sumptuous than pre-war—and by 1952 restaurant cars were called 'refreshment cars'. The trend established in the war towards self-service feeding was perpetuated;

on the ECML cafeteria cars were first introduced in 1952 on the 'Starlight Specials' to Scotland. The food in cafeteria cars was largely prepared before the journey, and minimal cooking facilities were needed. Much preliminary cooking for the ECML catering was done in the large kitchen under platforms 6–10 at King's Cross. There followed 'miniature buffet' cars, 'griddle' cars and more such labour-saving arrangements. For a while soon after Nationalisation, one of the new 'tavern cars'—named 'The Salutation'—ran on the ECML, and in January 1958 a 'miniature buffet' car was incorporated—in addition to the usual restaurant car set—on the 'Flying Scotsman'. The reorganisation resulting from the Transport Act of 1953, when catering was passed from Regional control to a new British Transport Hotels & Catering Services, did little to improve standards of catering on the move and the high pre-war standards never returned.

New catering vehicles introduced by BR in 1951 conformed to the new Mark I series of coaching stock, and comprised open first and third class restaurant cars with loose seating, also kitchen cars with anthracite stoves combined with electrical heating as on the later LNER cars. A limited number of these vehicles worked on the ECML in combination with LNER vehicles, until the introduction in 1956 of an entirely new series of (Mark I) catering vehicles on BR. The series included: a kitchen buffet with a bar section with seats, a kitchen restaurant (unclassed) car (33 seats) with full cooking facilities, and a kitchen buffet car capable of providing full meals to 23 seats and light refreshments from a self-service area. The cooking in all these vehicles was with propane gas, electricity being used only for refrigeration. With minor modifications these 1956 cars were built in substantial numbers between 1957 and 1963, and were employed extensively on the ECML.

Life for travelling catering staff was not easy, and is well described by Wooler (1987):

> On restaurant cars a crew is always out on its own, and at the mercy of unforeseen hitches and delays, for up to 13 or 14 hours at a stretch. In that time, its members will cook, serve and wash up for many hundreds of hungry and demanding travellers, not to mention the continuous coming and going at the buffet counter. Nearly everything is freshly cooked on board—and cooked in a kitchen smaller than that in the average suburban three-bedroom house, which by contrast would seldom prepare meals for more than six people. Much skill is needed by cooks and waiters working on a swaying train. It is a life of challenge, responsibility and variety. They are often called on to care for as well as cope with passengers and must be able to tackle equipment failures *en route*. There are no changeovers on the way, as for the locomotive men or guards, for restaurant car staff have a very long stint—preparing, cooking and serving two or three sittings per meal, then washing up, cashing up and clearing up. Catering cars are at once a grocer's store, wine merchant's cellar, tobacconist, hotel kitchen, store room and pantry. They must carry a refuse-bin area, and have a wardrobe, locker, and dressing space for up to eight staff, plus a toilet.

Pullmans

As referred to in Chapter 2, just before the war there were two regular Pullman expresses running down the ECML on weekdays: the 'Queen of Scots' to Leeds, Harrogate, Newcastle, Edinburgh and Glasgow, and the 'Yorkshire Pullman' to Leeds, Harrogate,[2] Bradford, Halifax and Hull, and one, the 'Harrogate Sunday' Pullman, on Sundays to Leeds, Bradford and Harrogate.[3] (The LNER also ran Pullman restaurant cars on certain trains in Scotland, including Perth–Edinburgh, Glasgow–Edinburgh, Carlisle–Edinburgh, and Glasgow–Dundee). These luxury trains vied with the 'streamliners' for comfort, and like them they called for a supplementary charge (30p first class, 15p third class, to Leeds in 1939) for which passengers enjoyed meals at their seats and

The pioneer Gresley Pacific, A1 Class No. 4470 *Great Northern*, passes through Doncaster station with the Up Yorkshire Pullman in the late 1930s.

Pullman third class carriage No. 107 was originally named *Kathleen* when entering service for the LNER in 1927; the change, made in 1946, was perhaps the reason the picture was taken at Doncaster Works. The carriage spent three years on the LMR from 1963.

other gratifications. The coaches belonged to the Pullman Car Company, which also provided the 'cabin' staff. Dressed in their distinctive uniforms and with an ingrained civility, the latter were more highly selected and probably even more skilled than the railway restaurant car staff. Each train had a conductor, who had under him one attendant for each coach and in addition the staff working in the kitchen compartments situated in each alternate car, and this team of men tended to remain with their own train set. The trains running on the LNER were made up from 31 all-steel cars built by the Metropolitan-Cammell Carriage & Wagon Co. in 1928.

During the war the Pullman trains were withdrawn, and after being stored for a while most of the coaches (repainted brown) were employed by the LNER as ordinary first class saloons in service trains. Some of the coaches were used in the special trains provided for the Prime Minister, for the Military Chiefs, and at times for the King and Queen.

The all-steel Metro-Cammell cars of 1928 comprised the following. Ten kitchen firsts, with names—female of course (*Belinda, Evadine, Ione, Joan, Lorraine, Nilar, Penelope, Philomel, Phyllis* and *Thelma*); seven parlour firsts (*Agatha, Eunice, Juana, Lucille, Sheila, Ursula* and *Zena*); four parlour thirds (Nos. 73–76) and 10 brake thirds (Nos. 67–72/7–80). It is of note that, unlike in the more modern LNER kitchen cars, cooking was still being done by oil-gas, but this was superseded by propane gas when the Pullman Car Co. pioneered the use of this safer fuel in the 1950s.

The consist of the 'Yorkshire Pullman' was 11 cars as far as Doncaster, where two firsts and two thirds were detached for Hull, two firsts and three thirds ran through to Harrogate *via* Leeds, and at Wakefield one first and one third were detached for Bradford. The 'Queen of Scots' had two sets of coaches, each comprising ten cars (four firsts and six thirds), two of each class being detached at Leeds and the remainder continuing to Glasgow. The new 'Tees-Tyne' Pullman was made up of eight cars of mixed origin including some still with wooden bodies: one kitchen first, two parlour firsts, two kitchen thirds, one brake third, one composite, and a newly-converted first class bar car named the 'Hadrian Bar'. The 'Master Cutler' had just six cars (three kitchen firsts, one kitchen second, and two brake seconds); these were still cars from the 1920s until the new ones built to the BR standard design were brought into service in 1960. In the meantime the BTC had bought themselves a controlling interest in the Pullman Car Company in 1954 and in 1959 the BRB bought up the rest of the shares.

Sleeping car facilities

On account of the long distances involved, especially to Scotland, the sleeping car trains on the ECML were of primary importance. Just before the war there were six regular sleeping car services from King's Cross,[4] including one (the 'Night Scotsman') that had very little seating accommodation at all. The 'Highlandman' conveyed sleeping cars to Inverness, Nairn (via Forres) and to Fort William, and the 'Aberdonian' included a car to Lossiemouth as well as those just to Aberdeen. On Friday nights, the 22.35 from King's Cross conveyed a first class car to North Berwick, which returned on Monday nights.

Apart from a period in the second half of 1940 when Edinburgh sleeping car services were diverted to the LMSR and Princes Street, during the war there were three on the ECML (one each to Aberdeen, Edinburgh and Newcastle); these services remained unchanged throughout the war—and until 1946. At the beginning of the war the REC stipulated a limit of one sleeping car of each class per train, but the demand for first class berths was so heavy that the limit soon had to be relaxed. Nevertheless from the beginning of the war, the 'number available to the general public is strictly limited', because most berths (including all first class) were reserved for civilian and military 'Top Brass' on Government business.

In 1947 a new third class sleeping car design was introduced and the interior of the first example, No. 1348, is depicted here. An interesting feature is that the berths in the adjoining compartment are placed under those in this one.

By April 1947 four[5] sleeping car services to Scotland (including Edinburgh, Fort William, and Aberdeen) and the one to Newcastle—named the 'Tynesider' in 1950—had been restored, with a relief (with first class car to Darlington) on Fridays which became nightly by 1949. In 1955 there was one more regular service to Edinburgh, by 1957 one more again, and in 1958 the 'Tynesider' formation—sleeping cars only—contained two cars that were transferred at Newcastle to the 07.05 semi-fast to Edinburgh, returning on the 20.00 Up mail train. That made seven sleeping car services to Scotland and one to Darlington and Newcastle. First class berths from King's Cross to Edinburgh cost £1.05 in 1939, rising to £2.00 by 1959. Several of these sleeping car trains to Scotland in peacetime made no stops on the way other than for locomotive and crew changes—usually at Newcastle—and the 'Aberdonian' would not even deign to deposit passengers at Edinburgh. The long non-stop runs made them all the more comfortable for their sleeping passengers.

The oldest sleeping cars in the 1930s were pre-Grouping—albeit renovated—first class single-berth[6] vehicles, but by 1939 most were of LNER vintage, some being articulated vehicles. They had single berth first class compartments—and one shower compartment per car; in third class there were four-berth compartments, in some of which the upper berths were capable of being folded back to give normal seating for daytime use. Naturally the third class had more primitive facilities. In those days neither class had 'en suite facilities', but the more modern first class cars had full pressure-ventilation with ducts leading warm or cool air by nozzles above the bed-heads. First and third class accommodation was usually—but not always—in separate vehicles, and there were two articulated sets (one half for each class) running on the ECML. Wash basins, with electrically-heated water; self-flushing 'pots de chambre' beneath were usual before the war only

Interior of a compartment in the Diagram 138 first class sleeping car introduced by Gresley in 1930. A total of four were built, the one pictured being No. 1154, which was one of two decorated by White Allom in the style of Louis XVI. The carriages also featured a new ventilation and heating system.

in first class, but were introduced in the two berth third class sleepers built by the LNER soon after the war.

Sleeping cars built to BR Standard Mark I design in 1957 were first class only, composites or second class only, both classes having full bedding and wash basins with hot and cold water. First class was now single berth and third/second class twin berth, but the charges for berths in the two berth second class cars were higher than those in the older four berth cars.

Post Office mail services on the ECML

The ECML had no 'Down Special' equivalent to that on the WCML. The principal mail service was the North-Eastern Down Travelling Post Office (TPO), comprising three carriages attached to the 'Night Scotsman', two of which came off at Newcastle, the third continuing to Edinburgh. The other TPO from London ran as part of the 20.25 express parcels, newspapers and mail train from King's Cross to Edinburgh. In addition there was the Bristol–Newcastle 'Midland' TPO, and also—before the war only—daytime (04.45) King's Cross–Leeds and York–Edinburgh TPOs. Only the London TPOs employed—mainly in the Down direction—automatic exchange apparatus, situated at New Barnet, Hatfield, Welwyn Garden City, Langley Junction, Hitchin, Biggleswade, Sandy, St Neots, Huntingdon, Peterborough, Pegswood, Alnmouth, Tweedmouth, Ayton, Dunbar, and Drem. After the war there were some changes in these locations, and of course like so much else they eventually disappeared. The TPO workings were taken off during the war in September 1940 and restored in May 1946, then remained essentially unchanged through the 1950s. Before coming south again on corresponding Up workings, the TPO vans had to be turned, at Newcastle by running them over the bridges round by Gateshead, at Edinburgh round the South Suburban line or the triangle at Niddrie; at the London end they were turned on the North London line Dalston triangle.

Newspaper trains ran overnight from King's Cross to Edinburgh and from Manchester to Glasgow, some of the papers being sorted on the trains by travelling newspaper staff, who completed their sorting on trestle tables provided on the platforms.

Trains for Royalty and other 'Very Important Persons' on the ECML; Royal Trains

The LNER's Royal Train, used in peacetime principally for Their Majesties to travel to and from Sandringham—normally down the ECML and *via* Cambridge,[7] and not for overnight journeys, dated from East Coast Joint Stock (ECJS) days. It consisted of one or two principal saloons, up to four 'semi-Royal' saloons and two full brakes (as staff accommodation and for luggage). There was no dedicated dining car as such—but the LNER kept one of their first class ones under cover at Bounds Green for Royal use when needed, and there was no sleeping car. The two splendid 12-wheel saloons were built in 1908–09 (one each by the GNR and the NER) for King Edward VII and Queen Alexandra, but in 1926 the King's saloon was converted for Queen Mary's day use, and was run either in the Royal Train or attached to a service train; it was later made use of by Queen Elizabeth (the Queen Mother). The Queen's saloon in 1926 became the King's principal saloon and had two separate dressing-rooms.

The LNER Royal Train made numerous journeys along the ECML between King's Cross and Hitchin on its way to and from Wolferton (for Sandringham). Journeys from London to Wolferton or elsewhere in East Anglia were made from King's Cross, because if the Monarch used Liverpool Street, He or She would have to obtain ceremonial 'permission' to enter the City of London. Probably the most memorable—and sombre—journey made during our period was on 11 February 1952, when (hauled by Britannia 4-6-2 No. 70000 from King's Lynn) after the death of King George VI conveyed the King's body from Wolferton to King's Cross. The train last ran in 1961, to York

Gresley A4 Pacific No. 60028 *Walter K. Whigham* heads the Royal Train through Harringay station on 8 June 1961. HM The Queen was travelling to York for the wedding of the Duke of Kent. *Picture: B. W. L. Brooksbank*

for the Duke of Kent's wedding, after which it was disbanded. Normally a pair of locomotives on Cambridge shed's allocation was maintained in tip-top and sparkling condition as 'Royal Engines', to cover the Royal Journeys to Sandringham, each maintained by its own picked crew. In LNER days they were D16/3 4-4-0s Nos. 8783 and 8787, until superseded in March 1946 by the B2 (rebuilt B17) 4-6-0 No. 2871 *Royal Sovereign* (formerly *Manchester City*), with B2 No. 61617 *Ford Castle* as stand-by. The two D16/3s were then transferred to Kings Lynn and employed when necessary on the Kings Lynn–Wolferton leg of Royal Train journeys.

During the war, King George VI and Queen Elizabeth made numerous journeys in one of the Royal Trains all over the country—44 on the LNER alone. On most journeys an overnight sleep was involved and therefore they employed the LMSR Train ('Grove') rather than the LNER Train described above. Although Euston was used most often for journeys to Scotland, many trips to Scotland and other places involved running over the ECML at least in part. Later, in the reign of the present Queen, Their Majesties sometimes travelled in other special coaches hired from BR and then these trains ran under what were known a 'Deepdene conditions'.

The LMSR Royal Train of 10 (or 11) cars comprised the King's saloon, the Queen's saloon, one (or two) saloon sleepers, three other saloons, a dining saloon, a dining car, and a first brake at each end. In the early part of the war the LMSR Train remained that inherited from the LNWR, but in 1941, on account of justifiable concern about Their Majesties' safety, three completely new all-steel armour-plated 12-wheel cars were built. Two were saloon sleepers, one for the King ('Mr Grove') and one for the Queen ('Mrs Grove'). They not only had double-glazed windows and air-conditioning but the windows were fitted with sliding armour-plated shutters. The third vehicle was a composite comprising generator, brake and staff sleeping compartments. When the King travelled without the Queen, the latter's saloon was left out of the consist, whereas when one or both of the Princesses (the 'Misses Grove') were travelling the extra saloon sleeper was added. In 1942 the LMSR also built two saloons (not armour-plated) for the LMSR chairman and other VIPs, equipped as self-contained mobile office/saloon/sleeping cars. After the war these two cars were converted into a lounge sleeper and dining sleeper for the use of Princess Elizabeth and Prince Philip.

On all these journeys the Royal Party included at least one private secretary, equerry, lady-in-waiting, maid, dresser, and valet, plus two footmen, and a chauffeur. Normally also various other VIPs, often in the war—military, would be travelling with the Royal Party. The Railway provided several senior officers (Mr Barrington-Ward—Divisional General Manager (Southern Area), often accompanied on LNER journeys), two senior police officers, as well as a number of attendants and engineering staff. Naturally, railway 'top management' were closely concerned with the supervision of the preparation, operation and safeguarding of the Royal Train and its occupants. (Before the war the driver of the Royal Train got a gratuity of £1, his fireman 50p—and officers concerned were sent pheasants at Christmas).

In peacetime the most detailed instructions and schedules were distributed in advance, and in wartime the instructions were much the same but not quite so widely circulated. Early in the war there was a great deal of concern—and discussion between the Palace, the railways, the REC and the Home Office—as to whether the plans for Royal Journeys should—as in peacetime—be printed and distributed to railway and other staff formally several days in advance. This was the 'Grove' Plan, favoured by the LMSR, GWR and SR; alternatively the schedules could be distributed as were those for an 'ordinary' Special, for the staff needed to check the route and ensure the safety of the Royal Train even on being informed only three hours ahead by telephone—the 'secrecy' plan, favoured by the LNER. Eventually, the 'Grove' plan, ensuring better physical security for Their Majesties but also less secret and more open to terrorism, was adopted.

Most of the instructions were aimed at the avoidance of any possible delay by other traffic, but Their Majesties' safety and comfort had to be safeguarded as well, by double-block signalling, but forbidding other trains to pass where they might come to a standstill beside the Royal Train—or splash it on water-troughs, and of course sites of possible terrorism such as bridges and crossings had to be guarded. Loud speakers on stations were not to be used as the train passed through, and—in peacetime—Air authorities were informed in advance, presumably to prevent disturbance of Their Majesties by low-flying aircraft. The Royal Train and its staff had to be as self-sufficient as possible, but detailed arrangements were made for its servicing—and heating, during stops. Provisions had to be made for replenishing the supply of gas for cooking and water for drinking,[8] but also ice for the pressure-ventilation system—which did not always work correctly. Also some other 'little essentials' had to be specially arranged:—'a supply of sanitary pans and steps will be required to be dispatched to York (addressed to R. M. Rutter, Esq., Superintendent, London & North-Eastern Railway, York) by the 2.12 p.m. train from Wolferton *via* Peterborough…' Charges made by the Railway were remarkably low: thus in 1959 HRH Princess Margaret was not charged more than the normal fares to attach her coaches to a service train, and only just under 10p/mile for her Special train from Newcastle to Barnard Castle.

Any amount of trouble was taken to look after Their Majesties. In the darkest days in July 1940, telegrams flew to top management of the LNER because the Queen had mislaid a book that slipped behind her bed on the Train: on another occasion the present Queen caused the train to be stopped twice in the night for examination because she heard an unusual noise under her compartment.

The LMSR Royal Train was kept at their Wolverton Works. For ECML journeys it was worked over *via* Bletchley and Sandy (reverse) to King's Cross,[9] to reach there some two hours before the scheduled departure. This was either too soon after 7 p.m. to allow dinner to be served *en route*, or departure was much later and the Royal Party slept while moving. Usually, at least the

Gresley B17/1 No. 1671 *Manchester City* was rebuilt by Thompson to B2 specifications in August 1945. By April of the following year the locomotive had been renamed *Royal Sovereign* and was allocated to Cambridge to work the Royal Train to Sandringham.

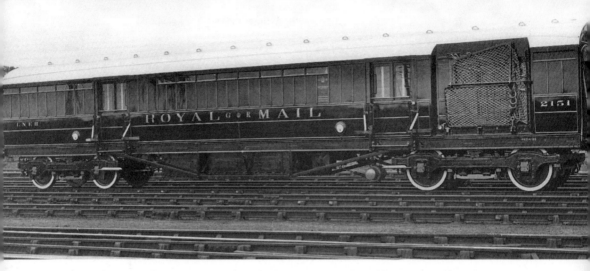

Above: Three new TPO cars were built in the late 1920s to replace old stock. These were soon sent to East Anglia and seven new cars took their place on the ECML. The first to be built was No. 2151 seen here in 1933.

Below: The armour-plated carriage constructed for George VI by the LMSR in 1941.

later part of the night was spent parked in some secluded—and well-guarded—siding, but also where Their Majesties could take a walk in the countryside. On journeys to East Anglia—other than Sandringham, the 'Night Halt' was made at Warren Hill (Newmarket), but on longer ECML journeys the site was quite often just north of Hertford on the Loop, or at Leadenham (Grantham–Lincoln line). Further north, night halts were made at Crimple or at Ripley Valley (both near Harrogate), or (after the war) at Baldersby (Melmerby–Thirsk line), Sledmere (Malton–Driffield line) or on the Wensleydale line from Northallerton. In Scotland, a favoured spot off the ECML was at Aberlady (on the goods-only branch east of Edinburgh); on the Royal Family's return from Balmoral in September 1944, they all ate and slept there on the Royal Train for two consecutive nights—although no doubt popping into Edinburgh for a few hours. On that occasion also, two

King George VI and Queen Elizabeth visiting Doncaster Works in October 1941. Fourth from the right is CME Edward Thompson and third is Assistant CME A. H. Peppercorn.

Royal Trains were assembled on 23 September, the main one to bring 'Mr and Mrs Grove' back to King's Cross and the other to take the 'Misses Grove' back to Ballater.

After the war and when Princess Elizabeth married Prince Philip they used a smaller set of LMSR Royal Coaches, made up into a train referred to as 'Deepdene', which comprised some of the 'Grove' stock together with the converted LMS saloons mentioned above, and for the less complicated journeys this train was also used after Elizabeth became Queen. Again, when one of the somewhat lesser Royal Personages such as Princess Margaret made a journey, just two or three of the Royal Coaches were run at the head of a service train, for example a night express from King's Cross to Edinburgh. On the other hand, while staying at Balmoral, the Queen several times used the whole Royal Train to pay a quick visit to friends at Bawtry, coming up from Ballaster overnight and returning the next night; the train was parked on the Misson branch and went to Doncaster for servicing after Her Majesty had alighted. Nonetheless, in peacetime some prolonged and elaborate tours were made by Their Majesties in the Royal Train, as when they toured in it—also in the Royal Yacht—around Scotland from 23 June until 7 July 1948.

Other Trains for Very Important Persons

During the war, the Prime Minister had his own train, which included two spare vehicles from the Royal Train, supplied at first by the LNER and then by the LMSR. Two special trains were

The interior of General Eisenhower's armour-plated saloon (code-named *Bayonet*), which was converted from a first class sleeper at Doncaster in early 1945.

also assembled for the operational use of Commanders-in-Chief. One train, already assembled in October 1941, was called 'Rapier'. It was made up of six coaches and three vans, comprising (in 1943): a first class sleeper with 10 berths and a shower, two first brakes for other ranks, a composite sleeper, a first saloon, a third restaurant car, one saloon being converted to an office—all LNER vehicles, an LNER generator van and two LMS motor car vans. 'Rapier' was used by the C-in-C Home Forces and his team, and was normally kept at King's Cross. The eight staff were all but one from the Army (including two ATS).[10] It ran 100,000 miles before it was disbanded in July 1945. The other train 'Alive', was a very heavy train of nine coaches, including two armour-plated cars (LNE No. 1591 and GW No. 574) as well as three sleeping cars, two carriage trucks and up to eight vans. It was assembled by the GWR at Swindon but incorporated an LNER sleeping car partly converted into a saloon and called 'Bayonet'. 'Alive' was created for the US Army and from January 1944, when he took over as Supreme Commander Allied Expeditionary Forces, the train was dedicated to General Eisenhower and his headquarters staff. It was kept at Old Oak Common and normally set off from Kensington Addison Road, until it was shipped over to the Continent in December 1944.[11] After the Victory in Europe, in July 1945 'Alive' was relinquished by the Americans and taken over by the War Office as Field Marshal Montgomery's special train, returned to England and eventually disbanded during the winter of 1945–46.

It would be most interesting to be able to detail the journeys made by both these trains, but records have not come to light.

Railway Hotels on the ECML

For the best-heeled ECML travellers—and for the 'Expense Account' ones—there were five major Hotels run by the LNER, the supervision of which came under a hotel committee appointed by the Board of Directors. All have survived to the present day, albeit since 1982 sold off by British Transport Hotels.

The Great Northern Hotel at King's Cross, like the station a Lewis Cubitt product, in spite of its five floors and an attic storey—making it unusually tall for its period, is yet almost dwarfed by the adjoining King's Cross and St Pancras stations. With a mere 69 bedrooms it was never one of London's best hotels, and as recently as 1950 a single bed & breakfast could be had for 95p. The Great Northern Hotel at Peterborough is likewise undistinguished, again in the severe style of GNR station architecture of the 1850s. Both these hotels have been demolished in recent years.

Altogether much more superior were—and still are—the NER's Royal Station Hotels at York and at Newcastle, and lastly there was the NBR's magnificent edifice adjoining Edinburgh Waverley and connected directly with it by lifts, the North British Hotel. All of these three great hotels were the principal and most prestigious in their cities. The North British Hotel (Balmoral Hotel since 1989) was built by W. H. Beattie in 1902, a magnificent pile of five storeys each with its own elaborate architecture, had no less than 400 rooms. Its palatial public rooms had splendid views over the sights of Edinburgh—and its own well-known clock-tower adding to them. Three of the storeys were below street level, and it had its own sidings off Waverley station. In 1939, bed, breakfast, luncheon and afternoon tea cost 92.5p at the Newcastle Royal Station Hotel, while a double-room with breakfast at the North British Hotel would cost £1.50 (a single room, £1.00).

These York, Newcastle, and Edinburgh LNER hotels were the general meeting places for society and business, renowned for their good food and wine, the resorts indeed of '*bon viveurs*'. With their banqueting rooms, ballrooms, and tea rooms of the 'Palm Court' variety, they were—and again to a large extent still are—the venue of countless dinners, conferences and other major events, and for innumerable important private assignations. In pre-war days and well into the 1960s, York and Newcastle boasted restaurants on the concourse. But, even in 1914 the hotels were catering for the 'opposition' by advertising their 'garages for motor cars'. In the Second World War these great hotels played a vital service to the myriad commissioned officers of the services, especially to those from the USA with their bottomless purses; the Royal Station Hotel at York being crowded with the more wealthy of the RAF officers from the numerous Bomber Command stations in the vicinity.

In LNER days, the hotels were managed by Area Hotel Superintendents responsible to the three Area General Managers. After Nationalisation, they came under the aegis of the BTC Hotels Executive (Chairman, Lord Inman until 1951, then Sir H. Methuen), which also ran BR's refreshment rooms and restaurant cars. When the Executives were abolished in 1953, they were taken over by the British Transport Hotels & Catering Services with its Board of Management (Chairman, Frank Hole). After the abolition of the BTC in turn in 1962, they were run by the nominally independent British Transport Hotels Ltd—still headed by Frank Hole. Following the election of the Thatcher government in 1979, and the deteriorating economic situation, pressure was put on British Rail to consider asset disposal. It was not long before the BT Hotels were under review. The hotels were sold by open tender, realising a much lower value for the UK taxpayer than the management buyout would have done. By 1984 the disposal was complete and the history of BTH was at an end.

5

Freight traffic on the ECML in 1939, in the war, and in the post-war period until the end of the 1950s

Pre-war, summer 1939 stations and yards

In commercial terms the freight traffic (in its broadest sense)[1] on the ECML was undoubtedly of equal value to that of passengers, but unlike on the other Northern main lines probably not more so. As a principal trunk route, the ECML had always been of great importance for the long distance carriage of the urgent traffic of parcels, mail and newspapers.

Yet it may not be appropriate to generalise about ECML freight, because even more than was the case with passenger traffic the flow was uneven along the length of the ECML. The middle section, Doncaster–Newcastle, passed through major industrial and coal- mining regions and connected with many other such areas and with east coast ports. That section therefore carried the greatest flow, while north of Newcastle freight flow was the least. Indeed, by far the greatest part of the freight passing along the ECML originated elsewhere than at the places directly served by the line. The possible flow of freight traffic along the ECML was also limited—a situation that arose originally from perhaps modest initial expectations of its nineteenth century builders, in that most of the route was only double-track, and moreover the four-track sectors were interrupted by stretches of double track which acted as bottlenecks and caused serious operating difficulties. When in the Grouping period the LNER wanted to speed up its expresses it had not the financial resources necessary for the elimination of these bottlenecks. Little more could be afforded than the breaking up of sections with automatic signalling, although with the assistance of a Government Loan Guarantee scheme parts of the busy section between York and Northallerton had been widened in the 1930s. Still, the elimination of the worst of the bottlenecks on this section was only carried out later, with Government funding, to cope with the great increase of freight traffic in the war.

The nature of the freight traffic in general varied somewhat along the ECML. Through trains for the conveyance of high class general merchandise, which was approximately equal in volume in each direction, ran between London and the major cities of Yorkshire, the north-east and Scotland, matching the primary flows of passenger traffic between these centres. One of its major predecessors (the GNR) having pioneered them, the LNER by the late 1930s was making major strides towards the provision of a regular and comprehensive service of fast braked freight trains—run mainly during the night, to cater for this important traffic which was already threatened by—and actually being lost to—road transport. In 1939 there were already about 75 partially or fully braked services running regularly on weekdays each way on all or part of the ECML.[2] The Class V2 2-6-2 locomotives were introduced specifically for these trains, and named the 'Green Arrow' class after the new designation of the premium, on the No. 1 Express Goods (fully braked) trains.

In the 1930s, merchandise—and livestock—was handled at the vast majority of stations, however small, on the ECML as in Britain generally. On a trunk line such as the ECML, on which many

BR 9F No. 92149 is at Hadley Wood on the down slow line, which was installed, along with the up slow, during the widening works of 1959. This abolished the bottleneck on the ECML between New Barnet and Potters Bar. *Picture: B. W. L. Brooksbank*

fast express trains were run and there was a dearth of relief lines, it was most unsatisfactory to try to operate slow goods trains that had to be backed out of the way into refuge sidings or stopping trains which needed to do shunting movements on to the through lines. Often the goods yards were only on one side of the main line, and at some places wagons from the conflicting direction had to be worked past to the next major yard and then back the other way. At some small sidings operated by a ground frame, the guard had to obtain a key to unlock it from the preceding signal box and arrange for the return of the key. After shunting was completed he had to ensure that all points and signals were restored for the main line. Operation of such sidings was normally forbidden at night or in fog or snow.

The only stations on the ECML which in 1939 did not cater for goods traffic were: the 'suburban' stations at Brookmans Park, Low Fell, Bensham, and Gateshead West, and the country stations at Dukeries Junction, Barnby Moor & Sutton, Moss, and Croft Spa. The goods traffic handled varied widely. Thus in the NE area, while the several Newcastle goods stations between them forwarded (in 1938) 170,000 tons of merchandise (Classes 7–21) and received 511,000 tons, Bradbury forwarded just one ton and received eight tons.[3] The goods station for Durham was not on the ECML at all, but across the city at Gilesgate, on a branch off the Leamside line; likewise, Croft Spa traffic was sent to the depot at the terminus of the Croft branch.

In the major cities there were of course large goods stations, providing employment for an army of men for the loading and unloading of many scores or hundreds of wagons each weekday, and to process piles of documentation relating even to the smallest consignment. Scores of other men drove railway-owned carts, hauled by live horses or the three-wheeled motor variety, which were driven round the town to collect or deliver, the LNER having in 1938 3,800 motor—and 4,300 horse-drawn cartage vehicles.

The major goods stations on or adjoining the ECML were the following:

King's Cross

By far the largest, this was located on a spur from Copenhagen Junction on the Down side between Gas Works and Copenhagen tunnels, next to the 'Top' locomotive depot. It comprised separate inwards (high level) and outwards depots and two satellite sheds on the south side of the locomotive depot. On the other side were substantial empties and coal yards; in the latter coal was dropped into delivery vehicles parked beneath the railway wagons, then were turned by capstans—as were merchandise wagons in the goods sheds. On the Up side, a great potato depot and market adjoined the main line. In 1939 over 1,100 men were employed in King's Cross Goods. They were supervised by the Goods Agent, F. C. Robbins (salary £650 a year), about 10 other managerial staff and over 45 foremen—some being 'working foremen'. In the Inwards Shed, 11 foremen controlled—on different shifts—123 porters, one 'underman', two lad porters and 57 loaders (who did the hardest work), five tracers, 60 checkers and 57 callers-off—all concerned with keeping tabs on the myriads of 'smalls' merchandise, while three number-takers checked the wagons for unloading. In the Outwards Shed, where work was even more complex, 17 foremen controlled 235 porters and 66 loaders who beavered away while the goods were checked by 72 checkers and but two callers-off, the wagons being recorded by five number-takers; there were also three 'undermen' and just one lad messenger—who must have been constantly on the run. Further similar men toiled away in the potato and granary sheds. Outside in the yards, six inspectors and 10 foremen oversaw the making up or breaking down of trains by 70 shunters and the marshalling of wagons by over 30 capstan-men, while 10 or so number-takers identified the wagons and containers—and of course work went on night and day. Finally, 152 King's Cross goods guards were in charge of trains on the move. Behind the scenes, a mere 35 or so clerks (one working all alone in the fish office)—less than 10 being women, documented all these operations, and just one time-keeper and one 'working foreman' kept order in the depot. Other goods depots had comparable but less numerous teams of men.

Continuing down the line, were the following: **Peterborough:** the goods station—also including a large tranship shed was on the Up side just south of Peterborough North station; **Grantham:** on the Up side just south of the station; **Newark:** on the Down side just north of the station; **Retford:** on the Up side north of the station; **Doncaster:** on the Up side just south of the station. **Selby:** on the Up side next to the station; **York:** Leeman Road, just north of the station on the Down side; **Darlington:** on the Up side of the goods lines passing Bank Top station on its east side; **Gateshead:** Eldon Street (also called Park Lane), on a spur from the Sunderland line west of Felling station; **Newcastle:** Forth Goods, adjoining King Edward bridge but on a spur from Forth Goods Junction off the Scotswood line,[4] and New Bridge Street Goods, adjoining Manors North station but on a spur from a junction on the Jesmond Loop; **Tweedmouth:** on the Up side, opposite the station. **Edinburgh:** South Leith, on the branch from Portobello; Leith Walk, on a spur of the North Leith branch just west of Easter Road station; Waverley (New Street), adjoining the east end of Waverley station on the south side.

Gresley A3 60092 *Fairway* hurries away with an Up express at Doncaster South Junction, passing St James Goods station on the right.

In the London area there were a number of other goods stations between which traffic was tripped in wagon-loads to and from the main ECML Yards at Finsbury Park (Clarence and East Goods) and at Ferme Park (between Harringay and Hornsey). Most of them belonged to other railways, but traffic also came from the LNER goods depots at Farringdon Street (on the Metropolitan 'Widened Lines'),[5] Royal Mint Street North (near Fenchurch Street station), Blackwall, Poplar, and Stratford Market.

In addition to the covered goods stations there were of course numerous goods and coal yards, usually serving a particular purpose, most commonly the discharge of coal. Subsidiary yards directly off the ECML in the London area included those before Finsbury Park at Caledonian Road, Ashburton Grove, and Highbury Vale. Wagons were distributed between the main ECML yards in London and a range of yards belonging to the LNER in East London, their coal yards on the SR at Elephant and Castle and at Brockley, and a number of small yards in the GN suburban area. In the London area there was of course also a great deal of interchange with the yards on the LMSR, GWR and SR.

In steam days, when there were relatively few fully-fitted freight trains running on the ECML—or on any other line—average freight train speeds were low (of the order of 25 mph for loose-coupled trains), and a round trip of about 75 miles out and back was a day's work for both locomotives and men. Therefore, quite apart from the necessity of having large marshalling yards (or sorting sidings) at major traffic centres, where wagons from many different outlets were assembled and sorted, it was necessary to have yards where engines and crews could be changed at key points roughly 75 miles apart on a main route. As the trains also had to be thoroughly examined—for safety of load, and especially for hot axle-boxes—it was convenient to combine these needs with remarshalling of trains at key junctions.

On the ECML, the principal marshalling and staging yards of this nature were at: Hornsey (Ferme Park), Peterborough (New England), Doncaster (Decoy and Mineral Yards), York (Dringhouses Yard, York Yard Down and Up, Skelton Sidings), Darlington (Croft Junction), Newcastle (Low Fell, and Heaton Down and Up Yards), Tweedmouth (superseding Berwick Yard, closed in 1939), Edinburgh (Niddrie West—supplemented by Meadows Yard from the beginning of the war until the late 1950s). Most of the above yards also served the vital parallel function of assembling and distributing wagon-load traffic brought from or dispatched to other yards, goods stations collieries etc. in their corresponding districts. Unlike at Whitemoor Yard at March or the yards at Woodford (Northants.) and elsewhere, their function was not in the first instance that of staging or remarshalling through traffic. Only at New England (one yard, of several) and at York Down Yard were there humps,[6] and none had the wagon retarders and other modern equipment of Whitemoor. Smaller marshalling yards were situated at: Tuxford, Doncaster area, Selby, Darlington (Bank Top), Ferryhill, and Portobello. The war brought into use the installations at Connington (between Abbots Ripton and Holme) and the reopening of Thirsk Yard and of Meadows Yard in Edinburgh, as well as considerable expansion of many of the major yards. After the war Dringhouses Yard at York was enlarged, and arranged specially for the preparation of braked trains.

Apart from Whitemoor, other major marshalling yards not far from the ECML which were the source of much ECML freight traffic were located at: Colwick, Welham, Annesley, Lincoln (Pyewipe and Holmes), Mansfield, Warsop, Worksop, Hexthorpe, Wath, Frodingham, Hull (Hessle Haven and Inwards), Gascoigne Wood (near Selby), Normanton, Lofthouse, Healey Mills (near Horbury & Ossett). Newport (between Thornaby and Middlesbrough), North Stockton, West Hartlepool, South Dock (Sunderland), Stella Gill, Consett, Gateshead (Park Lane and Norwood), Addison (Blaydon),[7] Tyne Dock (South Shields), and various yards in Central Scotland beyond Edinburgh.

At the larger towns down the length of the ECML, the following goods and coal yards—in addition to the principal marshalling yards named above, needed a shunting pilot at least for part of the day, a need that reflected the existence of a substantial amount of goods traffic:

Hatfield, Welwyn Garden City, Hitchin (South yard for Civil Engineer's depot, Cambridge Junction), Biggleswade, St Neots, Huntingdon North; Peterborough (Yaxley, Fletton, South yard, Westwood, Spital); Grantham (Down and Ambergate yards); Newark, Retford (Low yard, Whisker Hill and North yard); Doncaster (Belmont, West, and South yards, and Cattle Dock sidings, Carr Wagon Works, Locomotive Plant and Carriage Works, Cherry Tree, Marshgate and Wheatley Park Goods depots); Selby (Canal, Old, New, and Barlby Junction yards); York (Holgate Dock, Branches yard, Carriage and Wagon Works and Civil Engineer's yard, also Foss Islands Goods and Coal yards at the end of a branch off the Scarborough line at Burton Lane); Thirsk Junction Sidings—Yard from 1940, Thirsk Town Goods; Northallerton (Low and Castle Hills yards); Darlington (Croft and Darlington coal depots, West, Albert Hill, Northgate, Nestfield, Hope Town and Haughton Bridge yards, and various yards associated with the Locomotive and Wagon Works); Ferryhill (Old and New Sidings); Gateshead Oakwellgate, Lobley Hill, Hawks Siding, Park Lane Sidings, and Gateshead Warehouse, Redheugh and Redheugh Bank Foot, Dunston Staiths, West Dunston, Norwood and Blaydon West and North); Newcastle (Forth Cattle Dock and Infirmary yard, Trafalgar North and South, and Quayside yards); Morpeth, Alnmouth, Tweedmouth (Town yard and Tweed dock), Berwick (Goods and Cattle yards), Dunbar, Prestonpans; Edinburgh Rose Lane, between St Margarets and Abbeyhill Junction; Duddingston, Georgie sidings and cattle yard on the Suburban line, and St Leonards off it; several yards in the North and South Leith and Granton Dock areas, Lochend, Scotland Street, Heriothill).

Up and down the line, and especially in industrialised areas, factories, mills and plants sited—deliberately—near the railway were served by their own sidings. At these sidings raw materials and components could be directly off-loaded and outgoing products on-loaded by men employed by the concerns involved. Otherwise, in the case of coal mines and the largest industrial plants, branch railways were built to connect them with the main railway. The general provision of rail access to industry—wantonly removed since the 1960s—went a long way towards avoiding the necessity for rail-to-road transhipment of goods; the loss of them has been a major factor causing almost total transfer of freight from rail to road in recent times. Indeed, in the NE Area of the LNER (later to become the NE Region of BR), the tradition established by the NE Railway at the turn of the century of transporting coal in high-capacity (20-ton) hopper wagons, with bottom-discharge at coal-drops and staiths, was noteworthy for its relative efficiency—in an area where coal production and consumption was so great. Therefore, in addition to the principal marshalling yards named above, at numerous places down the length of the ECML there were groups of sidings either belonging to the railway or to other industrial concerns, and in the war military and other Government depots.

Although the ECML for parts of its length carried a great deal of coal, iron ore, and other raw materials destined for the heavy industrial plants of Humberside, South Yorkshire, Tees-side and Tyneside, and of the output of these plants and of the coal mines in the north Midlands, South Yorkshire, Co. Durham, Northumberland and East Lothian, very few of the mines and plants involved were directly on the ECML itself. Even in the Tyneside area, none of the great shipyards and works such as Vickers-Armstrongs actually had access directly to the ECML. Naturally, there was a wide variety of medium-size factories at principal towns down the ECML, such as engineering works at Peterborough, Grantham, Doncaster, York and Darlington, and sugar beet factories, breweries, flour mills etc. at Newark, Selby and Edinburgh. Nevertheless, the great bulk of merchandise on the ECML came on to it from its connecting lines.

Notable major industrial installations with their own sidings and (usually) private shunting locomotives, which were actually on or very close to the ECML included: Shredded Wheat Co. and Norton Grinding Wheel Co., at Welwyn Garden City; Little Barford electricity generating station, near Tempsford; London Brick Co. brickworks at Three Counties and, just south of Peterborough, the complex of 15 brickworks at Fletton and Yaxley, also British Sugar Beet Corp., at Fletton; Ransome & Marles Bearing Co., Newark; General Refractories, Bawtry; at Doncaster, Logan & Hemingway, British Bemberg Ltd, and Crompton Parkinson Small Arms, Wheatley Park, and Doncaster Gas Works; at Darlington, Cleveland Bridge & Engineering Co., English Steel Corp., Robert Stephenson & Hawthorn's and several other engineering works; at Birtley, Birtley Iron Co.; at Low Fell, a variety of factories at the extensive Team Valley Estate; at Gateshead/Newcastle, United Alkali Co., Vickers Armstrongs' Elswick Works, Robert Stephenson & Hawthorn's Forth Bank Works and various others.

In addition to the large independent locomotive works at Darlington (Robert Stephenson), and at Newcastle (R. & W. Hawthorn-Leslie), the LNER's own, locomotive, carriage and wagon works at Doncaster, York and Darlington, and the locomotive repair shops at Gateshead, together with wagon, engineering and masonry depots, were themselves major industrial installations.

The majority of collieries, including many quite close to the ECML, were served by lateral lines—usually built by the colliery companies, made connection only indirectly with the ECML itself, but during the war and after it provided tremendous coal traffic on to the ECML in Co. Durham and Northumberland. Coal mines adjoining and connecting directly with the ECML included the following:—Haworth (near Bawtry) and Rossington; Bentley near Doncaster; Mainsforth,

No. 4771 *Green Arrow* was the first engine of Gresley's V2 2-6-2 Class, which would eventually total 184 members. Only 25, including No. 4771, were constructed at Doncaster, the rest being the product of Darlington Works.

Thrislington and Tursdale near Ferryhill; Browney and Littleburn between Ferryhill and Durham; Kimblesworth south of Plawsworth, and Chester South Moor north of it. In Northumberland, several collieries near Killingworth, and at Dudley, Pegswood, Widdrington and Scremerston (Nesthill). In Lothian: at Seton, West Mains, Thornton, Walleyford and Preston Links near Prestonpans, and Monktonhall. In addition, during the war an open-cast site was opened at Cramlington, and soon after the war one at Widdrington. There were quarries and/or lime or cement works near the ECML at Aycliffe, Ferryhill, between Alnmouth and Little Mill, and Oxwellmains (near Dunbar).

There were several electricity generating stations very near the ECML, including Little Barford (between Tempsford and St Neots), Peterborough, Darlington, Portobello, etc. These consumed large amounts of coal, as did the numerous gas works up and down the country. After the war, mainly after 1959, new very large electricity generating stations furnished substantial and continuous additional traffic in coal on certain sections of the ECML, although only one—Cockenzie, near Prestonpans—actually had its extensive sidings beside the main line.

Apart from the transport of general merchandise and of coal and other minerals, the ECML—notably north of Doncaster, the GN&GE Joint line being a parallel artery south of there—was a trunk route for the exchange on the one hand of agricultural products (including livestock) from the highly productive lands of the eastern side of England, with on the other coal, fertilisers and farm equipment from the industrial regions further north. Naturally, agricultural traffic varied with the seasons, the ECML being concerned with one particular peak traffic during the winter, that of seed potatoes southwards from Scotland. The massive winter traffic in sugar beet was also borne on the ECML to a certain extent. North of York and especially between York and Northallerton, the ECML was virtually the sole carrier of the traffic in iron and steel from the great plants of Tees-side and Co. Durham to the consumers of steel—not least the motor car industry—of the Midlands. Furthermore, much of the enormous output of bulk chemicals produced at ICI Billingham, and in the 1950s also ICI Wilton, came away on to the ECML.

Freight Flows, Services and Routes

Focusing down on the working timetables (WTTs) of the period, interesting details of the operation of freight traffic on the ECML become apparent. Details of the freight trains and other comments given below refer—unless otherwise stated—to those given in the WTTs as scheduled to run on Tuesdays to Fridays. Schedules, and to an extent the number of trains, were often different on Mondays and Saturdays—especially at the peak summer weekends. Very few were scheduled to run after about 06.00 on Sundays. Furthermore it must be emphasised that this is in a peacetime context, whereas during the war large numbers of freight trains ran also on Sundays. Numerous freight trains were not scheduled in the WTTs but were run *ad hoc* under orders from Control. This applied particularly to the seasonal traffic and above all to the special trains in wartime.

Parcels, mail and newspaper traffic was a major source of income. Yet on the ECML most of the packages, bags and bundles were conveyed by passenger train in brake compartments or in vans attached, and there were few trains wholly devoted to this traffic. However, such trains ran at express train speeds. For instance, in 1939, there was the 21.30 SX Express Parcels from King's Cross to York, while the 22.50 King's Cross to York and Leeds was virtually a parcels and mails train, as it conveyed passengers only as far as Huntingdon. There was a daily early morning newspaper train to Grantham, and over Saturday night the 23.25 King's Cross to York took the *News of the World* etc. to the north of England. From York, on the other hand, there was one express parcels through to Edinburgh and four more of the same to Newcastle,[8] while Newcastle

After being run-in at Doncaster, No. 4771 was allocated to King's Cross and began working in the top freight links. The locomotive was also used a number of times for passenger trains.

sent one down to Morpeth as well as to Edinburgh. At Christmas time, these regular parcels trains were supplemented by many extra trains—and main platforms such as No. 1 at King's Cross and No. 8 at Newcastle Central were piled high with GPO parcels mail.

In addition, in the express but non-passenger category (Class C under BR), there were regular long distance empty coaching stock trains on the ECML. Before the war these were: Hornsey (Waterworks Sidings) to York (Clifton Sidings) and to Doncaster (both 'Q' trains), and King's Cross to Doncaster, with corresponding Up workings. After the war the principal regular train was the Newcastle (Delaval Sidings)–Holloway and the King's Cross–York trains. All these Class C trains were worked largely by the Pacifics and V2s, but often also by K3s. The importance of these regular parcels and other Class C trains not conveying passengers is underlined by the fact that many continued to run during the war; afterwards they were all restored virtually as in 1939.

Before further description, a few words about train classification are necessary. In the LNER system, No. 1 express goods trains were made up with vacuum-piped wagons only, 75 per cent of the train being fully braked, and could run at an average of 50 mph; under BR these trains came under the C classification that included parcels and other fully-fitted non-passenger trains. LNER No. 2 express goods trains were one-third braked, up to a maximum of 20 braked wagons behind the engine, and could run at an average of 40 mph; under BR these became Class D. The LNER also had two No. 3 express goods classes, braked (20 per cent of load) and unbraked (two or three wagons braked if possible), average speed 35 mph. No. 3 class was quite rare, the unbraked virtually overlapping with the Class A express freight (unbraked); average speed was 30 mph, and under BR they became Classes E and F. The other unbraked trains on the LNER were: through goods (Class B)—average speed 25 mph and class H under BR; mineral or empty wagon (Class C)—average speed 20—25 mph and class J under BR; finally, stopping freight (Class D)—was Class K under BR.

In the summer of 1939 there were scheduled times for 20 to 25 fully or partially fitted freights (Nos. 1 and 2 express goods) down and up the ECML from/to London, including three or four conditional. The majority of these trains ran in the night at times when the line was relatively free of passenger trains, but this was not so for some of them in the Down direction—all from King's Cross Goods. Representative of the rest, but varying between summer and winter, the Down day trains included:

> **321** 09.45 fish empties to New Clee, **389** 11.30 to Peterborough (Westwood), **527** 14.00 to York (Dringhouses), **584** 15.00 'fruit & veg.' to Manchester (Deansgate), **562** 15.35 to Niddrie West, **577** 16.05 to York (Dringhouses, **625** 17.15 to York Yard, and **669** 18.00 to Leeds. Train **562**, the 'Scotch Goods', was booked to stop only at Hitchin South (for water). Arlesey, Sandy, and St Neots (to be passed at each), Peterborough Westwood (for change of crews, not necessarily of engine), then to run non-stop to York Yard North, Newcastle Central, Tweedmouth, Berwick, and Niddrie West (arriving 02.40); in the 1950s this train was further accelerated. (Train **827** 23.00 King's Cross to York, which actually conveyed traffic only for Scotland, was also telegraphed as 'Scotch Goods').

Nearly all the Nos. 1 and 2 braked trains from and to London—with certain exceptions, like the 'Scotch Goods'—had to stop at both Peterborough (Westwood for Down or Spital for Up trains, or New England) and Doncaster, to change engines and/or take water. Unbraked trains stopped also at Hitchin (South Box on the Down, Cambridge Junction on the Up), Grantham and Newark, at least for water. Optional stops for water were designated at Offord, Essendine and Retford, also at Biggleswade in the Up direction, but stops for water at other places were strongly discouraged. Wagon examinations had to be made at both Peterborough and Doncaster.

Specific instructions laid down for many of the freight trains concerning conditional stops, shunting *en route*, make-up, load and traffic to be attached or detached make interesting reading, for example:

366 10.50 Class A goods and fish empties, King's Cross to Peterborough Westwood and No. 2 Braked from there to Doncaster Decoy: 'Worked by engine capable of hauling 60 wagons. May run at No. 2 speed by Control orders and if run main line may convey 75 wagons of goods and empties between London and Peterboro' when worked by a K3 engine. Stops Crews Hill when required to attach cattle for West Riding District.[9] Crews Hill advise control not later than 10.00 a.m. number of wagons. Room to be left accordingly. To be held Huntingdon North on Mondays for cattle from St Ives, on train due 4.11 p.m. On Mondays to Fridays inclusive to attach at Arlesey and Langford traffic for Manchester and the North which must be put off at Biggleswade for re-forwarding on **584**, **625** and **669** Down. May attach at Biggleswade vegetable traffic for Doncaster.[10] Convey from St Neots, when necessary, Mondays to Fridays fitted wagons containing market traffic for Huddersfield and West Riding, which must be detached Peterboro' the former for connection with **625** and latter for connection with **669**. Stops St Neots on Saturdays when necessary to attach traffic for Glasgow. When conveying tanks of petroleum for Botolph Bridge siding or important traffic for Fletton, train must stop at Fletton to detach.'

527 14.00 No. 1 Braked Goods, King's Cross to Dringhouses, Saturdays excepted 'Worked by "K3" engine. Load 60 wagons. Convey from King's Cross and Clarence Yard all Scotch wagons available. Load to be made up at Clarence Yard if necessary, with wagons for N.E. Area. Attach at Clarence Yard wagons off:– 1.49 p.m. from Farringdon Street, 1.0 p.m. from Victoria Dock, 1.5 p.m. from Royal Mint Street, 12.50 p.m. from Poplar Dock.'

584[11] 15.00 No. 2 Braked Fruit and Vegetable, King's Cross to Manchester, Saturdays excepted: 'Worked by engine capable of handling 60 wagons London to Colwick. Traffic for Blast Lane, Sheffield, loaded in fitted wagon and attached next engine. Convey vegetable traffic for Deansgate, C.L.C., Liverpool, Sheffield, Nottingham and West of Colwick. Convey from Biggleswade, Doncaster (Decoy) road van which must be transferred to **669** Down at Peterboro' Westwood. Also wagon for Chesterfield Central and road van for Peterboro' containing traffic for latter and L.M.&S. line. Convey from St Neots vegetable traffic for West Riding, to be transferred at Peterboro' to **669**. St Neots to advise control nightly number of wagons for north of Peterboro'. Guards to give St Neots necessary information. Perishable traffic from Tempsford for Deansgate and Liverpool is sent St Neots by suitable empties train which must reach latter by not later than 6.15 p.m. otherwise **584** must stop Tempsford to attach. Transships for Sheffield, Manchester, Liverpool and Cheshire Lines from Tempsford are forwarded from St Neots on **465** Down passenger, which must not be delayed in consequence.'

Of some interest also was that **23**, the 00.27 King's Cross Goods to Grimsby 'conveys mails, parcels and post hampers for Hitchin, Letchworth, Baldock, Royston, and Huntingdon.'

In the Up direction, with all the coal, fish, meat and vegetable needs of London and the south-east to be satisfied, the nature of the freight traffic was somewhat different from that on the Down, many of the Down trains being made up largely of empty wagons. The fast fish and meat trains with their specially equipped insulated wagons were a very important traffic all the year up the ECML, and in the winter so were the seed potato trains from Scotland to East Anglia. These traffics survived but little curtailed throughout the 1950s. In 1939 there were two booked express fish trains from Aberdeen, three from Hull and two from Grimsby, also one from Cowlairs (conveying Mallaig traffic), and there was an express meat train from Aberdeen and another from York. All these were No. 1 braked trains with fast schedules, and the motive power in 1939 was usually a K3. However, current new construction of V2s allowed a rapidly expanding utilisation of this more powerful class, which could take a load of 525 tons whereas a K3 was limited to 420 tons. One train at least, the 10.45 meat train from Aberdeen to King's Cross had 'to be given precedence over other trains as given express passenger trains.' (Similar special attention was given to the seed potato trains, from fear of frost damage). In addition, there were two regular vegetable trains from Lincolnshire, one starting from Sibsey, the other from Olde Leake, and in the sugar beet season—especially during and after the war, many special trains were run out of the eastern counties to the beet factories in the Midlands, four of which were on the ECML at Peterborough, Newark, Selby and York.

Lastly, an interesting train that joined the ECML at Grantham was the overnight milk train from Stafford Common *via* Eggington Junction, Derby Friargate and Nottingham Victoria to King's Cross. This train ran up at near express speed, but the empties went down (05.02 King's Cross to Derby) in more leisurely fashion—and also conveyed passengers after Hitchin. During the war the milk train started from Derby, and continued to do so until withdrawn in 1951.

As for coal, merely the LNER and private coal terminals on the GN line in the London area received about 32,000 tons of coal per month before the war, and a great deal more was consigned to other terminals in London or passed over to the SR for further transit to places in the southeast. Therefore, from New England Yard about 18 coal trains came up to Ferme Park—plus two to East Goods Yard, each Tuesday to Friday (slightly fewer on Mondays and Saturdays), and there

A Class H freight passes through Doncaster station, taking the Platform 3 Up Through line, on 17 July 1947 and is headed by Class O2/3 2-8-0 No. 3963. *Picture: B. W. L. Brooksbank*

was a corresponding number of empties trains on the Down. In addition, about five brick trains came up daily. Because of the constraints on line occupation, trains were usually made as long as possible, the 2-8-0s (2-10-0s in the 1950s) normally employed being allowed 80 loaded 10-ton wagons while 2-6-0s could take 70 (56 when running at class A speeds). For the brick trains from Fletton, the distinctive 50-ton bogie wagons were used; these were rated as equivalent to four 10-ton wagons when loaded, to three when empty. The two Gresley P1 2-8-2s were capable of handling 100 loaded coal wagons, but by 1939 such long trains were no longer run—on account of the dearth of loops of sufficient length; nor were they run during the war.

The standage in the sidings at both New England and Ferme Park was large (about 3,000 wagons), but this nevertheless did not allow for any great accumulation of traffic, 3,000 wagons corresponding to about 35–50 trains or only two to three days' traffic. The main limitation lay in the speed with which the coal traffic could be distributed when it got to Ferme Park, for each 80-wagon coal train required four transfer trips to take the traffic on further. It was vital therefore to keep the essential flows moving constantly, and to organise the marshalling in such a way as to keep shunting to the minimum. The latter was achieved by laying down for Up trains a fairly rigidly ordered grouping of wagons according to their destinations in the London area and on the SR beyond it.

Although severe gradients were not really a problem, the ruling gradient being 1-in-200,[12] it was not easy to work—along with many expresses including the high-speed streamliners—the slow, heavy loose-coupled trains on a main line with several two-track bottlenecks. Running times therefore had to be adhered to, and points where the trains had to stop and wait—sometimes for an hour or more—were clearly laid down. Running speeds and therefore overall times between New England and Ferme Park depended on the class of train and proportion (if any) of braked wagons. Running times varied between about 3½ hours for Class A and 5 hours for Class C trains. All these trains stopped at Hitchin, where normally New England crews changed over with Hornsey men, but some trains were scheduled not only to stop to detach/attach but also to shunt at certain other places on the way. Intermediate traffic however was largely catered for by the pick-up goods trains, which took anything up to 15 hours between King's Cross Goods and New England.

The Hertford Loop (Wood Green–Hertford North–Langley Junction) was used by several of the goods and coal trains, as a relief line avoiding the Greenwood–Potters Bar and Digswell–Woolmer Green bottlenecks. However, it suffered from a lack of refuge sidings and from a consequent restriction of its usefulness mainly to times outside that of the peaks of the important residential traffic on the stretch between Wood Green and Cuffley. There was also the daunting 1-in-57 of the Wood Green flyover to be surmounted by Down trains.

Apart from all the high-value merchandise, the food and the coal and brick trains that ran on the ECML into London, livestock was also carried in great numbers, varying according to market days. Cattle wagons had to be booked if possible by stationmasters in advance, and trains conveying these wagons when loaded were instructed to limit their shunting to a minimum; nevertheless, the unfortunate animals were often much buffeted around. Before and during the war, horses were still employed in large numbers as motive power for shunting and especially for delivery work to and from the goods stations. There were so many horses around King's Cross that a manure train was run daily at 03.55 from Ferme Park to Sandy—where the load was presumably distributed to numerous farms in the region, and other trains were scheduled to take odd wagons of manure to other country stations. But lasting into the 1960s was the daily 'dust train'—latterly of great 50-ton wagons, of household refuse, from Ashburton Grove to Blackbridge or Holwell Sidings on the branches from Welwyn Garden City.

The traffic each way over the ECML between Peterborough, Grantham and Doncaster included: firstly, the express goods trains from London already mentioned, some of which turned off at Grantham for Nottingham and further west. Secondly, there were a considerable number of trains that joined the ECML at Newark or at Tuxford and ran on down it to Doncaster and beyond, and *vice versa*. Thirdly, there was a sizeable flow of coal (or empties) and goods trains to and from New England Yard *via* Grantham to Colwick Yard or to Doncaster, and also one or two brick trains northwards from Fletton.

The New England loose-coupled trains were principally for the staging of the London and south-east coal traffic in transit from and to the collieries of the north Midlands (collected principally at Colwick) and south Yorkshire (collected mainly at Doncaster). Eight or so a day of these trains rumbled up and down the ECML, but owing to the limited capacity of the mainly double track line north of Stoke Summit, almost as many trains were sent round *via* Spalding. Sleaford (or in the war, Boston), and Lincoln.[13] These trains round the Loop were much increased during the war and its aftermath. The time taken on the relatively roundabout routes was only about 20 minutes more than straight down the ECML to Doncaster, but trains rarely had to be stopped to allow passenger trains to overtake, and there were no banks like Stoke to climb. Coal trains of 80 wagons could be run on the GN&GE, because not only were the gradients negligible but also many of the loops were long enough; O4 or other 2-8-0s could manage them, not only in terms of haulage power but also of braking. On the main line a stop for water was mandatory in either direction at Newark—even for fast freight trains if they were slowed too much to pick up at the Muskham troughs, and trains might be scheduled to wait there for an hour or so, also at Retford (Babworth). With through trains, prolonged stops were usually made at Doncaster Decoy for locomotive and crew purposes and for wagon examination.

Coal traffic between Mansfield Concentration Sidings and New England used the route *via* Lincoln in order to avoid Nottingham. Most of the trains between New England and Colwick went over the ECML over Stoke Summit as far as Grantham, but some went instead *via* Sleaford. The line that joined the ECML at Newark South Junction from Bottesford West Junction brought in about 15 regular daily trains to and from further north—Doncaster, Hull, York etc., a similar number to those leaving the ECML at Grantham. Both groups were mainly on their way to/from Colwick, but not least were the ale trains from Burton-on-Trent to Hull and to Newcastle. During and after the war, a number of trains—mainly of ironstone, off the GN&LNW Joint line also joined the ECML at Newark. Through Grantham passed also the ironstone trains from Highdyke, to Frodingham (for Appleby–Frodingham Steelworks at Scunthorpe) *via* Lincoln or *via* Doncaster, or to Parkgate & Aldwarke (for the Don Valley blast furnaces) *via* Retford,[14] or to Colwick (for onward working to Stanton Ironworks). During and after the war ironstone trains also ran to Tees-side and to Scotland.

Joining the ECML at Tuxford North was a flow of coal traffic to Hull, originating from Nottinghamshire collieries and marshalled at Mansfield Concentration Sidings or at Warsop Junction, and also the principal through freight and fish trains to/from the GC system at Kirkby South Junction by the LD&EC line through Mansfield. There were as well two express Fish trains daily from Hull southbound through Doncaster and by this route to Banbury, conveying fish consigned to destinations on the GWR as far afield as Swansea, Bristol and Penzance.

The ECML between Doncaster and York, the section linking the Southern Area with the North-Eastern Area of the LNER, was heavily utilised for freight as well as passenger trains. As well as many of the through express goods to York and beyond already mentioned, trains from Whitemoor *via* the GN&GE Joint Line (joining the ECML south of Doncaster) and those from

Grimsby and Frodingham (joining at Joan Croft Junction), ran over most of this stretch of the ECML, and it had 25 to 30 scheduled goods and coal trains each way per day. The line was very largely plain double track, so most extra trains—especially during the war, along with coal trains to Gascoigne Wood Yard assembled at Hexthorpe Sidings or from Bentley Colliery—had to be sent round *via* Knottingley and Church Fenton.

At Chaloner's Whin Junction, the ECML traffic was joined by all that coming into York from the Leeds, Normanton and Sheffield directions (also Hull *via* Selby), including the LMS trains. In 1939 this traffic comprised about 40–45 daily scheduled goods trains, of which about 15 were Nos. 1 and 2 express goods. The LNE trains originated principally from: Neville Hill (Leeds), Gascoigne Wood, Sheffield, Mexborough, Wath (plus *via* Woodhead from Mottram, Dewsnap, Brunswick (Liverpool) and Birkenhead), Colwick, Staveley, Annesley, Woodford, Neasden, Banbury and Park Royal (London, GW). The limited number of LMS trains came mainly from Wakefield, Sheffield, Masborough or Toton. Before the war, nearly all the freights from the Church Fenton direction terminated at either Dringhouses or York Yards, although two braked trains from Hull went on respectively to Heaton and Monkwearmouth and one train ran through from Normanton to Forth (Newcastle).[15] Notable were three No. 1 express meat trains from Huskisson (Liverpool) to Dringhouses, also three (conditional) cattle trains from Holyhead on the LMSR. One braked and two unbraked trains came from as far away as Woodford, but as stated already the pre-war pattern was generally based on loose-coupled trains running between yards not more than about 75 miles apart. During and after the war there were many more workings from yards south of York through to points in the north-east and Scotland. Northward destinations included: Newcastle (New Bridge Street and Forth Goods, Low Fell, Heaton, Addison (from 1942), and Park Lane), Edinburgh (Niddrie West Yard), West Hartlepool, Stockton, Darlington (Croft), and above all Newport Yard on Tees-side.

The freight traffic north from York, before the war consisting on the Down mainly of trains remarshalled there—but on the Up also the express meat and fish trains from Scotland to London already mentioned—all had to be funnelled along the line through Northallerton, which was four track for only part of the way at that time. Nevertheless, about 60 goods trains each way were scheduled over the stretch each weekday, the majority running at night, and no doubt as elsewhere this number was considerably swollen by various other trains running more or less *ad hoc* under the orders of Control. A substantial proportion of scheduled trains north of York in peacetime were No. 1 or No. 2 braked goods, otherwise almost all were either class A or class B, and thus timed to avoid holding up express trains. Nevertheless many of the freight trains were booked to stop at Pilmoor on the Down and at Thirsk (where they often watered) on the Up, to be passed by fast trains.

Many of the above, especially the unbraked trains serving the Tees-side industrial area *via* Newport Yard, but also including such braked trains as the 00.01 and 12.10 York Yard to Park Lane Yard, the 23.00 Hull to Monkwearmouth, and 01.15 Dringhouses to Forth (and equivalent trains in the Up direction), turned off at Northallerton to be joined by others coming up the Leeds Northern line through Ripon, leaving 25 to 30 braked and only about five unbraked goods trains to continue down the ECML to Croft Yard, Darlington, and beyond. Before the war there were just two goods trains in the WTT that joined at Northallerton from the Ripon line: the 18.51 No. 2 braked goods Armley (Leeds) to Forth, and the 22.00 Class A Starbeck to Croft, but during the war maximum use was made of the Leeds Northern line to relieve the main line through York, including traffic towards Darlington. Before the war the few freight trains passing through York stopped in the York Yards for examination or for water and crew and/or locomotive change. During and after the war the situation was quite otherwise with the majority running through York. The principal Down through trains being mainly handled at the expanded Holgate Reception Sidings. In the Up direction they were usually stopped at Clifton Box, used the newly-built Up loop and passed through the Passenger Station. From 1942 also, with the Skelton New Sidings in operation, through unbraked goods trains made prolonged stops there, in both directions. Between York and Newcastle there were few if any prolonged stops laid down, and crew changes, if they took place at all, were made at Croft Yard or Darlington.

Quite a number of freight trains started and ended their journeys at Croft Yard, which dealt not only with Darlington traffic but that to and from many of the branches of west Durham, and it was therefore much more than a staging point on the ECML. Thus on the ECML north of Darlington the total number of timetabled trains (and the small proportion of unbraked goods) were very much the same as south of Darlington. Of these 30 to 35 trains, before the war only four braked trains (22.35 Hull to Heaton, 05.05 Croft to Tyne Dock Bottom, and 04.10 and 07.55 York Yard to Park Lane) were booked to turn off at Ferryhill on to the Leamside line; the rest continued to and through Newcastle *via* Durham. The Leamside line catered mainly for the loose-coupled coal and steel traffic between Tees-side (Newport and Croft Yards) and South Dock (Sunderland), Tyne Dock, Park Lane, and Heaton, so only using the ECML through Ferryhill. During the war the Leamside line was used a great deal more–notably for convoy coal trains, and continued to be in the 1950s.

North of Newcastle, Heaton Yard was a major staging and marshalling yard and in 1939 nearly all the freight trains on the ECML began or ended their journeys there. In Edinburgh, ECML freight ended up (or originated at) the yards at Niddrie West, Leith Walk, Portobello, or—during the war and after Meadows. However, as many trains were to or from yards beyond Edinburgh, *i.e.* High Street or Sighill in Glasgow, Cadder, Townhill (Dunfermline), Thornton, or Craiginches (Aberdeen). The summer 1939 WTT shows 16 express braked trains running down to Berwick and Edinburgh of which only four were No. 1 braked—namely the 'Scotch Goods'—and its 16.05 'Q' relief, from King's Cross, the 21.40 from York to Niddrie West, and the 19.15 express fish Hull to Edinburgh. In the Up direction there were however 12 (two 'Q' conditional) express goods passing Heaton daily, including fish and meat trains: the 22.35 High Street (Glasgow) to Dringhouses, 20.35 Aberdeen to East Goods Yard, 03.40 'Q' Joppa to Dringhouses, 10.45 Aberdeen and 14.53 'Q' Edinburgh to East Goods Yard meat trains, 13.45 and 14.10 Aberdeen and 19.25 Edinburgh to King's Cross, 17.19 Leith Walk to York, 17.18 and 18.22 Niddrie West to Marylebone, and the 18.25 Niddrie West to Dringhouses. Tweedmouth was a staging point, and there or at Berwick Heaton crews changed over with men from St Margarets. There were some crew changes arranged at Alnmouth or Dunbar (a regular stop for water), and with the line before the war very much lacking refuge loops there were a number of stations where goods trains were scheduled to shunt off the main line and wait to be overtaken. This, and much else, changed radically in the war.

ECML freight traffic during the war

The effects of the war on ECML freight traffic reflected the changes on the railways have been outlined in chapter 3, but there were factors peculiar to this particular trunk route and to the regions it served. On the LNER the most marked change in traffic pattern arose from a very great reduction in the export through east coast ports of coal, steel and the products of heavy industry resulting in the diversion of these traffics to long inland hauls.

The ECML was naturally recognised as absolutely vital to the prosecution of the war. When in May 1940 the German Blitzkrieg raised the real threat of a German invasion of Britain, the major

Above: An up Class F freight is brought over Selby swing-bridge by Thomspon B16/3 Class 4-6-0 No. 61418. On the left is Selby North Box, which controlled traffic on the lines over the bridge. An additional signal box, seen in the background, was placed on a gantry above the lines to move the bridge for river traffic. *Picture: B. W. L. Brooksbank*

Below: Peppercorn K1 Class 2-6-0 No. 62061 passes through York station with a Class H freight on 13 April 1957. The engine was built by the North British Locomotive Co.'s Queen's Park Works in December 1949 and was in service until December 1964. *Picture: Bill Reed*

Above: Ex-WD 2-8-0 No. 90434 (ex-WD No. 7474, LNER No. 3113) takes a typical train of special wagons for steel plates back to the great steelworks at Middlesbrough. The locomotive is leaving the ECML just south of Northallerton and taking the Low Level Loop to Eaglescliffe and Tees-side. *Picture: B. W. L. Brooksbank*

Below: Passing over the Scarborough line flat crossing over the ECML at the north end of York station is Ivatt Class 4MT 2-6-0 No. 43130. The engine is in charge of a freight service from the coastal resort on 29 December 1952. *Picture: Yorkshire Post*

bridges, tunnels, junctions, yards and depots along the whole length of the line were designated as vulnerable points (VPs)—as were those on the other key routes across the country, susceptible to attack by enemy airborne troops or to saboteurs. The VPs were therefore assigned armed guards, initially from the Field Army but soon taken over by the Home Guard—especially at night-time. From mid-May 1940 when the menace of a German invasion on the east coast was taken quite seriously—until instructions were rescinded in mid November 1940, locomotives (and breakdown cranes) in steam were moved inland at night from places on the east coast. Railwaymen were anyway given quite precise instructions about what to do with trains on the move and with locomotives if the enemy came, instructions that included derailing locomotives to block the exits from sheds and their immobilisation. It is not clear what effect these desperate measures had on the ECML in particular, but one report mentions 99 locomotives being moved from the coast every night on the GE section.

The ECML—directly or indirectly—was affected by wartime conditions in certain respects particularly. It served some of the greatest concentrations of the iron and steel industry (in South Yorkshire, Humberside, Tees-side, Tyneside and Clydeside) on which all war production ultimately depended, and the traffic on the NE section of the ECML was probably the most radically affected. In peacetime most of the huge coal output of Northumberland and Co. Durham was consumed by heavy industry in the region or shipped from local ports. Freight traffic in general on the main line north of Northallerton was relatively light, but this was to change notably from the outbreak of the war as the short haul traffic diminished and that on the main line expanded.

The convoy coal train plan introduced on 26 February 1940 entailed a programme of up to 200 block coal trains per week from Northumberland and Co. Durham, and 71,500 tons of coal was to be conveyed to London and the south-east each week. (The gas works alone needed 51 train loads weekly, and electricity generating stations, 49). All the block coal trains as well as everything else had to run on the ECML certainly through Northallerton and mostly along the whole stretch between Ferryhill and York. Most convoy trains joined the ECML at Ferryhill, but some went *via* West Hartlepool and Stockton. The number of freight trains passing daily through Northallerton in March 1941 was 56—double that in March 1938. The capacity of the main line through York was already overstretched, especially by the traffic to and from the heavy industries of Tees-side, that of the Leeds Northern line down to Harrogate being limited by its rather severe gradients. The programme still involved running 94 extra coal trains per week south of Doncaster; 54 up the GN&GE Joint Line and still 30 up the ECML all the way. The remaining ten were routed *via* Newark, Bottesford and the GN&LNW Joint line on to the WCML. A mere four were sent up the GC London Extension main line, the capacity of which had yet to be radically enhanced before it could carry the extra traffic that had to be sent that way as the war progressed. The massive programme meant that drastic cuts had to be made in passenger services. The demand for paths, wagons, men and locomotives resulting from the convoy coal trains and other wartime freight traffic on the ECML was alleviated little by the decline in the traffic through east coast ports. Later in the war, these ports came back fully into use for traffic in troops and war equipment from America.

The enormous production by the Tees-side plants of semi-finished iron and steel sometimes overwhelmed the railways. The number of wagons dealt with daily at Newport Yard doubled, to 4,500 in each direction, and hundreds of wagon-loads had to be held back, or else the ECML relieved by dispatching output over to Manchester (by rail) to be forwarded from there to South Wales by sea. Fertiliser output from ICI Billingham was very large, although varying according to the season, while over 15,000 tons per week of Durham coke were sent south in addition to the convoy coal. The output of Consett Ironworks in 1942 amounted to an average of 230 wagons per day, and that of Vickers-Armstrongs in Newcastle to 60 a day. The NE Area coped in part by bringing in its scheme of rewarding men with bonuses for speedy working, hard as this was on locomotives, which had to work flat-out almost continuously, seven days a week and 24 hours a day with boiler wash-outs delayed often until the engines almost broke down. Further south, the steelworks of Lysaght, Appleby–Frodingham, and Richard Thomas in the Scunthorpe area were turning out (in 1942) 1,000 wagons a day, as were the steelworks in the Sheffield/Rotherham area on to the LNER alone, and much of this output was carried on to the ECML.

From the beginning of the war, there was a very great increase in freight traffic to and from Scotland by the ECML, which by mid-1942—*i.e.* before *Bolero*—was about double that carried before the war. Under the *Bolero* programme the LNER was called upon to cope with an average of eight troop trains and four supplies trains per day from Scotland to the south and east of England throughout 1943 and much of 1944. The transfer of much import traffic from east coast to west coast ports, extensive use was made of over-side discharge of ships in the Clyde and landing from lighters at Craigendoran, together with traffic from the Faslane Military Port No. 1, led to great increases in freight traffic on the LNER at Glasgow. There was consequently a large expansion on the ECML of English traffic to and from Clydeside, which could not be carried by the LMSR because of the bottleneck at Carlisle. This was an inter-company arrangement begun during the great freeze of January 1940.

About five trains a day from the Glasgow area to Lancashire which would normally have come up by the LMSR were handed over to the LNER and run *via* Berwick, York and Leeds or Woodhead. Also, two a day for London and one a day for Birmingham were sent over the LNER from Carlisle to Newcastle and thence south. In the Down direction, trains of iron ore and dolomite for the steel works at Rutherglen were carried on the ECML. In a May 1941 report it is recorded that while on one day 5,940 wagons from Scotland were awaiting acceptance by the LMSR, in addition as many as 4,326 were to come south by the LNER *via* Berwick. The average diversion of traffic across the border from the LMSR to the LNER in 1941 was 5,600 wagons per month.[16] In addition to this extra traffic from Glasgow, the ECML also had to handle a great deal more traffic to and from Leith Docks, which were heavily engaged in military traffic.[17] As well, from October 1941 Leith became a major port for shipping supplies to Russia.[18]

The LNER also relieved the LMSR of some of its traffic to London and the south-east from Merseyside *via* the CLC and from Manchester. In winter 1940–41 four goods trains a day and three trains of meat and one of whale oil, which had previously run up the WCML to Willesden, were routed *via* Woodhead and Colwick to King's Cross instead. Also, by the use of the GW/GC axis through Banbury and Woodford, the LNER relieved the LMSR to a similar degree by taking over traffic from the south-west to Scotland normally routed by the WCML—but this traffic also still came on to the ECML at York. In winter 1941–42 the ECML was overloaded. Some of the iron ore trains from Highdyke to Rutherglen, together with some that had been taken off the LMS at Codnor Park also coke and dolomite trains from Scotland to London, had to be routed by the LMSR Settle & Carlisle Line, while straw trains from the GE section to Leith were now handed over to the LMSR at Peterborough. This situation persisted, and even in the autumn of 1946—well over a year after the end of hostilities—traffic to Scotland was being diverted from the LNER to the LMSR.

In 1944 the ECML carried an extra burden, because as well as military supplies from Scotland additional coal was once again being moved from the north-east. Additionally, most of the east coast ports were now being used as points of entry for US military supplies and after D-Day for stores shipments to the Normandy beaches.[19] By this time the route over the GC main line,

Woodford and Banbury was saturated and supplies for the American Army in the south and west were already having to be diverted over the ECML and through London. At the beginning of 1944, imports through Immingham—mainly of steel and military supplies from America—was three times those of a year before and continued at that rate until September 1944. In May 1944 compared with the previous peak month of November 1943, the extra traffic southwards up the ECML balanced out as follows.

Through Berwick about 280 wagons a day extra military stores and 30 a day of coal had to be passed south, and this was offset only by a reduction of 230 wagons a day: 100 of timber, 15 of iron and steel, 65 empty lime wagons, plus the equivalent of 50 wagons by withdrawal of passenger trains. Between Newcastle and Northallerton, 2,350 extra wagons per day had to be moved south (made up of the 310 coming from Scotland, 390 of imports through north-east coast ports and 1,650 extra wagons of Northumberland and Durham coal); the extra was offset by a reduction of a mere 645 wagons (230 from Scotland, 145 of iron and steel, 235 empty ore wagons, 10 of basic slag and 25 of lime from Billingham). Through Northallerton a maximum of 5,850 wagons could pass per day, but the above extra burden coming from the north was further increased by 25 wagons a day of fertiliser from Billingham. Southwards from Doncaster, the new burden amounted to a net increase of 1,115 wagons a day: 750 from north of York, swollen by 365 of imports through the Humber—mitigated only by reductions of passenger services equivalent to 100 wagons per day. Up from Doncaster all the three principal routes were already working to full capacity. Earlier in the war the GN&GE Joint Line had some spare capacity, but in 1944 this line was fully occupied with the heavy traffic to the eastern counties air force bases, and the GC main line southward was also working to the full. The LNER was therefore obliged not only to cut passenger services severely but also to reduce southward movements of the less essential freight and it was compelled to apply extensive embargoes. Thus about 25 regular trains (passenger and freight) per day had to be cancelled on the ECML to allow the extra *Overlord* traffic to get through.

During the first six months of 1943, British and American Army depots dealt with 2.1 million wagons, but in the first half of 1944 the figure rose to a staggering 3.1 million. In the three months April–June 1944 railways ran 45,538 special trains (passenger and freight) on Government account, and in the period July–September 1944 55,787 trains; 3,150 trains being handled by the NE Area—which gives a measure of the number on the ECML. Despite the reduction of convoy coal trains after the winter of 1941–42, the total wagon-miles on the LNER Southern Area—of which at least half would be on the ECML, reached peaks of 89 million in September 1942, 88 million in November 1943 and 94 million in July 1944. The climax in traffic came in June 1944, total traffic moved nationwide in the four weeks after D-Day (6 June) at 2,027 million ton miles exceeding even the previous peak in September 1943 of 1,977: in the week ending 9 June 884,000 loaded wagons were dispatched. The peak week for special trains was that ending 17 June, when the railways ran 3,063 special trains for troops and stores: also 86 ambulance, 21 military postal and 25 prisoner-of-war trains. Of the specials, 180 troop trains and 364 supplies trains originated on the LNER, while 528 troop and 932 supplies trains travelled at least in part over the LNER. It seems likely therefore that about 1,000 military specials ran on the ECML or part of it that week, and it would be interesting to know the figures for traffic passing major ECML junctions—let alone details of trains, but these can only be imagined.[20] The extra *Overlord* traffic continued for at least three months after D-Day, and even in October 1944 the LNER was still running twice as many military specials as in the same already busy period a year before. The net ton-miles of freight remained near 2,000 million per month until the end of 1944, and the number of military specials did not fall off appreciably until the end of the war in Europe in May 1945. Indeed freight traffic in general on the LNER did not decline until after VE- Day, for during the first six months of 1945 it was 10 per cent above even the 1944 level.

The stretch of the ECML from Northallerton to York was a major worry. After two extremely difficult years of working greatly augmented wartime traffic through two exceptionally severe winters and the Blitz, a Government Central Transport Committee (CTC) produced a special report in January 1942 on North-East Area traffic. Earlier, a systematic traffic count on a typical day in March 1941—one of many made at key points up and down the country—revealed that at Thirsk (Green Lane) a total of 57 passenger trains—and no troop trains on that day, 184 freight trains and 49 light engines (with/without brake-van) passed in the 24 hours. Such an intensity over a small partially two track stretch was unmatched anywhere else in the country. (At Stevenage on the same day there were 97 passenger and 88 freight trains in the 24 hours). This drew attention to a 70 per cent increase over peacetime levels of main line freight through the NE area. The total number of freight trains passing through Northallerton per week each way was 722 in June 1941 and 796 in December 1941,[21] the larger number in winter being attributable to greater traffic of coal, seed potatoes, sugar beet and fertilisers.[22] The figures of 100–110 freight trains each way per day on the line through York did not increase further during the war,[23] despite line widenings increasing capacity, because other factors—availability of locomotives and crews—became limiting. The Tees-side yards alone (in October 1942) dispatched no fewer than 66 trains every weekday (49 from Newport Yard), and the majority of these would run on the ECML. Besides, fewer fast braked freight trains were being run in wartime and average speeds were very low—20 mph for convoy coal trains.

The latter presented a major problem. The report spelled out the existing limitations of the lines south through York or through Harrogate, with 72 per cent using the former and 28 per cent the latter (double the pre-war level), although by concentrating on bulk train-loads, the LNER had been able to ensure that 63 per cent of the traffic passing through York did not have to be remarshalled there. By passing traffic through Harrogate—to Leeds or to Church Fenton, York could be avoided altogether, but the Harrogate route was hampered by severe gradients: maximum loads were 32 per cent less than on the York route and/or double heading was necessary. South and west of Harrogate or York, traffic dispersed to various routes. About 40 per cent of the coal went to Lancashire but 32 per cent came south to Doncaster (much of it *via* Church Fenton and Knottingley), but in doing so it conflicted with other flows across Yorkshire and the North Midlands. Further south, there was a heavy flow of coal from the Nottinghamshire coalfield joining at Grantham, although the ECML south of Doncaster was relieved to some extent by sending traffic down the GN&GE Joint main line not only for East Anglia but also for London *via* Whitemoor or New England. In turn, this route was relieved by running trains all the way round from Lincoln to Spalding *via* Boston. Of course, the capacity of all these lines had to be expanded by the building of new and longer loops, as was done at innumerable places all over the country. The WTT for summer 1942, for example, lists paths for 23 Up convoy coal trains on the ECML through Doncaster—only four of which were routed to Whitemoor, seven days a week (*i.e.* 161 per week) with just as many on Sundays as on weekdays.[24] Routes and destinations were not specified, except that four were designated 'Whitemoor coal' and 19 'South coal', this impression typifying the way most freight trains were run on an *ad hoc* basis during the war.

When the coal eventually got to London at Ferme Park Yard, there was then the problem of distributing it in small trips on to the other railways, the trips to the SR alone amounting to over 60 per day (and at least 20 on Sundays) in 1940, compared with 34 a day pre-war. By the beginning of 1941, 1,000 wagons each way per day were being exchanged with the SR over the widened lines, and 120 with the GWR at Acton. The problem became acute in the Blitz and was tackled by extensive diversions,[25] in part making use of the ex-GC lines, the traffic through the Woodford Yards at the end of 1940 being 32 per cent up on pre-war. Eventually, in 1944 the burden on Ferme Park Yard was relieved to a small extent by the link put in between the GN Hertford Loop and GE Section at Bounds Green, and some coal trains were then diverted by the Palace Gates branch to Temple Mills—although that yard was already handling an abundance of coal traffic routed through Whitemoor. In July 1944, on Sundays alone, four coal trains—and return empties—were scheduled to use the new link.

The Arctic weather of the first two winters of the war was particularly disruptive. In 1940, the first of several Restriction Orders during the ensuing month was put on ECML traffic through York and Doncaster on 22 January. After that the weather and other troubles forced the LNER to restrict coal traffic for the south through Peterborough intermittently during the next ten days, applying a complete embargo from 1 February for five days. Then the cumulative effect of diversion of Scottish traffic due to blockage by snow of the WCML and the Settle–Carlisle line at the end of the month, coupled with the LNER's own difficulties that included staff sickness, led on 14 February to a three-day embargo being put on the loading of all but food and the most essential Government traffic from Scotland and the north-east to the GN and GE sections. During a period when there was flooding due to a sudden thaw and then more snowstorms followed by more flooding—this time in the south of the country, severe restrictions were again put on traffic over the southern portion of the ECML on 29 February and for four days from 4 March. Flooding was particularly bad in the lower Trent Valley, Gainsborough being under several feet of water for a week.[26]

The general dislocation during the 1940–41 winter was compounded by more severe weather in February 1941, bringing about congestion of crisis dimensions. Even in early October 1940 about 300 coal trains were already immobilised in yards owing to interruption of SR lines in London by the Blitz—without any snow. Then blizzards on 19–21 February and the extensive damage caused to signalling installations brought about complete paralysis on the ECML from north of Newcastle down to Darlington for a week. This disaster naturally caused immense disruption of goods traffic along the ECML and elsewhere, in a period when the Blitz was in progress. During the next winter heavy snow again caused congestion of Anglo-Scottish traffic sufficient for at least a brief imposition of loading and/or acceptance restrictions by both the WCML and the ECML in the third week of January 1942, the first week of February and on 7 March, also on the ECML southwards from York a week later. The last three winters of the war were not particularly severe. This was fortunate because, owing to the limitations on the use of coal and mineral wagons for merchandise anyway, there was a shortage of wagons for the coal, as well as of locomotives and above all of staff. Therefore the greatly increased calls for the movement of merchandise made it impossible to run anything approaching the number of convoy coal trains that had been dispatched out of the NE Area during the first three winters.

The weekly output of coal from Northumberland and Co. Durham mines in the winter of 1941 was running at 735,000 tons (about 20 per cent of national output), of which about 105,000 tons was sent south by rail (mainly in convoy trains) and over 210,000 tons per week by sea. Up to 30 train-loads a week were also sent up to Scotland.[27] The CTC believed that coal consumption for electricity generation would increase by over 20 per cent in the coming year, and therefore more coal would have to be conveyed, mainly by rail, out of the NE Area. They concluded that, even on the assumption that the physical enhancements of line capacity currently in hand were completed by the following winter, the routes south from Northallerton could take a maximum of 595 trains per week through York, and 230 per week *via* Harrogate. It was estimated that 'demand' might

Above: View south-eastward towards the Portobello Yards on the ex-North British section of the ECML, with Craigentinny carriage depot off to the right. The freight train is headed by Reid N15 Class 0-6-2T No. 9148, which was built by the North British Locomotive Co. in August 1912. Pictured on 13 August 1948, the engine would be in service until June 1958. *Picture: B. W. L. Brooksbank*

Below: Thompson's mixed traffic B1 Class 4-6-0 design was built in numbers between 1942 and 1952 when 410 were in traffic all over the ex-LNER system. No. 61273 has a mixed freight train on the levels near York during March 1956. *Picture: Yorkshire Post*

Above: Just back on the four track main line after coming through the two track bottleneck at Welwyn, a typical Down train of mineral empties on the busy Ferme Park (Hornsey)–New England (Peterborough) shuttle is seen at Woolmer Green behind WD 2-8-0. No. 90613 on 19 May 1956. *Picture: B. W. L. Brooksbank*

Below: BR 9F Class No. 92040 takes the down slow through Offord & Buckden station on 28 April 1956. The engine was based at New England from new in December 1954 until June 1963 when a move to Colwick occurred. *Picture: B. W. L. Brooksbank*

reach 5,500 wagons per week—10 per cent above the calculated capacity, and therefore at times the capacity of the lines might be exceeded after either abrupt increases in forwardings or problems with severe weather. In practice, over 200 convoy trains per week were run in 1941, but thereafter they fell markedly to 115 per week in 1942 and 87 in 1943, rose to 104 in 1944, and then fell away to 78 in the first six months of 1945. The widenings completed in 1942 between Northallerton and York eased congestion a certain amount, but then—despite the installation of new loops—the mainly two track section between Ferryhill and Northallerton through Darlington became a bottleneck, and many convoy coal trains had to be re-routed to start from West Hartlepool and run *via* Eaglescliffe. In fact but for the continuing limitations of the ECML, even more industrial expansion would have taken place in the north-east, because the labour needed was indeed available. Convoy coal trains did not end with the war, for there were 60 per week in the second half of 1945, and still 41 per week in 1946. After the war, on occasions demand over the critical stretch of the ECML still exceeded capacity, and temporary embargoes had then to be applied.

So there were a number of occasions during the war when the capacity of the railways for one reason or another reached saturation, and temporary restrictions—total or partial—had to be imposed on acceptances, and this situation arose especially on the LNER's ECML. Firstly, there were the problems caused by the very severe weather in early 1940, 1941 and 1942 (also less so in early 1944), and of course the Blitz in 1940–41. Then there was the burden imposed by the large new requirement to relieve the LMSR of some of its greatly swollen Anglo-Scottish traffic and to some extent its traffic from Merseyside—also to help the LMSR during the Blitz. There were occasions when LMSR Scottish traffic had to be transferred to the ECML, notably during the great blizzards of early 1940, but also at other times such as on 15 May 1944 when a major derailment at Mossband (between Carlisle and Gretna Junction) blocked the WCML completely.

The construction and operation of the numerous new airfields in eastern England added to the burden of the ECML. It resulted in much heavier traffic entering East Anglia through Whitemoor and Peterborough, and quite often during 1943 and early 1944 led to the imposition of embargoes on acceptances of general goods that way. In fact, there was an abrupt increase of traffic in October 1942 which overburdened Whitemoor Yard to the extent that convoy coal trains to east London and the LT&S section had to be diverted on to the ECML. Finally, the ECML was of course heavily engaged in the traffic for *Overlord*, and this demanded severe cut-backs not only in ECML passenger trains but also a reduction in regular freight movements—including coal trains. The LNER somehow managed in the first three years of the war with a reduced number of freight locomotives, by employing passenger locomotives on freight work probably more than any of the other Groups. The loan from early 1943 of substantial numbers of the British and American 2-8-0s, built for military purposes on the Continent alone made possible the satisfaction of the imperative additional demands for freight motive power in 1943–44. In the end the limit to the amount of traffic that could be moved was set by the shortage of engine-men.

The importation of iron ore was curtailed in the war, and requirements were made up by great expansion of home production. This came from Oxfordshire, Northamptonshire and Leicestershire. Therefore great tonnages of ore had to be carried from the Midlands not only to the blast furnaces of the Rotherham and Scunthorpe areas but down the ECML north of York, at the rate of 75 trains per week to those on Tees-side and in Co. Durham, and also even up to Whifflet in Scotland. Earlier in the war, three-quarters of these trains came off the LMSR and joined at York, but by 1943 a third of them were from points on the LNER and running mainly down the ECML. They continued to run in the first years after the war, if at a lesser frequency and more predominantly from the LMSR. To save shipping space, the importation of foreign timber also was radically reduced in the war. As a result the felling of British woodlands was accelerated, and gave rise to especially heavy traffic in softwoods from Scotland up the ECML, for building work, pit-props, etc. and for paper-making. The last also gave rise to a remarkable traffic in straw from East Anglia to mills in Scotland.

Wartime rail traffic in farm products was greatly augmented, on account of curtailment of imports and increased home production, as well as diversion from road and from sea. Nationwide, railway traffic in agricultural commodities rose by 70 per cent between 1938 and 1945 to 1.85 million tons. Vegetables and potatoes figured largely, of which 3½ times as many tons were conveyed in the war period. Even between 1939 and 1940 the tonnage of East Anglian potatoes conveyed was doubled and that of grain multiplied four-fold although perhaps less than in peacetime. During each winter of the war up to 250,000 tons of seed potatoes were carried down from Scotland— under two sheets per wagon, to protect against frost, while 130,000 tons of sugar beet came out of the eastern counties: much of all this must have been conveyed on the ECML. Nevertheless, the ECML was relieved to some extent of seed potato traffic during the war: normally thought too precious to shovel into boats, they were now transported partly by coaster—and coasters were also loaded with apples on their return from the south.

Between 1939 and the end of 1944 the number of military airfields in Britain rose from 158 to no less than 623 including 133 built for the USAAF in 1942–44. By February 1944 they covered in all 250,000 acres and had cost £615 million. A high proportion were located in the eastern half of England and Scotland and therefore would be served at least in part by the ECML. The total area of paved runways, perimeter tracks and hard standings laid during 1940–44 (the peak being in 1942) was 175 million square yards—equivalent to about 10,000 miles of 30 foot roads.[28] Numerous wayside station goods yards on and off the ECML became their railheads and so dealt with unprecedented traffic. The construction of each standard bomber airfield consumed 90,000 cubic yards of hard core and 18,000 tons of cement, and together with prodigious amounts of sand, bricks, timber and steel; most of all this was brought to the locality by rail. A five-fold multiplication in the goods traffic of country stations supplying airfields was average, and at some stations the increase was 20-fold.

After the airfields were in operation, the supply of armaments and fuel entailed the running of hundreds of special freight trains that had to pass over parts of the ECML and especially over the GN&GE Joint Line.[29] A 1,000-bomber raid was estimated to require the equivalent of 28 trains of petrol and eight of bombs. Raids by the RAF and the USAAF with over 250 aircraft were mounted at least twice a week from late 1942, from March 1943 the sizes of the armadas were usually well over 500 aircraft and during 1944 and early 1945 operations with up to 1,000 aircraft were mounted frequently. The explosive stocks for the RAF were held underground in Main Reserve depots, in remote but rail-served sites each having a planned turnover of 60,000 tons per month (84 wagons per day). Then, especially in eastern England and near the bomber bases—and served by the ECML—were the Forward Ammunition Depots and Air Ammunition Parks (AAPs), which mainly received by rail and issued by road but still required to handle over 100 rail wagons per day. From late 1943 this traffic soared as the number of AAPs mushroomed and the turnover of the RAF No. 42 Maintenance Group, responsible for the supply, rose to over 3 million tons in 1944—and meanwhile the traffic in ordnance for the VIII and IX USAAF would have been of the same order.[30] The airfields and the numerous depots for military stores and ordnance tended to be situated in rural areas and to be served by rail on branch lines, but several were sited not far from the ECML—notwithstanding the potential danger. In any case their traffic would be on or off the main line at some point. The Doncaster–York section, with three airfields (Snaith,

Burn and Riccall) and a large bomb depot (Escrick) very close to the main line, was particularly vulnerable: apart from the several occasions when aircraft crashed on the line it was closed—to passenger trains—for 10 days in 1943 after the dump at Snaith blew up.

There were a large number and variety of Government depots served by the ECML—many being close to it. Probably the largest military installation entirely dependent on the ECML for rail-borne traffic was Catterick Camp, on a steeply-graded military branch off the Eryhome–Richmond line, while not far off the ECML at Prudhoe (between Blaydon and Hexham) there was a huge Ministry of Supply depot turning out about 150 wagons a day. Although of necessity supplied principally by road, there was a great RAF Maintenance Unit (No. 60) beside the ECML at Beningbrough, to which were brought the remains of most of the 1,500–2,000 aircraft that crashed in Yorkshire. The same Maintenance Unit had a factory nearby at York (Clifton) Airfield, where up to 4,000 people were employed repairing damaged Halifax bombers. The Ministry of Aircraft Production (MAP) had a factory at Urlay Nook (near Darlington) engaged in breaking up damaged aircraft and this dealt with several trains a day. Of the many huge depots built up and down the country for the *Bolero* supplies, those feeding traffic more or less directly on to the ECML were at Bottesford, Boughton (near Ollerton) and at Histon (Cambridgeshire), while the VIII USAAF had its 2nd

Although designed exclusively for express passenger traffic, the A4 Class were equally adept at handling freight trains. No. 60021 *Wild Swan* has just emerged from Welwyn South tunnel for this photograph to be taken on 2 June 1951. *Picture: B. W. L. Brooksbank*

Strategic Air Depot served by a branch from Abbots Ripton dealing with an average of 45 wagons a day from December 1943. Lastly, it must be remembered that much of the traffic to and from naval bases in Scotland and on the east coast was conveyed on the ECML: the Admiralty Depots at Rosyth and Charlestown alone dispatched 200 wagons a day.[31] At the end of the war, stored ammunition was disposed of by sending it all the way up from the south to the military ports in Scotland to be dumped out at sea, the vast surplus stores of the US Army had to be sent to the ports for export back to North America, and so on.

Another new major source of traffic during the war were the vast Royal Ordnance Factories (ROF), for the manufacture of guns, shells, bombs, mines and other armaments, the production of explosives and the filling and assembly of explosive devices. There were eventually 44 ROFs up and down the country, so the transportation of many thousands of tons of explosives and ordnance was a vital but hazardous task taken on by the railways. The principal ROFs on or near the ECML were as follows: in Co. Durham, Birtley (engineering, used in the First World War and reopened in 1937), Aycliffe (filling, opened in 1941) and Spennymoor (opened 1938); in Yorkshire, Thorp Arch (near Wetherby, filling, opened 1941), Barnbow (near Garforth), and Maltby (near Rotherham); in Nottinghamshire, Ranskill (explosives–cordite, opened 1941). These added very considerably to the ECML freight traffic, with hundreds of wagon-loads per week at each, both inwards and outwards. In February 1944, per day Birtley was turning out about 30 wagon-loads, Aycliffe 70, Thorp Arch 45, and Ranskill 20. Most of the factories very quickly ceased work after the war, but maintained a modicum of rail traffic as they were transformed eventually to civilian trading estates. However, Thorp Arch remained in use—on a much reduced scale, as a Military Stores Depot.

Trains of petrol tank wagons were a major traffic. They were almost as dangerous as those of bombs and presented their own operating problems. During 1940 the British railways as a whole ran 1,158 special trains of aviation spirit, but this tally rose to no less than 9,235 in 1944. Because so many of the operational airfields lay in eastern England the LNER carried a high proportion, but to minimise enemy strafing the tank wagons were kept if possible 30 miles away from the east coast and not allowed to stand overnight in that area. During the early years of the war, much of the aviation fuel was sent from Stanlow and from Avonmouth through Peterborough to a stabling and distribution point at Whittlesea. The burden on the ECML of petrol traffic was eased to some extent when a major distribution depot was built in September 1943 at Sandy Heath, on the LMSR line between Sandy and Potton. This was supplied by pipelines from Stanlow, from Avonmouth and later from Thames Haven. In the three months after D-Day, 634 train-loads of petrol were sent from Sandy to railheads all over East Anglia, but the latter also still received another 498 train-loads from the ports in that period. The ECML also continued to handle petrol coming in through Hull for the RAF depot at Ripon. From 1943, at certain airfields across the country the fog-dispersal system, FIDO, was installed. This used such enormous quantities of petrol that special sidings for its supply were put in at the local railway station; on the ECML, one at St Neots supplied Graveley Airfield.

The movement of other military traffic, notably that of AFV also presented particular problems. British tanks had to be designed to fit the restricted British loading-gauge and required special Warflat and Warwell wagons, on which they had to be loaded with extreme care. The loaded wagons were barred from branch lines with weak bridges, and there was a long list of places where they could not pass anything on an adjacent line—partly because at a considerable height above the rail they were in fact too wide. Trains dedicated to the transport of AFVs were assembled and stationed at many places up and down the country, usually adjacent to Army depots.[32] There was also a chronic shortage of bolster-wagons, used for carrying steel plate and other large loads—including small naval craft, also (from 1943) the large crates of vehicles sent over for the US Army. The transport of explosives—full of potential danger—required elaborate regulations and instructions, not least when wagon-loads of ordnance were stored—as they often were—on the railway. The requirement for special dedicated wagons was not large, but an example on the ECML was the provision of designated wagons (with supports for protective sheets), for transporting corrosive nitre-cake in large quantities away from Ranskill ROF.

Thus direct military needs, for airfields, camps, and storage depots etc. for the armed forces, who numbered 3.5 million by mid-1941—even before the arrival of any US servicemen—brought about a large increase in freight as well as passenger traffic over routes lightly loaded in peacetime. As it supplied three airfields, the freight traffic on the Easingwold Light Railway from Alne mushroomed in 1943 to 37,000 tonnes—nearly five times its pre-war level. Likewise, the Derwent Valley Light Railway had its carryings multiplied three-fold at that time, and the North Sunderland Railway from Chathill carried 3½ times the peacetime traffic.

In considering the locomotive workings in wartime, it must be borne in mind that to the staff, who had to run the railway, a locomotive from an 'unusual' shed normally meant trouble: some shed-master or running foreman was short of his normal stud of motive power, on account of 'failures' or extra traffic. Under wartime circumstances the return of such 'foreigners' to their home depots was not ensured by the District Controller with the same diligence as was normal in peacetime. After the war this was done much more conscientiously.

For the footplate-men and guards, wartime freight working might mean a lot more overtime, but also long frustrating hours out on the road, perhaps crawling along from block to block, or queuing interminably on Permissive Block stretches waiting for a path or for space in a yard. Even without bad weather, men might work a whole shift queuing and not moving their train an inch—and this still occurred to some extent just after the war. A serious problem in these circumstances was that engines held up for hours in sidings could run out of water and their fires would have to be dropped. To avoid this, Controllers tried to have trains backed into sidings to allow the engines to uncouple and go off to replenish their tanks, although water-columns were installed at many of the new wartime loops. Being out in the black-out was eerie, and could be dangerous: it was much easier to get lost, and men anyway might have to work on lines with which they were not familiar—and under the sheets draped over from cab to tender to hide the glow of the fire from enemy aircraft, it was claustrophobic. Then again they might quite likely be handling a load of ordnance—like the brave men who were blown up at Soham in June 1944, at Gascoigne Wood in April 1945, and elsewhere. Still at least train crews were issued with 'tin hats'.

In terms of timetabled freight services, there were really remarkably few changes during the war compared with pre-war. Even the braked freight trains were not markedly reduced, and the paths provided for non-fitted trains were essentially the same, in routes and in numbers. Perhaps the most obvious difference was the insertion of paths for the convoy coal trains and for certain corresponding empties trains from New England to the NE Area in the Down direction, also for some ironstone trains from Highdyke to the NE and Scottish Areas. Undoubtedly the intention remained, even in the middle of the war, to have a schedule of regular freight workings much as in peacetime. Of course it was very often not possible to adhere to the WTT, and the innumerable extra trains on Government account had to be fitted by the District Control officers into the WTT in the best way they could.

Empty 'Blue Spot' fish vans are worked north on the Down Fast through Harringay station by 9F Class No. 92174. *Picture: B. W. L. Brooksbank*

Post-war freight until the end of the 1950s

Once the war was over in Europe in May 1945, there was an easing up in the volume of freight traffic—but this was relative. For example, in the LNER Southern Area freight tonnage originating in the 12 weeks to 20 October 1945 was only 7.2 per cent less than in the same period of the hectic previous year,[33] coal traffic being 9.8 per cent higher; moreover, fish traffic was double that of pre-war. In November 1945, congestion again forced the LNER to place embargoes from time to time on the dispatch of traffic for south of Peterborough. Then in the winter of 1946–47 embargoes once again had to be put—even before the Great Freeze began, on account of shortage of serviceable locomotives.

Commencing as early as July 1945, the LNER built up—again as in 1939, an extensive service of fast fitted and semi-fitted trains between the main goods depots of the principal cities, running mostly at night. However, study of the WTTs for freight trains on the ECML in winter 1945 shows that immediately after the end of the war, the majority of trains were still running unbraked, but much of the New England—Ferme Park coal traffic, which persisted at a high level in the first ten post-war years, had already been up-rated to class A speed. There were significantly more scheduled unbraked trains than before the war, and both braked and unbraked trains were running between a greater variety of yards, and often for longer distances than pre-war. A number of trains were still instructed 'to run under Control orders', which had applied to so many during the war. The new destinations included Connington Sidings, to which as well as to New England Down empties trains ran from London. Of the 16 daily Down empties between New England and Doncaster, half

Doncaster-allocated V2 No. 60876 travels homeward through Arksey on 26 June 1952. The engine spent several years at York before being condemned at the shed in December 1965. *Picture: Yorkshire Post*

ran *via* Sleaford or *via* Boston. Furthermore, the legacy of wartime left through workings between Doncaster and West Hartlepool or Heaton, and a number of conditional paths between Doncaster and York (some *via* Knottingley). There were several through workings over the Hertford loop, which included at least one train each way to/from Temple Mills Yard *via* the Bounds Green link. Also certain braked trains continued to come through York from the Yard at Thirsk which had been reopened in the war. By the early 1950s these paths had been taken out of the WTTs.

In 1953–54 five daily express parcels trains ran from King's Cross to York, while Marylebone sent one to York which joined the ECML off the former GC at Tuxford North, and one ran down the GN&GE Joint line from March joining the ECML at Doncaster. York ran two express parcels trains to Edinburgh and no less than five to Newcastle, while one other ran from Newcastle to Edinburgh. Up services were similar, although at least one express parcels ran through from Edinburgh to King's Cross. There was one express meat train from Aberdeen to East Goods Yard, and nine express fish trains to King's Cross Goods: two from Aberdeen, one from York, three from Hull, two from New Clee, and one from Grimsby. Actually, Grimsby dispatched daily eight fish trains and Hull five, all running at least briefly on the ECML. The urgency of the fish traffic after the war is exemplified by the fact that one of the Aberdeen–London trains was given priority over the Up 'North Briton'. The equally urgent seasonal seed-potato traffic from Scotland continued to be very heavy, the ER handling no less than 300 trains between November 1950 and January 1951. All these Class C trains were worked largely by the Pacifics and V2s, but often also B1s or K3s. To smooth their ordered assemblage, the refrigerated and insulated wagons needed for these express fish and meat trains was arranged by the Central Freight Rolling-Stock Control office at BR headquarters. This office superseded the wartime ICRC, and collated nationally the information sent to Regional Freight Wagon stock control offices (a combined office at York for the ER and NER) by the district offices, to which individual depots and yards sent daily details of their stock positions. The same system was conducted with respect to mineral wagons at collieries, quarries, etc.

The ECML in the 1950s was still a very important freight artery, and as late as 1958 the total on the ER was still 3,300 million ton-miles, of which respectively 56 per cent of the merchandise, 75 per cent of the minerals and 91 per cent of the coal originated on the (new) Great Northern Line (London–Doncaster, inclusive).

By 1953–54 the number of braked freight trains down the ECML was now similar to that before the war, although the proportion that was fully-fitted was much larger. Their destinations were likewise similar, except for the notable omission of any to Manchester or Liverpool, and four instead of one going down north from Whitemoor plus one from Thames Wharf. With all new freight and mineral wagons from 1957 being fitted with power-brakes, changes that were made between 1953–54 and 1959 comprised primarily the introduction of more express freight trains, including some engaged in the new 'Assured Arrival'—usually overnight—service now offered to traders. Also many of the workings between Ferme Park and New England, New England and Doncaster—and certain others, were speeded up to Class E (limited load with or without at least four piped wagons next to the engine). Entailing in several cases the reintroduction of lodging-turns for the footplate-men, the new fast braked train workings included, for example, King's Cross to Hull,[34] to Sheffield *via* Retford, and to Aberdeen, from Clarence Yard to Colwick, to Heaton and to Niddrie, from Woodford to Hull (via Tuxford), from Boston to York (via Doncaster), from Immingham to Consett, and from Hull to Glasgow High Street—dubbed the 'Humber-Clyde'; the Aberdeen–Newcastle overnight train was the 'Geordie'.

No. 60862 was one of seventy-one V2s to have separate cylinders fitted between May 1956 and March 1962, being an early recipient in 1957. The engine was in the minority when a Kylchap blastpipe and chimney was installed in late 1961 as only seven others were similarly treated. *Picture: Malcolm Crawley*

Above: A total of 40 9F Class 2-10-0s were allocated to New England shed for varying periods during their careers. No. 92044 was initially to work on the LMR but went to March in January 1955 before moving on to Peterborough in June 1957. The engine is seen at Hitchin with a Class F train five months later.

Below: Gresley K3 Class 2-6-0 No. 61883, built at Doncaster in October 1929, enters the north end of Doncaster station with a Class C train on 13 August 1953. The locomotive was allocated to Hull Dairycoates and would be withdrawn there in December 1962.
Both Pictures: B. W. L. Brooksbank

There was a deliberate policy during the 1950s of running through trains further between remarshalling. The outstanding example on the ER of this kind of rationalisation in the period was the scheme undertaken at Peterborough in 1953, when three yards were closed, saving the shunting and tripping of 2,000 wagons a day and an average of six hours in the transit time of these wagons—and this was at a time when rail freight was still booming and not being lost to road to any great extent. In this period, existing marshalling yards were being modernised and even new ones were being built. Examples of new long distance freight workings on the ECML included, from Mansfield to Uphall (West Lothian), and from the upgraded new marshalling yard at Healey Mills near Wakefield—and from Normanton—to destinations in the north-east.

The output of iron and steel in the Scunthorpe area increased by over 50 per cent in the 1950s, providing more traffic on to the ECML. The Highdyke–Frodingham ironstone workings flourished, and came to be re-routed *via* Sleaford, Boston and Grimsby—or by the ECML and Doncaster, to obviate reversals at Lincoln and Barnetby. Workings between Frodingham and York and thence to the north-east expanded, and in the reverse direction much larger tonnages of coking coal than formerly were passing from north-eastern pits to Frodingham.

With the radical changes on the ECML in winter 1957, there was a revision of the freight services as well as the passenger timetable. The celebrated 'Scotch Goods', which a few years earlier had been diagrammed to run non-stop to Retford (Babworth), was now made non-stop to York (Skelton)—a record non-stop run for a British freight train, and conveying wagons for Scotland only. In addition, the 02.55 King's Cross to Niddrie was also made non-stop to Skelton, and the 16.30 King's Cross to Dringhouses non-stop to Selby. By this time a quarter of the ECML freight workings were express, comprising almost all long-distance trains other than coal, minerals, and iron and steel; there was now also a fully-fitted brick train from Fletton to York.[35] Merchandise— as well as meat—was now coming to London in only four hours from Leeds, six hours from Newcastle and eight hours from Edinburgh, with 70–80 per cent not more than 30 minutes late on schedule. Such performance depended largely on the employment of Pacifics and V2s, and latterly the powerful and fleet-footed Standard 9F 2-10-0s.

By winter 1959 there were 30 regular braked freight trains running down the ECML and originating at points between London and Doncaster, compared with 19 in winter 1953; almost a half of these were class C and many involved top link engines and men. There were also about 12 coming off the Joint Line at Doncaster (six in 1953), and another six joining at Newark or Tuxford (four in 1953). More noteworthy was that the number of braked trains (mainly empties) from the London District down to New England was only half those run in winter 1953, although there were four more braked empties trains down to New England in 1959—enabling more economical out-and-home rosters. North of York the pattern in 1959 was still quite similar to that in 1952, but with a tendency towards longer overall journeys and many more trains from Healey Mills Yard. Otherwise, the reduction—such as it was—in traffic up to that date must have been reflected in the loading of trains and in the number of unscheduled or irregular workings.

Undoubtedly, apart from the traffic in domestic coal,[36] little change occurred in the 1950s in the nature of the freight carried on the ECML. The movement of coal to east coast ports, for export or bunkering, never again came anywhere near to the pre-war level, and much more coal was still moved inland. Indeed—by 1957 already, coal was being imported through these ports. The annual consumption of coal by public utilities nationally at this time was 40 million tons more than before the war, and some 3,000 wagons a day of coal still left the Doncaster, Nottingham, and Lincoln Districts for the south and East Anglia. Over half of this coal was conveyed on the ECML, while heavy lateral flows continued through Doncaster, Selby, York, Ferryhill, Newcastle and Edinburgh. The ironstone traffic from the East Midlands had rather fallen off, but on the other hand the heavy traffic in ore from Tyne Dock to Consett was transported with the latest modern equipment.[37] Indeed, under the Modernisation Plan, in addition to the standard 16-ton steel wagons built to replace the old 10- or 12-ton wooden ones, 21- and 24½-ton steel hopper wagons for coal and minerals were now being used extensively, the hopper wagons being introduced without difficulty in the NE Region where they had been used traditionally. Trials were undertaken also in the late 1950s between New England and London of vacuum-fitted coal trains (hauled by 2-10-0s), but they proved premature. As well, wagons specialised for particular bulk traffics came into widespread use, and the loading methods at goods depots were mechanised, with pallets, fork-lift trucks and conveyors. All these facilities, along with the radical reduction of intermediate marshalling and trip working, were leading to substantial reductions in overall transit times. Yet the railways were by this time already under-utilised by about 30 per cent, and the construction of motorways was soon to abolish any advantage they had—even over long distances—in speed of conveyance of merchandise.

Appendix A

Background facts relevant to the ECML, 1939–1959

The circumstances of the railways of Britain in general just before the outbreak of the war, during it and in the 15 post-war years have been described in chapter 3. However, to complete this description of the ECML it is necessary to record some facts about the LNER and the successor Regions concerned with the line. It would be interesting, but is not possible, to give statistics relating to the ECML separately, to show how this essential part was affected. At a rough estimate, perhaps some 60 per cent of the passenger and freight traffic of the LNER as a whole was handled at some stage on the ECML; after Nationalisation a similar proportion of the combined ER and NER traffic and perhaps 10 to 20 per cent of that of the ScR would be ECML-related (south of Edinburgh).

Mainly on account of road competition, the net operating revenue (adjusted to the price index) of the LNER had fallen since Grouping in 1923 from £9.5 million to £6.1 million in 1938. When road transport was severely restricted during the war—by 1943 lorry numbers were down to only 120,000 nationwide, and the LNER's revenue rose dramatically to a peak of £18.8 million, although the Company was only allowed to retain the 'agreed revenue' of £9.9 million. The operating ratio—traffic expenses/revenue, which before the First World War had been about 60 (on the NER), was as high as 87.0 in 1938, falling to 71.6 by 1943. In the 16 years between Grouping and the end of 1938, rail passenger journeys had declined on the LNER by 27 per cent to 288.2 million, and the freight tonnage originating had fallen by 23 per cent to 104.0 million. Total freight tonnage carried by the LNER was 121.3 million made up of 78.7 million tons of coal, 18.3m tons of other minerals (merchandise classes 1–6),[1] and 20.3 million tons of merchandise classes 7—21 (plus livestock).

Expressed in ton miles, total LNER freight traffic in 1938 was 5,642 million (3,385 million in the Southern Area, 1,483 million in the North-Eastern Area, and 774 million in the Scottish Area). The Southern Area moved 1.934 million ton-miles of coal, 699 million of 'other minerals' and 752 million of merchandise (Classes 7–21); in the NE Area, 672 million ton miles of coal was moved, 269 million of 'other minerals', and 542 million of merchandise; in the Scottish Area, 364 million ton miles of coal were moved, 131 million of 'other minerals', and 279 million of merchandise. Included in the 104.0 million tons of freight originating on the LNER in 1938 were (million tons); iron ore 4.77, iron and steel (finished and semi-finished) 4.40, bricks and tiles 1.66, grain and flour 1.22, pig-iron 0.69, fertilisers 0.66, timber 1.61, vegetables 0.99. Lastly, 0.83 million head of cattle and 1.40 million of sheep were conveyed. Moreover, the revenue (in 1938) of merchandise traffic (Classes 7–21), at 60.7p/ton, was much greater than for minerals (22.3p/ton) or coal (15.9p/ton), and therefore the loss of merchandise traffic to road haulage was commensurately more serious.

On the LNER in 1938 total passenger-journeys had been 288 million, rising slightly to 290 million in 1939. Wartime at first brought a fall to 227 million in 1940, but then there was a progressive rise, to 240 million in 1941, 286 million in 1942, 315 million in 1943, 316 million in 1944, and a

After being constructed at Darlington in October 1937 V2 No. 4785 was sent south to King's Cross. The locomotive is seen a short time later with a fitted freight at New Barnet.

peak of 322 million in 1945. Meanwhile, coaching train-miles (loaded and empty) on the LNER fell from 74 million pre-war to a constant 52 to 53 million during 1940–44.

In terms of mileage, freight traffic on the LNER as a whole increased from 454,000 pre-war (1938) to 545,000 in 1940 but then rose only a little more to a peak of 551,000 in 1943. Thus by far the greater part of the increases on the LNER occurred in the first year or so of the war. (The trends were similar on the LMSR, but on the GWR and the SR on which increases in tonnage of freight were even greater, the greatest expansion occurred later in the war). On the LNER, net ton miles of all freight climbed eventually to 8,200 million in 1944 (43 per cent above pre-war)—and fell only to 7,400 million in 1945.

All-line forwardings of loaded wagons reached their peak (929,000) in the week ending 24 September 1943; on the LNER the peak was 328,000 in the week ending 22 October. After the war, by September 1947 the figures were respectively 772,000 and 267,000. Total loaded wagon-miles on the LNER had attained 1,395 million in 1944 (33 per cent above pre-war), while empty wagon miles had gone up by only 5 per cent to 551 million. The shift from short-haul to longer-haul movement was revealed most starkly in the LNER Scottish Area, where loaded wagon-miles had increased by the peak period of mid-1944 to about 70 per cent above pre-war, although at that time loaded mineral wagon-miles were 87 per cent above pre-war in the Southern Area and 37 per cent up in the NE Area. The combined loaded plus empty wagon ton-mile figure on the whole LNER was only 25 per cent above mid-1938 (21 per cent up in the Southern Area, 29 per cent up in the NE Area, and 33.5 per cent up in the Scottish Area).

Relatively, the greatest wartime expansion was in merchandise traffic. On the railways as a whole, from 1941 the ton-mileage figure for class 7–21 merchandise rose at the phenomenal rate

Five A4 Class, Nos 4488–4492, were primarily intended to work the 'Coronation', but as two engines tended to monopolise the Up and Down trains, one was kept spare and two were left free to be used elsewhere. No. 4490 *Empire of India* is in charge of the 'Flying Scotsman' as the train rushes through Doncaster in the late 1930s.

of 15–20 per cent per year. The trend applied as much to the traffic on the LNER as to any other railway, although on the GWR the growth was considerably greater. It is interesting also to note that the tonnages of freight being handled at the main city goods stations were in fact lower than in peacetime, further emphasizing the enormous increases in traffic loaded elsewhere. Already in the last quarter of 1939 on the LNER merchandise ton-miles were no less than 29 per cent up on those of the same quarter in 1938. By July 1940 the four-weekly ton-mileages on the LNER of merchandise, minerals and coal were increased by 35, 42 and as much as 62 per cent respectively over the average 1939 figures; in the NE Area, the corresponding increases were 33, 54 and 102 per cent. The tonnages of merchandise class traffic originating on the LNER then increased—trends being very similar in all three areas—during the course of the war to peaks of respectively 25 million tons (in 1944) in higher-rated merchandise and of 23 million tons (in 1943) in minerals, while its originating coal class traffic decreased by 15 per cent from 74 million tons in the last pre-war year to 63 million tons in 1944. The reason for this decrease in tonnage of coal, which also applied to the other three railways, is probably largely accounted for by the profound drop in the traffic of coal for export and for the bunkering of foreign ships, nearly all this export coal being hauled only over short distances between mines and ports. The tonnage of coal shipped from east coast ports—excluding Scotland—fell from 17.0 million in 1938 to 7.9 million in 1943; it never recovered after the war to the pre-war level, but had risen in 1946 to 10.2 million tons.

In spite of the upheaval of the war, there were remarkably few changes in the parameters of the LNER system between 1938 and 1947. The total miles of track, the numbers of stations and depots, and of locomotives and rolling-stock, remained almost unchanged. The greatly increased traffic during the war had been hauled by very much the same number of total locomotive stock: the loss of 92 2-8-0s requisitioned early in the war was roughly compensated by new construction. During 1943–44—but not in 1945—vital extra needs were met by the loan of 518 2-8-0s from the Ministry of Supply (War Department) and the US Army. In fact, the LNER managed its extra traffic with a considerably larger proportion than before the war of locomotives laid up under or awaiting repairs. The LNER had quite the worst figures of the Big Four: in August 1945 20.6 per cent of its locomotives were not available for traffic, a year later the proportion was 24.6 per cent (32.5 per cent of engines of tractive effort above 25,000 lb). The rate of locomotive repair actually fell directly after the war, thanks to shorter working-hours, and extended holidays, but also more work was needed on each locomotive. Moreover, most of the WD 2-8-0s coming back in 1946 from service on the Continent, on which the LNER depended so heavily to meet its needs, required heavy general repairs before they could be taken into traffic. Locomotive shortage on the LNER was a prime factor in its failure to capture the market and improve receipts after the war to the extent that the demand was there.

With the markedly enhanced carryings of passengers and freight during and after the war, the efficiency of locomotive utilisation, in terms of passenger miles and freight ton-miles per engine-hour, was considerably increased and was still high in 1947. During the war, LNER rolling stock vehicles destroyed amounted to 1,583[2] (with 9,120 damaged) but the coaching-stock losses (278) were not made good, and in spite of new building directly after the war the number of coaching vehicles (16,400) was still in 1947 16 per cent below the 1938 total. (In January, the LNER had to convert some 85 first class (three-a-side) coaches to third class, to ease the overcrowding. One year after the end of the war, 2.5 per cent of the LNER fleet of passenger coaches were over 50 years old and 14 per cent were 40–50 years old, figures much higher than on the other three railways. The Company's wagon fleet, at 241,600 in 1947, was 6.5 per cent less than in 1938, but there had been some new construction. This was of larger-capacity wagons, and the average wagon capacity in 1947 became 13.77 tons (10.6 per cent up on 1938).

In staff, there had been an increase on the LNER during the war of 10 per cent (to 195,000), and not surprisingly the number of women had almost doubled (to 15,744), their proportion of the whole having risen from 4.5 per cent in 1938—after a maximum of 14.6 per cent in 1945—to 8.1 per cent in 1947. Efficiency in terms of labour had changed little, for the total 'Conciliation' labour force in 1947 (at 108,500) was 11.6 per cent higher than in 1938, locomotive grades being 20.5 per cent up, and traffic grades 15.2 per cent higher—reflecting the extra demand for Operating staff.

Just after the war, with traffic still buoyant, the LNER was able to maintain its next operating revenue at least up to the 'agreed' figure, but after allowing for charges on capital the true net revenue fell back to £4.8 million in 1946 and then to a deficit of £0.75 million in 1947. Nevertheless, in 1947 the net revenue from its operations was still 71 per cent above that in 1938, roughly in line with inflation. The post-war increase in the Operating Ratio, which had risen to 101.4 in 1947, was due to inflated costs of labour, fuel and materials compounded by unusually heavy expenditure on maintenance that had run into arrears during the war. At this time (July 1947), the LNER Board seriously considered a daring plan to introduce main-line diesel traction on to the ECML expresses, but Nationalisation—which the Board strenuously opposed—intervened, nothing was done and the plan remained a pipe-dream for 10 years.

At £26.1 million, LNER passenger receipts in 1947 were 104 per cent above those in 1938. As fares were only 33 per cent higher (55 per cent from October 1947), the figures represented a substantial increase in passenger carryings, in spite of the fact that travel by servicemen and the number of special trains on Government account were coming down by 1947 to near the normal peacetime level. The proportion of first class receipts (13.0 per cent) in 1947 was significantly

Above: WD No. 77274, BR No. 90349 from March 1951, has been photographed at Potters Bar on 3 July 1948 with a Class F freight train. The locomotive was built by the North British Locomotive Co. in August 1944 and was condemned in June 1965 at Retford shed. From March 1947 until November 1963 No. 90349 worked from New England.

Below: No. 90309 was only a couple of weeks out of Darlington Works after a General repair when pictured heading south at Metal Bridge (Tursdale) with this freight on 12 June 1954. Surprisingly the engine had managed to remain quite clean in the meantime. *Both Pictures: B. W. L. Brooksbank*

Above: No. 1347 was the prototype third class carriage designed and built at Doncaster in 1945 in preparation for new construction after the end of the war. A first, No. 1531, was also built. Both featured steel panels, teak frames, larger windows and a new compartment layout.

Below: The interior of one of No. 1347's compartments. These were split into groups of two and three with a passageway installed between to facilitate passengers' exit at stations. The quality of the interior was subject to some criticism at the time.

above the 9.2 per cent of 1938, probably owing to the continuing restrictions on private motoring. Passengers on the LNER in 1947 were still travelling a good deal further on average than in 1938, for revenue per passenger (overall and corrected for fare increases) was double that in 1938, and that from excursion and weekend reduced fares was up 2.4-fold. After the great holiday rush of the summer of 1945, there was nevertheless a considerable falling off in passenger-journeys on the LNER immediately after the end of the war in August 1945; in 1946 the figure was down to 299 million journeys, then 269 million in 1947. This was due not only to the rapidly diminishing numbers of servicemen, but also to the release of fuel oil for both buses and private cars, the bus services especially quickly expanding their share of the passenger market. Broadly indicative of the trends of ECML traffic are the figures for passenger journeys originating in the NE Area, which fell by 24 per cent in 1946 to 48.1 million.

Although rates for most of the year were only about 33 per cent above those being charged in 1938, the LNER's freight revenue in 1947 was £40.0 million (at 1938 prices), compared to £28.9 million in 1938. Freight tonnage originating in 1947 was 80.6 million, or 18 per cent less than in 1938, the decrease being mainly in coal carryings for shipment, but total net ton-miles of freight had fallen in 1946 from its peak in 1944 by only 16 per cent to 6,890 million and to 6,675 million in 1947, and were thus still 18.3 per cent above the figure for 1938. Total wagon-miles on the LNER in 1947 (1,558 million) were almost the same as in 1938, as was coal traffic, but there was considerably less empty wagon mileage while minerals traffic was still half as much again as it had been before the war.

After Nationalisation, in terms of net operating receipts the ER did better than BR as a whole, showing a profit every year until 1957, while the NER fared very much better, showing operating profits every year (ranging from £7.11 to £14.1m); on the other hand the ScR made a loss every year except in 1948 and 1951. The best of these years was 1952 when BR as a whole made £39.6 million. The ER's working expenses in the same period fell just from under 17.8 per cent of the total for BR to 16.15 per cent, while those of the NER rose from 8.0 per cent to 11.2 per cent—no doubt as a result of boundary changes, and on the ScR they remained constant at 11.1–11.2 per cent.

As a proportion of the total for BR, which increased by about 10 per cent in the period, passenger-journeys on the ER rose suddenly—due to the incorporation of the Tilbury section, from 101.9 million in 1948 to 158.6 million in 1949, after which they went up gradually to 179.8 million in 1957. Those on the NER tended to parallel those on the ER whereas on the ScR passenger journeys remained constant. During that ten-year period, total BR passenger train-miles rose only from 363 million to 384 million. The proportion on the ER rose slightly from 16.2 per cent to 17.5 per cent, while that on the NER was constant at 7.5 to 8.0 per cent until after 1955, when (in an enlarged region it rose to 10.5 per cent. Train-miles on the ScR fluctuated only between 11.1 per cent and 12.4 per cent in the period.

A major census of passenger traffic in a week in October 1952, covering all the regions individually, revealed some differences relevant to the ECML and its associated traffic. Thus the operating ratio (movement costs/revenue) for fast trains on the ER, NER and ScR (0.26, 0.28 and 0.28 respectively) were close to the average, but higher than on the WR and lower than on the LMR. On Edinburgh–London ordinary express trains the average load factor (passengers/seats) over different portions of the ECML was 56 per cent for first class and 83 per cent for third class (73 and 71 per cent respectively on Pullman trains), but was only 26 and 49 per cent respectively on Edinburgh–Leeds services, and 25 and 74 per cent on Edinburgh–Colchester trains. For semi-fast trains the operating ratios (about 0.70) were well above the average, and the ratios (about 2.2) for stopping services—roughly 40 per cent of train-miles run—were not only appallingly high but double those on the SR with its many electrified services. The October 1952 analysis revealed that the best load factors on branch line services in East Anglia were 22 per cent and the worst 6 per cent—*i.e.* about two people on a three-coach train. All these figures give a pointer to the level of passenger loadings and profitability on the ECML and some of its feeder services at non-holiday times, and were probably the best that were achieved at any time after the war, as 1952 was one of BR's 'Best Years'. In 1955 just before the DMUs were introduced, detailed surveys were made on East Anglian branches in March (winter service) and September (summer service); they showed that the operating ratio on these services averaged 2.4, and fell to 0.73 when DMUs were brought in.

The RE's response to these telling exposures of the loss-making local steam services was slight. The inertia maintaining the status quo took more than another ten years to overcome, the substitution of the much more economical DMUs later in the 1950s coming too late to prevent the radical reshaping of the network in the 1960s. By 1959 stopping passenger trains, in spite of the introduction of DMUs to many of them, were calculated to be producing an operating loss of £39.0 million a year, and more than the corresponding profit of £31.3 million being made by the fast and semi-fast trains; suburban trains were breaking even. Meanwhile, before the eventual proliferation of the private car, public bus services grew rapidly in the early years after the war. These included long distance coach services, such as on the London–Edinburgh route on which—in spite of their being much slower than the trains, carryings doubled between 1947 and 1951, but fares were considerably lower than by rail.

Approximately 18 miles from York and 12 miles from Northallerton, Sessay station was opened by the Great North of England Railway on 31 March 1841. Speeding through the station with a Colchester to Newcastle passenger service is V2 no. 60974. *Picture: Yorkshire Post*

As we have seen, net ton-miles of freight on BR as a whole was constant (at 20,880–22,900 million) between 1948 and 1957. The traffic on the ER, NER and ScR also remained remarkably constant over the period, at 20.3–21.9, 9.1–10.3 and 10.1–11.6 per cent of the total respectively—except that in 1956–57 the proportion on the now larger NER rose to 13.8–14.0 per cent. (The NER was second only to the LMR—by far the largest Region—in the originating tonnage of coal, and in 1957 this was 43.6 million tons—26.2 per cent of the BR total). At the close of the 1950s the ECML could not yet have been in decline, for in 1959 freight traffic on the GN section (3.6 million loaded wagons forwarded) was slightly up on 1958, as were passengers (at £6.68 million) with the King's Cross and Doncaster Districts showing significant increases.

Efficiency expressed as net ton-miles per total engine-mile rose on BR as a whole by 18 per cent from 543 to 643 in the period. It differed however between Regions. On the ER, thanks to widespread adoption of out-and-home engine and crew diagrams and strict scheduling,[3] the figure went up by 30 per cent, whereas on the NER it rose by 22 per cent and on the ScR by only 6.8 per cent. Total staff numbers on BR fell from 648,300 in 1948 to 519,300 in 1959; after boundary changes in 1950, a constant 15–17 per cent of these worked on the ER, 11–12 per cent each on the NER and on the ScR.

The very detailed studies made in the late 1950s, culminating in the test week ending 23 April 1961, formed the basis of the Beeching Reshaping Report of 1963. They underlined but greatly amplified the findings of the earlier post-war traffic surveys, and by extension provide a measure of traffic on the ECML and its branches. It seems appropriate therefore to summarise them here, for although modernisation was well underway—especially in the shape of dieselisation—there would have been little change in traffic patterns in the 16 months after the end of 1959, and the findings indicate levels at the end of the period covered in this book—prior to the falling of the 'Beeching Axe'. The reader must bear in mind that the figures are basically flawed in at least one vital respect: they take no account of seasonal variations in traffic. The third week of April is an almost totally 'non-holiday' week. On main lines passenger traffic fluctuated by a factor of two between 'high' and 'low' seasons, while on branches serving holiday resorts it varied by more than ten-fold.

From King's Cross as far as Hitchin the ECML was carrying 100,000 to 200,000 (100k–200k) passengers per week (p/w); the number fell to rather less than 100k p/w on to Doncaster and were of the same order between York and Darlington. Between Doncaster and Selby, and from Darlington through Newcastle to Edinburgh, carryings were about 50k p/w, rather less between Selby and York. Of the feeder and branch lines of the ECML, Wood Green–Hertford North, Hitchin–Cambridge, Retford or Doncaster–Sheffield, Doncaster–Hull, Doncaster–Leeds or Bradford, York–Malton, Darlington–Redcar, Darlington–West Hartlepool–Newcastle, Newcastle–Hexham, Newcastle–Tynemouth, and the main lines west and north of Edinburgh Waverley, were all carrying more than 10k p/w and were therefore not candidates for closure under the Beeching Plan,[4] nor were Doncaster–Leeds or Darlington–Middlesbrough/Sunderland–Newcastle (all more than 50k p/w). The lines Peterborough–March–Ely*, Peterborough–Grimsby, Grantham–Sleaford (as far as Honington)*, Grantham–Nottingham*, Retford–Lincoln*, York–Hull, Northallerton–Harrogate, Northallerton–Eaglescliffe*, Darlington–Bishop Auckland*–Crook, Hexham–Carlisle*, Drem–North Berwick*, and Edinburgh–Hawick,[5] were carrying only 5–10k p/w. The remaining ECML branches still operating passenger services all had densities of less than 5k p/w, and were undoubted candidates for closure, namely: Hatfield–Dunstable, Hertford North–Stevenage*, Hitchin–Bedford, Sandy–Bedford (as far as Willington), Sandy–Cambridge, Peterborough–Northampton or Rugby, or Leicester* (as far as Manton), Honnington–Lincoln or Sleaford and Boston*, Doncaster–Gainsborough*, Selby–Goole, Selby–Market Weighton, York–Harrogate* (as far as Knaresborough), Darlington–Richmond, Bishop Auckland–Durham–Sunderland, Tweedmouth–St Boswells, and the Edinburgh South Suburban line.

English Electric DP1, or Deltic, was built in 1955 and subsequently tested extensively on the LMR. After being rejected there, the ER took the locomotive in 1959 and soon an order for 22 others, later BR Class 55, was placed. Deltic is seen at Doncaster station.

The freight traffic data in the Beeching Report showed that London–York and Newcastle–Edinburgh on the ECML were carrying 50–100k tons per week (t/w), the higher levels being on the Sandy–Grantham and Newark–Doncaster stretches, while Newcastle–Morpeth was at the lower end of the range. Not surprisingly, the density on the York–Northallerton stretch was well over 200k t/w, while along the Northallerton–Darlington–Newcastle axis it was about 100k t/w. Of the connecting lines, Sheffield or Barnsley–Doncaster–Scunthorpe was carrying over 200k t/w, and also very healthy (with more than 100k t/w) were: Peterborough–March, Sheffield–Retford–Lincoln, Shirebrook–Lincoln, Doncaster–Lincoln,[6] York–Normanton, Northallerton–Tees-side, Tees-side–Ferryhill, and the Edinburgh South Suburban line. Traffic was satisfactory (more than 50k t/w) on: Hertford North–Stevenage, Sandy–Bedford, Peterborough–Rugby or Leicester, Peterborough–Spalding–Boston–Grimsby, Nottingham–Grantham–Sleaford, Newark–Bottesford, Doncaster–Hull, Leeds–Selby–Hull, Eaglescliffe–Darlington–Bishop Auckland, Ferryhill–Leamside–Newcastle, Durham–Bishop Auckland or Consett, Newcastle–Carlisle, Morpeth–Bedlington, and the South Leith and Granton branches in Edinburgh. Lines carrying between 5k and 10k t/w and therefore on the margin of being unprofitable, were: Hatfield–Dunstable, Sandy–Cambridge, Doncaster–Knottingley, Selby–Goole, York–Malton, Ferryhill–Bishop Auckland, and Newcastle–Tynemouth. All the remaining branches connected with the ECML on which either passenger services had been discontinued already or were those listed above with very low passenger densities, carried less than 5 t/w.

Most of the lines conveying less than 10k passengers (or less than 5k t/w of freight) were closed in the 1960s. (Those that were not are marked above with an asterisk*). In many cases they were

A train of high-capacity coke wagons is headed by Q6 0-8-0 No. 63458 on the ECML near Metal Bridge, Tursdale. The locomotive was the penultimate member of the class, which totalled 120, to be built in March 1921 at Armstrong Whitworth. Construction had begun in 1913, to Raven's T3 design, and the engines were employed mainly on the many mineral trains being moved around the north-east and beyond. *Picture: B. W. L. Brooksbank*

kept open because they were part of a through route, and in any case their wayside stations were closed, virtually all having passenger receipts of less than £5,000 per year and/or goods turnover of less than 5,000 tons per year—as were those on the ECML itself not already closed. There were very few lines where freight traffic density alone justified their being maintained. Exceptions included: Peterborough–Leicester, Peterborough–Grimsby, the lines from Shirebrook or Retford, or Doncaster to Lincoln, Northallerton–Eaglescliffe, and several lines in Co. Durham; conversely, Hitchin–Cambridge and Newcastle–Tynemouth were saved by their passenger traffic. On the other hand, Sandy–Bedford, Peterborough–Rugby, and Peterborough–Grimsby, which all seemed to have sufficient freight but were only marginal for passenger traffic, succumbed eventually to the 'Beeching Axe'—probably largely because alternative routes were available, whereas York–Malton–Scarborough has remained open, no doubt on account of the heavy summer traffic and the absence of alternative routes.

It is interesting to note that the Beeching Report identified very substantial flows of freight (50–100k t/w)—not including coal—that was 'favourable to rail but not on rail' passing along the Great North Road artery, especially southwards. This was so even in 1961, when almost the only motorway then in use was the M1 (London–Birmingham).

Capital expenditure on the ER was relatively high in the first decade of Nationalisation, with the completion of the Liverpool Street–Shenfield electrification early in 1950,[7] its extension to Chelmsford in June 1956 and to Southend Victoria in December 1956, the completion of the electrification from Manchester to Sheffield and Wath in June 1954,[8] and work in hand on the

London, Tilbury & Southend electrification. However, none of these relate directly to the ECML, where the only major works carried out in the period before January 1960 were the York and Newcastle re-signalling and the quadrupling between New Barnet and Potters Bar.[9] But just after the war the advantages in financial terms of converting principal ECML expresses to diesel traction were not seen to be very great, and while the ideas were resurrected immediately after Nationalisation it was to be over ten years after that before the diesels came, nearly 19 years before the GN London Suburban lines were electrified, and 40–42 years before the wires were carried down the main line through to Edinburgh. Earlier schemes in the 1955 Modernisation Plan had had to be shelved for the lack of funding—and of confidence in the financial benefits to be derived from the plan itself. Indeed in September 1960, Ernest Marples had cut planned investment on BR by 30 per cent—in favour of more Motorways.

Changes on the ECML before the end of 1959 related principally to motive power. Many of the 218 main line diesels already ordered (for £21.4 million) to replace 400 steam locomotives on the ECML were at work, and the prototype 'Deltic' was showing its potential, but it was two to three years into the 1960s before a radical acceleration of ECML express schedules could be brought into operation with the new diesels. Meanwhile, DMUs were taking over in wholesale fashion almost all the suburban and local passenger services by the end of the 1950s. In fact the NE Region forged ahead faster than any other Region with conversion of regional passenger services to DMU operation. Commencing with the Bradford Exchange–Leeds Central–Harrogate–Knaresborough service in June 1954, by October 1958 most of the Region's stopping and semi-fast services had been converted and 24.3 per cent of its coaching mileage was diesel–double the all-BR average. In 1955 it could be said that receipts (internal branch bookings only) had risen 300–400 per cent in the West Yorkshire scheme, 50 per cent on the Newcastle–Middlesbrough service and 30–35 per cent on the Newcastle–Carlisle and Darlington–Saltburn services, but strangely hardly at all on Darlington–Richmond/Crook. Indeed, with the rapid proliferation of private cars in the 1960s, the upward trends in receipts were not sustained, and some dieselised branches (e.g. Hull–Hornsea/Withernsea, where initial improvements in receipts were 55–80 per cent) were closed in the Beeching Era.

Appendix B

Causes of serious delay to ECML expresses October 1944

2nd: 10.15 Edinburgh to King's Cross: 34 min. late—time lost at Newcastle in detaching a defective guards van and transferring contents.
        16.00 King's Cross to Leeds: 63 min. late—defective brake on engine, necessitating change of locomotives at Dukeries Junction.

4th: 10.00 Edinburgh to King's Cross: 37 min. late—engine short of steam between Peterborough and King's Cross because of injector trouble.

9th: 10.15 Leeds to King's Cross: 48 min. late—delayed between Wakefield and Grantham through locomotive trouble on relief train ahead.
        13.10 Edinburgh to King's Cross and 17.30 King's Cross to Newcastle: both 26 min. late—diverted *via* Askern and Knottingley owing to aircraft crash on line near Selby.

13th: 10.00 King's Cross to Edinburgh: 50 min. late—train lost 25 min. through engine failure at Hitchin (hot driving box) involving change of locomotive and 25 min. between Peterborough and Grantham from shortage of steam caused by inferior coal.

16th: 07.50 Leeds to King's Cross: 44 min. late—delayed by military special ahead.

17th: 07.50 Leeds to King's Cross: 33 min. late—time lost between Huntingdon and Hitchin through reaction to goods train ahead being stopped because of hot axle box on wagon.

18th: 07.50 Leeds to King's Cross: 41 min. late—delayed near Hitchin through goods train ahead having become divided.

23rd: 07.00 Newcastle to King's Cross: 46 min. late—delayed by military special ahead which lost time through locomotive trouble.

25th: 10.30 King's Cross to Leeds: 45 min. late—delayed by derailment at Holbeck of three coaches on the 16.00 parcels train from Doncaster to Leeds.

27th: 17.30 Leeds to King's Cross: 49 min. late—failure of points at Hatfield.

28th: 07.50 Leeds to King's Cross: 31 min. late—reaction from delay caused to goods train ahead through defective wagon.

30th: 17.50 King's Cross to Leeds: 52 min. late—delayed between Wakefield and Leeds because of defective sand pipe and priming of engine.

31st: 10.00 Edinburgh to King's Cross: 48 min. late—engine short of steam, requiring an assisting engine from Retford.

Appendix C

Excursion Trains and their Routes

1939

Study of the special traffic notices (STNs) along with the WTTs relating to the ECML for some key dates in 1939 reveals the great extent and variety of special trains worked in those days. Maundy Thursday was always one of the busiest days of the year on the railways. On 6 April 1939 51 relief trains were dispatched from King's Cross down the ECML—42 of them in the nine hours from 15.00 to midnight, mainly by dividing normal trains into many (up to seven) separate portions.

Their destinations were: Aberdeen (two trains), Glasgow (four, one to Fort William also), Edinburgh (six, in addition to the above—one with coaches for Perth, another for Inverness), 13 (apart from the Scottish trains) to Newcastle (one *via* West Hartlepool); one each to Darlington, South Shields, Sunderland, and York; one to Ripon *via* Knottingley and Church Fenton, 14 to Leeds and/or Bradford (including one through to Halifax); five to Hull, one just to Doncaster and another just to Grantham. Most of this parade of trains were balanced by corresponding Up reliefs, but not so the six parts of the (unadvertised) overnight trains from Marylebone to Newcastle, the empty stock for most of which had to be worked up from Doncaster *via* Tuxford and the GC main line.

Further down the ECML many other relief trains ran on 6 April 1939. One each ran from Hitchin to Doncaster and from Letchworth to Manchester (Central) *via* Retford. Through Retford ran reliefs from Manchester (Central) to Ipswich, Liverpool (Central) to Harwich and another to Cleethorpes, and through Doncaster a relief ran from Liverpool (Central) to Hull. At York, four reliefs were run to Newcastle, and other reliefs ran from Bournemouth to Newcastle, York to Bournemouth, Newcastle to Swansea (via Bourton-on-the-Water), and no doubt a number on the Sheffield, Leeds and Scarborough lines (see below for Easter 1955), several services from Newcastle to Lancashire, to Carlisle and to Edinburgh were duplicated, and a number of extras were run on the other more local services.

The relief trains run down the ECML in the day or two before Christmas were comparable to those on Maundy Thursday. Perhaps of more interest were the extra and excursion trains run over the August Bank Holiday in 1939, for not only were there a remarkable number of relief trains on Saturday 5 August 1939 in addition to the Saturdays only (SO) ones in the timetable, but a host of excursions were put on, mainly on the Sunday and Bank Holiday Monday (6 and 7 August). A measure of the immense number of people expected to be going on their seaside holidays on the Saturday is indicated by the notes on strengthening the SO 07.52 Burton-on-Trent and 09.48 Basford (North) trains to Mablethorpe to each accommodate 1,000 passengers. Down the ECML from King's Cross 27 relief trains were run, principally by the division of normal trains into several portions, and many others ran on part of the ECML or passed through its major centres.

From King's Cross, there was one overnight extra to Aberdeen and another to Glasgow and Perth, one to Newcastle and one to Leeds/Bradford. During the day there were: one relief to Edinburgh, five to Newcastle, two to Saltburn, seven to Leeds/Bradford, three to Hull, one to Doncaster, one to York, and one to Grimsby, while the 15.00 Down was also divided to give separate portions to Cromer, Boston, and Cambridge. In addition, the overnight Marylebone–Newcastle train ran in eight portions. Through Doncaster or through Retford ran extras from: Liverpool (Central) to Yarmouth/Lowestoft, Manchester (London Road) to Skegness, and Sheffield to Boston, while two extras were run from Peterborough to Cleethorpes. Up specials were very similar, and included an overnight troop special from Newcastle to Bude which ran *via* Canonbury and the North London line on to the SR.

Further down the ECML the reliefs included: Rugby (Central) to Scarborough, Nottingham (Victoria) to Bridlington, March to York, Skegness *via* Grimsby to Newcastle, three overnight trains from Birmingham to York plus one from Leicester (LMS) to York, and (in daytime) one each from Birmingham, King's Norton, and Heeley to Scarborough, also three extras from Leeds to Scarborough; one each from Castleford to Scarborough and Leeds to Whitby and five extras from Leeds to Bridlington, one each from Leeds to Hull and to Saltburn, and York to Newcastle. Corresponding reliefs were run in the opposite direction, but some extra-long-distance empty stock workings were needed. If one had been observing the ECML, where it crossed the LMS lines to the east coast resorts near Little Bytham, the Nottingham–Sleaford line near Barkston, or the West Riding & Grimsby line near Shaftholme Junction, one would have seen also numerous extras and excursions going to the resorts from the Midlands and West Yorkshire. For example there were seven reliefs just from Nottingham (Victoria) to Skegness or Mablethorpe on 5 August.

Over the long weekend 5–7 August, numerous return excursions were run, mainly but by no means entirely on the Sunday and Monday. For many of these trains non-corridor stock was employed, and the LNER even found it necessary to borrow stock from the LMSR.

On Monday 7 August they ran the following:– To King's Cross from Bradford/Leeds (two trains); to Skegness from King's Cross (two trains), and one each from Hitchin, Letchworth, Peterborough North, Doncaster and Leeds (Central); to Yarmouth/Lowestoft from Luton *via* Cambridge, to Yarmouth from Peterborough North; to Hunstanton from Peterborough North *via* King's Lynn and March; to Newcastle from Doncaster: to Cleethorpes one each from Barnsley, Castleford, Morley/Leeds (Central), and three trains from Leeds (Central) to Bridlington/Scarborough *via* Selby, one each from Bentley Crossing/Wakefield (Westgate)/Bradford, Drighlington *via* Castleford, Normanton, Moorthorpe, Castleford, Bolton-on-Dearne, Chapeltown (LMS), Knaresborough *via* Wetherby, and Leeds (City); to Liverpool from Hull; to Bridlington from York; to Scarborough from York (two trains); to Scarborough *via* York one each from Heeley, Bradford (Forster Square), Leeds (City), Morley, Batley, Castleford, Halifax/Keighley, and also from Sunderland and Newcastle (two trains); to Whitby one each from Sheffield (Victoria) and from York, and from Leeds (City) (two trains); to Blackpool from York (two trains); to Ripon from Hull *via* York; to Harrogate one each from Newcastle, South Shields, Seaham, and York; to Saltburn one each from Bradford (Forster Square), Leeds (City), Harrogate, and Crook; to Redcar from Liverpool; to Balloch Pier from Saltburn (overnight); to Middlesbrough from Edinburgh *via* Darlington; to West Hartlepool from Liverpool; to Edinburgh one each from Durham and from Newcastle; from Newcastle two each to Alnmouth/Alnwick and to Carlisle, and one each to Glasgow (Queen Street), Berwick-on-Tweed, Rothbury, Warkworth, Brampton Junction, Bellingham, and Hexham; from Sunderland one each to Alnwick and Carlisle (Total, 77 excursions).

As already mentioned, several race courses were served by the ECML, and all the year horse-boxes (with their compartment for the groom or trainer) were conveying racehorses between racing stables and training centres such as Newmarket.

Also in the hunting season horses travelled by train to major meets such as the East Midlands and the Vale of York. Before the war, but to a rapidly diminishing extent after it, the ECML at Doncaster had its St Leger Week each September. For the whole week the LNER Plant works and other works closed down, coal traffic was diverted as much as it could be, and the sidings at the Plant, at Decoy, at West Yard and at Bentley Colliery were cleared in order to accept the empty stock of numerous race specials. On St Leger Day itself these came from far and wide, as much from the LMSR as from the LNER. In 1936 their origins were as follows. LNE:– Cambridge, March, Barnsley (2), Peterborough, Arkwright Town and Kirkby-in-Ashfield, King's Cross (2, one Pullman), Leeds (Central) (4), Bradford (Exchange) (2), Darlington, York (2), Hull (2), Newcastle (2), Halifax/Keighley, Cleethorpes, and Harrogate; LMS:– Heeley, Gloucester (2) and Hinkley, Northampton (via GN&LNW Joint), Luton (via Sheffield), Coventry, Kidsgrove, Low Moor/Wyke, Colne, Meltham/Holmfirth, Leeds (City), Southport, Blackpool, Manchester Victoria, and Barrow-in-Furness.

All these 39 Specials arrived between 09.15 and 13.15, and along with 29 normal trains dealt with in the same four hours made a frequency of one train every 3½ minutes. Apart from the St James' excursion platforms, two special extra platforms in the Plant locomotive sidings had to be brought into use for their discharge. Almost as many specials were run on the three other days of St Leger Week. Moreover horse-box specials were run, mostly each on several days, to and from Waltham (on the GN&LNW Joint), Witham (Essex), Newmarket, Newbury, Thame and Lambourn, Cheltenham, Battersea, and Holyhead.

Finally, an indication of the trains run for horse races even well off the ECML, those for the Grand National Handicap at Aintree provide another sample. The ECML itself carried as far as Retford two first class only trains (one consisting entirely of Pullmans) from King's Cross to Aintree, also a special from Newcastle *via* Sunderland, York, Sheffield and Manchester, and another by the same route from Darlington. That morning Doncaster dispatched its own special to Aintree and passed through another from Hull, and through Retford passed one from Cleethorpes and Skegness and one from Colchester *via* March and Lincoln.

1955

The STNs show that the numbers and destinations of relief and excursion trains were virtually the same on Maundy Thursday in 1955 as in 1939. Thus on 7 April 1955, King's Cross dispatched 46 reliefs (25 of them third class only), a high proportion running overnight, and rather more to Scotland than in 1939; the similarity applied also to those further down the ECML away from London.

Major Football fixtures still needed countless specials across the country, and even justified the opening of new (primitive) stations—one built in 1950 for the Hibernians at Easter Road Park on the Leith Central branch served arriving fans only. For the F.A. Cup Final on 26 April 1951 (Newcastle United *v*. Blackpool), 18 specials ran up to London from Tyneside, and when Newcastle United played Manchester City on 7 May 1955 14 Excursions were sent up overnight to King's Cross from Newcastle alone (returning between 19.00 and 02.15), two to Marylebone and three to Wembley Hill. In addition there was one each from Newbiggin, Monkseaton, and Bradford/Leeds, to King's Cross, and from Edinburgh, Blyth, Hebburn, and West Hartlepool to Marylebone; Marylebone also handled some from the Manchester and Sheffield areas.

The Illuminations at Blackpool and at Morecambe drew numerous evening excursions (Evex) not only from the north-west but also from the north-east, 170 in August to October 1952. (In 1953 the NE Region also ran 85 specials for Ladies Only, with restaurant cars, many to the Hockey at Wembley. A further example of their enterprise in the post-war era was the running of an Evex from Morpeth to Rothbury, a line already closed to passengers, in September 1953 for a cocktail party, with stops between stations to pick up guests!

The STN for the GN section for the August Bank Holiday week in 1955 ran to 157 pages. The programme for Saturday 6 August 1955 included pigeon specials from King's Cross to Newark and to Pinchbeck, and from York to Retford and to Grantham. In addition to advertised SO trains, there were 11 Down reliefs (9 third class only) from King's Cross; there was also a programme of extra holiday trains to and from east coast resorts quite as prolific as in 1939, as were also the excursions to the seaside and elsewhere on the Sunday and Monday.

On Sunday 7 August 1955—when considerably more were run than on Bank Holiday Monday (1 August), there were 74 scheduled excursions on the GN lines, of which the following went through ECML centres:– One each from Hull, Bradford, and Leeds to King's Cross and one from King's Cross to Hull, one to Southend from Hertford North (*via* the Palace Gates link), one to Clacton from Hitchin (*via* Canonbury), one to Yarmouth Beach from Peterborough North *via* the M&GN, and one from Newcastle. There were 18 ER excursions to Skegness, 10 to Mablethorpe, two to Woodhall Junction, 21 to Cleethorpes, four to Bridlington, six to Scarborough and one from Scunthorpe to Buxton. Most of these latter passed through Retford or Doncaster, or crossed the ECML at Barkston or near Shaftholme Junction. In fact the pattern was remarkably similar to that of excursions in summer 1939. Moreover, Nationalisation of the railways seems to have had only a slight effect on through running of trains from former LMSR stations to the east coast. One can only conclude that in regard to special passenger traffic, as to regular passenger and freight flow, the railways were still being operated very much as if Nationalisation had not occurred, and the ER and LMR, for example, were still isolated entities.

Although the number of relief and excursion trains was beginning to decline by the end of the 1950s, examination of STNs for 1958 and 1959 show few differences in routings from those of 1955. The NE Region STN for the 1958 August Bank Holiday Sunday (3 August) was typical: it showed four overnight Starlight Specials from Marylebone to Edinburgh plus one to Cardenden, overnight trains (probably military) from Whitby to Carlisle and from Ollerton to Edinburgh, and there were the following day excursions: three to Newcastle (from Bradford (Forster Square), Leeds and Hull), one to Glasgow (from Seaburn), one to York (from Altrincham), one to Edinburgh (from Newcastle), one to Dumfries (from Morpeth), two to Saltburn (from Bradford and from Leeds), one to Leyburn (from Spalding), one to Monkseaton (from Nottingham), five to Bridlington, 24 to Scarborough (some *via* Selby and including four from Leeds plus one from Kippax and one from Penda's Way, also—the furthest—from Burton-on-Trent), and lastly one from Sheffield to Whitby.

Appendix D

Military and other Government installations served by the ECML in the Second World War (mid-1942 to mid-1945)

The following is a list of depots established just before and during the war for military and other Government purposes which would have contributed substantial traffic, either passenger or freight, to the ECML more or less directly. Many had rail access with sidings and dealt with at least 10 to 100 wagons a day, for example the cold stores for the Ministry of Food listed below had 6.8 miles of sidings between them. Depots known to be rail-connected are printed in italics, but there were many others. Those that still existed in 1956 are marked '#', with where applicable the department or firm to which they were handed over after the end of hostilities.

The list is collated from—secret—lists compiled during the war for the REC, with additions from other sources including—at mid-1944—for the RAF the secret Locations of Units documents.[1] Table I lists depots served by main-line ECML stations, Table II those by stations on its connecting lines. The distinction as to which were or were not important to the ECML is naturally subjective. The criterion for inclusion in Table II broadly was that traffic to the rest of the country would have to pass along the ECML or through one of its major junctions, such as York or Doncaster. Depots in all of Lincolnshire, East and North Yorkshire (excluding the Hull & Barnsley line), Co. Durham, most of Northumberland, and some in the borders counties are included. Not included are depots beyond Seaton on the LMSR lines going west from Peterborough, in East Anglia (other than those served by the M&GN west of King's Lynn), east of Cambridge, St Ives or March, those in much of the east and north Midlands, the West Riding of Yorkshire, on the western part of the Newcastle—Carlisle line, and nearer the Waverley route in the Borders, and—most importantly—those in Scotland beyond Edinburgh. The lists[2] cannot be vouchsafed to be entirely complete.[3] At the very least it constitutes a representative sample of all the numerous depots established for war purposes all across the country, and it is interesting to note how many of the HM Government Sidings were extant in 1956.

Table I
Depots on the ECML

Station: Depot.

King's Cross: RAF No.232 MU4 Equipment Depot, White City, west London.
New Barnet: POW Camp, Trent Park, Cockfosters; Militia Training Camp, Whetstone; WD Records and Pay Office, Barnet.
Hatfield: *Ministry of Food Buffer Depot, Marshmoor Siding*; RAF (MAP, De Havillands) Airfield, Hatfield; No. 64 MU (Ammunition Park and Oxygen Depot).

Welwyn Garden City: RAF Airfield & Training Depot, Holywell Hyde (Panshanger). RAF Airfield Construction Depot.

Knebworth: WD Signals Development Branch.

Stevenage: Dept. of Education Stores Depot.

Three Counties: *RASC Duplicate Supply Depot, RASC Siding, Arlesey.*

Biggleswade: RAOC No. 27 Sub-Depot, Shefford (also served from Sandy).

Tempsford: RAF Airfield, Tempsford.

St Neots: RAF (later USAAF) Airfield, Little Staughton; Ministry of Food Slaughterhouse, Eynesbury; Eaton Socon Militia Training Camp.

Offord & Buckden: RAF Airfield, Graverley; War Hospital, Diddington Hall, Buckden. **Huntingdon North**: RAF Airfield, Wyton; HQ 2 Group (later HQ 8FF Group), Castle Hill House; Ministry of Works Depot; RE Stores Depot (Mail); US Army Engineers' Depot; HQ USAAF 1 Bombardment Division; RAF Petroleum Depot.

Abbots Ripon: *USAAF 2nd Strategic Air Depot, Abbotts Ripon; RAF (later USAAF) Airfield, Alconbury.*

Holme: USAAF (later RAF) Airfield, Glatton.

Fletton Sidings: RAF Petroleum Depot, Fletton; Ministry of Food Cold Store,[5] Botolph Bridge Siding.

Yaxley & Farcet: Royal Engineers' Camp, Yaxley.

Peterborough: *RAF Station, Peterborough (Westwood);[6] AA Training School, Peterborough; #RAOC Depot, Sage's (WD) Siding, Walton.*

Essendine: RAF Ammunition Park, Park Farm.

Little Bytham: RAF Airfield, Woolfox Lodge; Army Tank Corps Training Centre, Grimsthorpe Park.

Corby (Lincs.): RAF (later USAAF) Airfield, North Witham; RAF Airfield (later USAAF Airfield and Maintenance Base), Folkingham; RAF Landing Ground, Swinstead (Swayfield).

Great Ponton: RAF (later USAAF) Airfield, Saltby (later Waltham-on-the-Wolds); RAOC Dump, Waltham-on-the-Wolds.

Grantham: RAF Airfield, Grantham—Spitalgate from 1944 (HQ 5 Group—later HQ USAAF IX Troop Carrier Command—was adjoining, at St Vincent); RAF Airfield Harlaxton; RAF Regiment Depot, Belton Park.

Claypole: RAF Emergency Landing Ground,[7] Claypole.

Newark: RAF (later USAAF) Airfield, Balderton; Bowbridge Militia Camp; RAF Depot, Coddington Hall; *RAF Maintenance Depot, Lincoln Road*; RAF Airfield, Winthorpe; RASC Depot, Winthorpe Hall; MoS Home-grown Timber Depot, Stapleford Wood; RAF No. 203 Maintenance Unit.

Carlton-on-Trent: RAF Airfield, Ossington.

Tuxford North: Militia Training Camp, Tuxford.

Retford: RAF Airfield, Gamston.

Ranskill: *#ROF (explosives), Torworth, later MoS Siding: 2nd Armoured Division, Barnby Moor.*

Bawtry: RAF Airfield, Bircotes; *#RAOC Dump (later, Ministry of Works).*

Rossington: Royal Engineers' Barracks, Rossington Hall.

Doncaster Carr: Brigg's Sidings, *MAP Depot, Brigg's Motor Bodies Ltd.*; Crompton-Parkinsons' Siding; SPC Wagon Repairs Ltd; MoS Depot.

Heck: RAF Station, Snaith.

Henwick Hall Sidings, Selby: *#RAF Airfield, Burn, later WD Siding.*

Selby: Militia Camp, Brayton; *Royal Ordnance Depot, Selby.*

Riccall: RAF No. 80 MU Holly Carrs Wood Ordnance Depot, Escrick; RAF Airfield, Riccall; Skipwith Common Ordnance Dump.

York: *#Ministry of Food Cold Store, Eason View, Dringhouses; #RAF Airfield (RAF No. 60 MU, Salvage & Repair), Shipton, later WD Siding; No. 87 MU Equipment Park*; Northern Command HQ Depot.

Beningbrough: RAF Maintenance Unit No. 60, Beningbrough (Shipton).

Tollerton: RAF Station, Linton-on-Ouse; RAF Airfield, East Moor.

Raskelf: RAF Airfield, Tholthorpe.

Sessay: RAF Airfield, Dalton Moor.

Thirsk, or Topcliffe: (Thirsk-Melmerby); RAF Station, Topcliffe; RAF Station, Skipton-on-Swale.

Northallerton: *#Ministry of Food Cold/Food Stores, Boroughbridge Road*; RAF Hospital. **Darlington**: *#RE Depot, Black Banks WD Siding; RAF Repair Depot, Geneva Works*; RE Stores, Nestfield.

Birtley: *#ROF, Birtley Ministry of Supply Siding.*

Gateshead, Team Valley Estate: Ministry of Works Store.

Killingworth: 7th AA Division Ordnance Depot; Mobilisation Stores, Killingworth.

Chevington: RAF Airfield, Northstead.

Acklington: RAF Station, Acklington; RAF Airfield, Eshott.

Longhoughton: RAF Airfield, Boulmer.

Chathill: RAF Airfield, Brunton.

East Fortune: RAF Airfield, East Fortune. Drem: RAF Airfield, Fenton Barns (Drem). **Longniddry**: RAF Airfield MacMerry.

Edinburgh: *RAF No. 205 MU Universal Equipment Yard.*

Table II
Depots fairly directly served by the ECML, with approximate locations.

LNER Southern Area and LMSR connections

Aby (Firsby–Louth): RAF landing-ground (later, Airfield), Strubby.

Alford Town (Firsby–Louth): Military Camp, Well.

Ancaster (Grantham–Sleaford): RAF Airfield, Barkston Heath.

Ashwell & Morden (Hitchin–Cambridge): RAF (later USAAF) Airfield, Steeple Morden.

Aslockton (Grantham–Nottingham): Militia Training Camp, Walton-in-the-Vale.

Bardney (Lincoln–Boston): RAF Airfield, Bardney.

Barnetby: RAF Airfield, Elsham Woods; RAF Airfield, Kirmington, Ulceby.

Barnstone (GN&LNW, Saxondale–Harby & Stathen): RAF Airfield (later USAAF), Langar.

Bingham (Grantham–Nottingham): RAF Airfield, Newton; RAF Airfield, Syerston.

Blankey & Metheringham (Lincoln–Sleaford): RAF Airfield, Metheringham.

Blyton (Gainsborough–Barnetby): RAF Airfield, Blyton.

Bottesford (Grantham–Nottingham): RAF (later temporarily USAAF) Airfield Depot, Bottesford/ Normanton; *#No. 17 RASC Petrol Depot, WD Siding.*

Boughton (Lincoln–Shirebrook: *#US Army Stores Depot, Boughton WD Siding.*

Brigg (Retford–Barnetby): RAF Nos. 207 and 209 MU, Broughton Equipment Park.

Carcroft & Adwick-le-Street (Doncaster–Wakefield): Ministry of Food Store, Carcroft.

Cardington (Hitchin–Bedford): *#Air Ministry Siding; RAF No. 26 MU Repair Depot.*

Cole Green (Hatfield–Hertford): RAF Training Depot, Hatfield Hyde.

Collingham, LMS (Newark–Lincoln): *Air Ministry Sidings, Swinderby.*

Coningsby (Lincoln–Firsby): RAF Airfield, Coningsby.

Digby (Lincoln–Sleaford): RAF Airfield, Digby.

Doddington & Harby (Lincoln–Shirebrook): RAF Airfield, Wigsley.

Doncaster, Edlington (LMSR): Wadworth Woods Ordnance Depot.

Doncaster, Hexthorpe Sidings: MoS Depot, Sprotborough.

Doncaster, Marshgate or York Road: RAF Airport, Doncaster.

Doncaster, *Wheatley Park Sidings: MoS Depot (Crompton Parkinson Ltd); #Ministry of Food Cold Store, Churchill Road.*

Donington-on-Bain (Bardney–Louth): RAF No. 23 MU Forward Ammunition Depot, Market Stainton.

Dunstable (LNER): *#Ministry of Food Cold Store, Luton.*

Enfield Chase (Wood Green–Hertford): Home Office Regional Store, Great Cambridge Road, Enfield; Military Training Camp, Great Cambridge Road, Enfield; Military Training Camp, Slades Hill, Enfield.

Eye Green (Peterborough–Sutton Bridge, M&GN): Ministry of Food Grain Silo, Dogsthorpe.

Finchley Central (Highgate–High Barnet): AA Unit Station, Territorial Army.

Finningley (Doncaster–Lincoln): RAF Airfield, Finningley; RAF Airfield Lindholme. **Firsby**: RAF Airfield, Spilsby; *RAOC Ammunition Sub-Depot.*

Gainsborough (Central): Ministry of Food Buffer Depot.

Gamlingay, LMSR (Sandy–Cambridge): RAF Airfield, Great Gransden.

Great Dalby (GN&LNW): RAF Airfield, Melton Mowbray.

Grimoldby (Louth–Mablethorpe): RAF Airfield, Manby.

Grimsby Docks: *#Admiralty Siding.*

Haxey & Epworth (Doncaster–Lincoln): RN Mines Depot.

Henlow Camp LMSR (Hitchin–Bedford): *#RAF Airfield and Army Camp, Henlow WD Siding, RAF No. 13 MU Repair Depot.*

Hertford North: RAOC Dump, Hertford.

Hill End, or Smallford (Hatfield–St Albans): *#Ministry of Food Cold Store Butterwick.* **Histon** (Cambridge–St Ives): WD Technical Stores Depot; *USAAF Equipment Depot.* **Holbeach** (M&GN): RAF Bombing Range, Gedney Drove End: RAF Bombing Range, Long Sutton.

Honington (Grantham–Sleaford): RAF Works Repair Depot, Honington.

Horncastle (branch from Woodhall Jct): *RAF Petroleum railhead*; RAF No. 233 MU Chemical Weapon Depot, Hemingby.

Immingham Dock: RN Depot.

Killingholme, Admiralty Halt (New Holland–Immingham): *#Admiralty Oil Fuel Depot, East Halton; Admiralty Siding; RAF Petroleum Depot.*

Kimbolton, also Long Stowe Siding (Huntingdon–Kettering, LMSR): RAF Airfield Longstowe.

Kingscliffe (Peterborough–Market Harborough, LMSR): RAF station, Collyweston; RAF Camp, Kingscliffe; MAP Depot, RAF Airfield, Wakerley (later USAAF, Spanhoe).

Kirton Lindsey (Gainsborough–Barnetby): RAF Airfield, Hemswell (Harpswell); RAF Airfield, Kirton Lindsey.

Langworth (Lincoln–Barnetby): RAF Airfield, Dunholme Lodge.

Langworth, or **Reepham** (Lincoln–Barnetby): RAF Airfield, Fiskerton.

Lea (Doncaster–Lincoln): RAF Airfield, Sturgate.

Leadenham (Grantham–Lincoln): RAF Airfield (later USAAF), Fulbeck.

Letchworth (Hitchin–Cambridge): WD AFV Depot, Letchworth.

Lincoln (LNER): RAF Airfield, Scampton; RAF Airfield, Ingham; Boultham Gate Siding *Ministry of Food Cold Store*; Rushton & Hornsby Siding *RN Armament Depot, Sheaf Ironworks.*

Lords Bridge LMSR (Sandy–Cambridge*): RAF Sidings, and No. 95 MU Ammunition Park and Oxygen Supply.*

Louth, or *Ludborough* (Louth–Grimsby): RAF Airfield, Kelstern.

Lowesby (GN&LNW Leicester branch): WD Ammunition Distribution Centre, Lowesby.

Luffenham (Peterborough–Manton, LMSR): *RAF Depot, Luffenham*; Militia Camp, North Luffenham.

Luton (Hatfield–Dunstable): *Admiralty Victualling Depot & Salvage Stores*, Balmforth's Siding.

Maltby (Kirk Sandal–Dinnington: *#ROF Maltby, later Ministry of Supply.*

Market Rasen (Lincoln–Barnetby): RAF Airfield, Binbrook; RAF Airfield, Ludford Magna.

Melton Mowbray (GN&LNW): Militia Training Camp; US Forces Ammunition Dump.

Mill Hill East (branch for Finchley): *Mill Hill Barracks Depot and Ammunition Dump.* **Misterton** (Doncaster – Lincoln): *Air Ministry Petroleum Depot.*

Moortown (Lincoln–Barnetby): RAF Landing Ground, Caistor

Navenby (Grantham–Lincoln): RAF Airfield, Colbey Grange; RAF Airfield, Wellingore.

Netherfield & Colwick: *MoS, Colwick Depot WD Salvage Unit Siding.*

Newark, LMSR: RAF No. 58 MU (Salvage & Repair) and No. 203 MU (Supply); Hawton Road Militia Camp; RAF Petroleum Depot, Langford.

New Holland: RAF Airfield, Goxhill, Barton-on-Humber; WD Site 'F'.

North Thoresby (Louth–Grimsby): RAF Airfield, North Coates.

Old North Road (Sandy–Cambridge, LMSR): RAF Airfield, Bourn; RAF Station, Caxton Gibbet; Royal Ordnance Depot, Caxton.

Ollerton (Tuxford–Mansfield): Militia Camp, Ollerton; Militia Camp, Rufford Abbey. **Oundle** LMSR (Peterborough–Northampton): RAF (later USAAF) Airfield, Polebrook. **Peterborough** (LMSR), Crescent Wharf Sidings: *RAOC sub-Depot.*

Potton, LMS (Sandy–Cambridge): WD Stores Depot, Belle Vue.

Ramsey, North or East: RAF Airfield, Upwood; Militia Training & Cemetery Camps.

Rauceby (Grantham–Sleaford): RAF Hospital.

Redmile (Bottesford–Harby & Stathern, GN&LNW Joint); *RAF Petroleum Depot.*

Royston (Hitchin–Cambridge): Militia Camp, Royston; *#Ministry of Food (WD 1943) Depot, The Drift*; RAF (later USAAF) Airfield, Basingbourn, *WD Petroleum Depot.*

Sandtoft (Axholme Joint): RAF Airfield, Sandtoft.

Sandy (LMSR): *Air Ministry Petroleum Depot, Sandy Heath.*

Saxondale Sidings, **Bingham** (GN&LNW Joint): *RE Stores Depot, Bingham Road.*

Scawby & Hibaldstow (Gainsborough–Barnetby): RAF Airfield, Hibaldstow.

Shefford (Hitchin–Bedford): RAF Depot, Creaklands Priory Hutted Site.

Shepreth (Hitchin–Cambridge): RAF (later USAAF) Airfield, Fowlmere.

Skegness: RN Training Establishment, HMS 'Royal Arthur'.

Skellingthorpe (Lincoln–Shirebrook): RAF Airfield, Skellingthorpe.

Sleaford, Cranwell Sidings: *RAF Training Establishment, Cranwell.*

Snelland or **Wickenby** (Lincoln–Barnetby): RAF Airfield, Faldingworth; RAF Airfield, Wickenby.

Spalding: RE Searchlight Corps, Fulney Park.

Stamford (branch from Essendine, or LMS Peterborough–Manton): RAF Airfield, Wittering.

Stickney (Lincoln–Firsby): RAF Airfield, East Kirkby.

Stow Park (Doncaster–Lincoln): *Air Ministry Petroleum Depot, Brampton.*

Sutton Bridge (M&GN): RAF No.3 Armament Training School, Sutton Bridge (Holbeach).

Swinderby, LMSR (Newark–Lincoln): *RAF Depot, Swinderby; #RAF No. 93 MU, Norton Disney (Oxygen Supply and Chemical Weapons Dump).*

Theddlethorpe, or **Salterfleetby** (Louth–Mablethorpe): RAF Airfield, Donna Nook.

Thorne South (Doncaster–Scunthorpe): Militia Camp, Hatfield.

Thorp Culvert (Firsby–Skegness): RAF No. 233 MU Satellite Ammunition Depot. **Thrapston**, or **Kimbolton** (LMSR Kettering–Huntingdon): RAF (later USAAF) Airfield, Molesworth.

Thurlby (Essendine–Bourne): AA Searchlight Co HQ, Obthorpe, near Bourne.

Tumby Woodside (Woodhall Junction–Firsby): RAF No. 93 MU Equipment Park.

Ulceby (Barnetby/Immingham–New Holland): RAF Airfield, North Killingholm. **Waddington** (Grantham–Lincoln): RAF Airfield, Waddington.

Waltham (Louth–Grimsby): RAF Airfield, Waltham.

Waltham-on-the-Wolds (Mineral branch from Scalford, GN&LNW): RAF (later USAAF) Airfield, Saltby; Military Hut Storage.

Wansford, LMSR (Peterborough–Northampton/Market Harborough): RAF Airfield, Sibson.

Warsop (Lincoln–Shirebrook): RAF No. 66 MU General Equipment Park, Cuckney.

Whittlesea (Peterborough–March): *WD 38th VR Depot, Saxon Sidings, Pingle.*

Woodhall Junction, or **Woodhall Spa** (Horncastle branch): RAF Airfield Woodhall Spa (Tattershall Thorpe).

Worksop (Harriecroft Sidings), Ollerton or Checker House (Retford–Sheffield): Royal Ordnance Depot, Clumber Park.

Worksop, or **Checker House** (Retford–Sheffield): RAF Airfield, Worksop; RAF Training Station, Firbeck.

North Eastern Area

Akeld (Alnwick–Coldstream): RAF Airfield, Millfield, Wooler.

Alnwick (Alnmouth–Coldstream): RAF Petroleum Depot.

Amble (branch from Chevingon): RAF Marine Base, Warkworth Harbour.

Arram (Hull–Driffield): RAF Airfield, Leconfield.

Barlow (Selby–Goole): *#WD Mobilisation Depot.*

Barnard Castle (West of Darlington): Barnard Castle Training Camps.

Bedale (Wensleydale branch) RAOC No.23 Sub-Depot.

Benton (Newcastle–Backworth): RAF Balloon Centre, Benton.

Boroughbridge (Pilmoor–Knaresborough): RAF Airfield, Dishforth.

Bowes (Barnard Castle–Kirkby Stephen): RAF Chemical Weapons Store, Bowes Moor. **Brafferton** (Pilmoor–Knaresborough): *RAF No. 92 MU Air Ammunition Park, Brafferton*; Cundall Oxygen Depot.

Brancepeth (Durham–Bishop Auckland): Durham Light Infantry Training Camp. **Brandon Colliery** (Durham–Bishop Auckland): *#Ministry of Fuel & Power Sidings, Broom Park.*

Brough (Doncaster/Selby–Hull): RAF (also Blackburn Aircraft Co.) Airfield, Brough.

Bubwith (Selby–Market Weighton): RAF Station, Gunby (Breighton).

Burton Agnes (Driffield–Scarborough): RAF Airfield, Lissett.

Callerton, or **Woolsington** (Gosforth–Ponteland): *RAF No. 83 MU Salvage & Repair Depot, Woolsington.*

Carnaby (Bridlington–Driffield): RAF Emergency Airfield, Carnaby.

Castle Eden (Ferryhill–Hartlepool): Air Ministry Experimental Station, Old Shotton. **Catterick Bridge** (Richmond branch), also **Richmond**: *#Catterick Camp Military Units and Depots, NAAFI canteens etc., including traffic over Catterick Camp Military Rly*; RAF Station, Catterick.

Cawood (branch from Selby); RAF Bomb Dump.

Church Fenton (York–Leeds/Sheffield: RAF Station, Church Fenton.

Copmanthorpe (York–Church Fenton): RAF Airfield, Acaster Malbis.

Cottingwith (DVLR): MoS Mustard Gas Factory.

Croft Depot (Croft branch): RAF Airfield, Croft.

Danby (Picton–Battersby–Whitby): RAF Wireless Station, Danby Beacon, Leelholm.

Darlington, Fighting Cocks: RAF Station, Middleton St George.

Driffield: RAF Bomb Dump, Cottam; RAF Airfield, Eastburn, Driffield; RAF No. 91 Maintenance Depot, Southburn; Watton Siding; WD Site, Watton Crossing.

Eaglescliffe: *MAP Factory and Metal Products Recovery Depot, Urlay Nook; #Admiralty Siding*; HQ 59 Division.

East Boldon (Newcastle–Sunderland): 7th AA Division, Advanced Ordnance Depot.

Elvington (DVLR): RAF Airfield, Elvington; WD Ordnance Depot (from 1952).

Everingham (Selby–Market Weighton): RAF Airfield, Melbourne.

Fangfoss (York–Market Weighton); RAF Airfield, Full Sutton.

Fencehouses (Ferryhill–Pelaw): #Ammunition Depot, Finchale WD Sidings.

Filey: RAF Airfield, Hunmanby Moor; French Air Force Depot.

Garforth (York–Leeds): RAF Bomb Dump, Parlington.

Gilling (Pilmoor–Malton): *RAOC Ammunition Sub-Depot.*

Goldsborough (York–Knaresborough): *#MoS Cold Store.*

Goole: RAF Petroleum Depot, Hook.

Greatham (Stockton–West Hartlepool): RAF Landing Ground, Greatham.

Guisborough (Middlesbrough–Whitby): Militia Camp, Hulton Lowcross.

Harrogate: Militia Camp, Harrogate.

Haxby (York–Malton): RAF Mines Depot, Haxby.

Heighington (Darlington–Bishop Auckland): *ROF (Filling Factory), Aycliff; #Ministry of Works Siding.*

Hedon (Hull–Withernsea): New Mobilisation Store, Paull, Hedon, Hull.

Hessay (York–Harrogate): *#Ordnance Stores Depot, Hessay WD Siding*; RAF airfield, Tockwith (Marston Moor); RAF Airfield, Rufforth.

Hetton (Ferryhill–Murton–Sunderland): Lambton, Hetton & Joicey Works; *MAP No. 1 Store.*

Hexham: *#Ministry of Food Cold Stores, Tyne Mills.*

Holme Moor (Selby–Market Weighton): RAF Station, Holme-on-Spalding Moor.

Hornsea: RAF Airfield, Catfoss.

Hull, Wilmington: Balloon Barrage Depot, Sutton, Hull.

Hutton Cranswick (Hull – Driffield): Mobilisation Store; RAF Airfield, Hutton Cranswick; *RAF Petroleum Depot, Watton.*

Kenton Bank (Ponteland branch): RAF No. 13 Group Depot, Kenton Bank.

Knaresborough: Farnham Small Arms Factory.

Leeming Bar (Wensleydale branch): RAF Station, Leeming.

Market Weighton: *RAF Reserve Supply Depot, Market Weighton.*

Marske (Middlesbrough–Saltburn): *#25th Medium Heavy Regt., RA Training Camp, Marske Airfield.*

Masham (branch from Melmerby): RAOC No. 23 Sub-Depot.

Melmerby, **MoS Sidings**: *#Ministry of Supply Ordnance Storage & Inspection Depot.*

Middlesbrough: *#Post Office Telegraph Pole Yard.*

Murton Lane (DVLR): *WD Northern Command Petroleum Depot.*

Nawton (Gilling–Pickering): *#Ministry of Food Cold Store; RAF Airfield, Wombleton.*

Norham (Tweedmouth–Kelso): RAF Airfield, Winfield.

Norton (Shaftholme Junction–Knottingley, LMSR): Askern Brick & Tile Co. Siding; *MoS MT Depot.*

Norton-on-Tees, Bells' Siding: Mobilisation Depot, Stockton.

Ripon: Militia Camp, Ripon.

Ryhope (Ferryhill–Sunderland): 7th AA Division Advanced Ordnance Depot, Ryhope. **Scorton** (Richmond branch): RAF Airfield, Scorton; RASC Depot and Kiplin Air Ammunition Park, Scorton.

Scruton (Wensleydale branch): Engineers' Store Depot, Scruton.

Sedgefield (Ferryhill–Stockton): Hardwick Militia Camp, Sedgefield.

Slingsby (Malton–Gilling): *WD Ordnance Dump.*

South Bank (Middlesbrough–Redcar): *#Admiralty Depot.*

Southburn (Selby–Driffield): *RAF No. 91 MU Air Ammunition Park.*

Spennymoor (Ferryhill–Bishop Auckland): ROF Spennymoor.

Staddlethorpe (Doncaster/Selby–Hull): RAF Relief Landing Ground, Bellasize.

Starbeck (York/Leeds–Northallerton): *RAF Aviation Fuel Depot.*

Stocksfield (Newcastle–Hexham): RAF Station, Ouston, Stamfordham.

Stockton, South: RAF Station, Thornaby.

Stokesley (Picton–Battersby): Mobilisation Depot, Stokesley.

Strensall (York–Malton): Mobilisation Store, Huntington, York: RAF Airfield, East Moor.

Tadcaster (Church Fenton–Harrogate): Air Ministry Contracts Depot.

Thirsk Town (goods branch): *#Ministry of Food Cold Store.*

Thorp Arch (Church Fenton–Harrogate): *#ROF (Filling Factory No. 8), Thorp Arch (Boston Spa).*

Topcliffe (Thirsk–Knaresborough): Mobilisation Store, Topcliffe.

Usworth (Ferryhill–Pelaw): RAF Station, Castleton (Usworth), Sunderland.

Waskerley (Crook–Consett): *#MoS Ordnance Storage Depot, Burnhill.*

West Auckland: *#Ministries of Food, Works and Home Security Stores, Bishop Auckland; RASC and NAAFI Stores.*

Wetherby (Church Fenton–Harrogate): RAF Repair Depot, Wetherby.

Wheldrake (DVLR): RAF Airfield, Melbourne, also Petroleum Dump for FIDO (fog dispersion); *#Ministry of Food Cold Store.*

Whitby: Mobilisation Depot.

Whitedale (Hull–Hornsea): WD Site, Rise Park, Skirlaugh.

Willington (Durham–Bishop Auckland): *#Ministry of Food Stores, Sunnybrow; #MoS, Bowden Close Siding.*

Willington Quay (Riverside line): Militia Camp, Willington Quay.

York, Layerthorpe (DVLR): WD Ordnance & Supply Depot, York; *Petroleum Depot for RAF Linton-on-Ouse and RAF Full Sutton; Rowntree's Siding: Ministry of Supply Depot No. 14, Haxey Road.*

Scottish Area

Duddingston & Craigmillar (South Suburban line): *#RE Dump, Duddingston.*
Haddington (branch from Longniddy): RAF Landing Ground, Lennoxlowe.
Granton, East: *#Northern Lighthouse Commissioners' Siding.*
Leith: *RN Base.*
Marchmont (Reston–Duns): RAF Station and No. 54 OTU, Charterhall.
Edinburgh, Leith Walk or **Waverley Goods**: Ministry of Works Store, McCleod St.

Appendix E

Sidings and works on the ECML, 1938–1962

The following list is compiled largely from the *Railway Clearing House Handbooks of Stations* for 1938 and 1956, and from the Appendices published between those dates as well as that for 1962. (As no Appendix was published between 1956 and 1962, the precise situation at 31 December 1959—the cut-off date for the rest of this book—could not be used).

In general, sidings and works belonging to the railway are not listed here. The entries are headed by the name of the railway station having charge of the siding. All the facilities (other than railway installations) listed in the Railway Clearing House (RCH) Handbooks under the heading of an ECML station are given below. Those added by the RCH after 1938 are marked '*' and those not in the 1956 *Handbook* (and/or closed before 1962) are marked '#'. In a number of instances the establishments operating the installation changed during this period, and this is indicated in most cases. The designation 'Siding' is left to be inferred in many cases.

At the larger towns, many of the Works and Sidings listed were not directly adjacent to the ECML and only those coming under the auspices of an ECML station are cited. Where the location was on a branch this is indicated.

King's Cross Goods:
Camley Street coal bays;
*Rowntree & Co Ltd, Blundell Street Siding.

Holloway:
Islington Electric Light Works (later Central Electricity Authority, CEA)*, Tuner, Burns & John Inns Ltd (Holloway Mill), Ashburton Grove Sidings—Islington Borough Council.

Finsbury Park:
#Clarence Yard Siding (public);
LNER Engineer's Siding;
*MacFisheries Depot.
*Stoneyard Siding.

Hornsey:
Hornsey Gas Works (later North Thames Gas Board).

Wood Green:
Metropolitan Water Board; Alexandra Park Siding.

New Southgate:
LCC Colney Hatch (later Friern) Hospital;
Standard Telephone & Cables Ltd, Southgate & District Gas Co. (later Eastern Gas Board).

New Barnet:
Barnet Gas Works (later Eastern Gas Board).

Hatfield:
Marshmoor Siding: Calder & McDougall's Ltd, *Holland, Hammen & Cubitt's Ltd, *Massil & Sons (Wood Turners) Ltd, *Measures Bros Ltd, *John Mowlem & Co. Ltd; Sherriff & Sons Ltd, Smart's Siding;
Blackbridge Siding (Dunstable branch);
Fiddle Bridge Public Siding (St Albans branch);
Mount Pleasant (Hertford branch).

Welwyn Garden City:
*Associated British Picture Corporation (Welwyn Studios), *Crown Macaroni Co., Hertfordshire Gravel & Brick Co., *Lincoln Electric Co. Ltd, Mouldrite Ltd, *Nabisco Foods Ltd, *Roche Products, Shredded Wheat Co., Twentieth Mile Siding, Unity Heating Co.;

Dunstable branch:
#Horn's Siding, Welwyn Garden City Co.

Hertford branch:
Attimore Hall Public Siding, Dawnay's Ltd, New Town Trust Ltd, *Norton Grinding Wheel Co.

Knebworth:
#Rowe's Lime Siding.

Stevenage:
#Ellis & Everard Ltd, #Inn's Coal & Grain Siding, W. Pearman Ltd., Langley Public siding, Wymondley Public Siding.

Hitchin:
Cadwell Public Siding, Hitchin Gas Works (later Eastern Gas Board).
Ransome's North Siding: P. H. Barker & Sons Ltd.
Ransome's South Siding:*Concrete Proofing Co., Wallace & Bros Lime Works, *Wilmott & Sons.

Three Counties:
Arlesey Brick Co (later London Brick Co.), #Associated Portland Cement Manufacturers, Three Counties Mental Hospital.

Arlesey:
#Gault Brick Co., #London & Arlesey Brick Co.

Biggleswade:
#Gas Light & Coke Co. (later Eastern Gas Board), Tidman's Ltd (Wisbech).

Sandy:
#Love's Brick Yard (H. Cope), #Pym's Sand Sidings.

Tempsford:
*Little Barford Power Station, Beds. Cambs. & Hunts. Elec. Co. (later Edmondson Electricity Corp.) (later CEA).

Huntingdon North:
Huntingdon County Council Siding: *Chivers & Sons Ltd.
Fuel Oil Installation Siding, #Thackray & Co.

Holme:
Highney Estates Co.
*Lark Ltd (formerly H. H. Knighton & Co.).

Fletton:
*AEI Hotpoint Electric Appliance Co. Ltd., Beeby's Brick Co.;
Botolph Bridge Siding (Botolph branch):British Sugar Corporation, *British Thomson-Houston Ltd., Eastwood's Ltd, Yaxley Brickworks, Farrow & Co. Siding, Hicks & Co. (Fletton) Ltd Nos. 1, 2 & 3 Sidings, #Kemil Ltd., Celta Works, London Brick Co. Ltd.
Farcet Brick Works; Fletton Crown Siding; New Peterborough Nos. 1, 2, & 3, *Noble & Mushroom's Ltd, Norman Cross Siding; Peterborough District (later Midland) Tar Distillers Ltd., Plowmans' Brickfields Ltd., Yaxley Brickworks Siding.

Peterborough North:
Peterborough Corporation Electricity Works (later CEA), Southeast England Electricity Siding (LMS, Mid.), Spital Cattle Docks; Air Ministry Siding (M&GN): Baker, Perkins Ltd, Arktos siding; *Baxter Guion Ltd., W. P. Hartley Ltd., *Post Office Siding, Crescent Cattle Docks (LMS, Mid), Crescent Wharf Public Siding (LMS, Mid), S. Thomson & Sons, LMSR C&W Siding; Brotherhoods; Gilstrap, Earp & Co., Paston Siding.

New England:
Burnett & Co., *Cambrian Wagon Works, Peterborough Cooperative Equity Co. (later Co-op Wholesale Soc. Ltd), Cripple Sidings; *New England Anglo Siding (public), Sage & Co.'s Siding, Walton; Shell Mex & BP Co. Ltd.

Tallington:
*Dow Mac Products Ltd.; Etton Siding: Peterborough Corporation Water Works.

Essendine:
#Wilsthorp Siding (Bourne branch).

Little Bytham:
Lawnwood Siding: Adamantine Clinker Works, #T. E. Gray & Co. Bulk Storage, Highdyke Ironstone Sidings, etc. (Stainby branch).

Grantham:
Saltersford Siding; Lee & Grinley's Siding, *Lion Emulsions Ltd.
Ambergate Yard (Grantham Canal Station, Public Siding, on branch from Nottingham line): H. Bell's Siding, #Grantham Gas Works (later East Midlands Gas Board); Bristowes, Tavia Siding; Barnstone Cement Co., Little Ponton Siding. #Gonerby Public Siding: W. F. Swallow & Son (Wheeldon's Siding); Grantham Water Works, Ruston & Hornsby Siding: Aveling Barford Ltd., *Ransome's, Simms & Jeffries Ltd., Shell Mex & BP Ltd.

Newark:
Bottesford Branch: Bowbridge Siding; Cross Street Siding; Abbot & Co.'s Siding, Hugh Baird & Sons Ltd, Cliff Nook Kilns; Barnston's Maltings, British Glues & Chemicals Ltd. Siding: *Calfoss Ltd., *Croid Ltd., Kerol Ltd. Cafferata & Co. Siding: Pure Bone Phosphate Co. Ltd.; Jericho Siding: Lowfield Siding; T. W. Ward Ltd., Worthington, Simpson Ltd., Newark Gas Co. (later East Midlands Gas Board).

Balderton:
Newark Gravel & Concrete Co.; Gilstrap, Earp & Co.'s Maltings. Joint Curve (GN & Mid): H. Baird & Co., Spital Kilm No. 1, Branstone's Riverside Malt Kilns and Farrar's Boil Works, Fish Meal Plant, Gilstrap, Earp & Co.'s Cow Lane and Massey Maltings, *W. Peach & Co., Cow Lane and Spital Maltings; Ruston & Hornsby Ltd. Ironworks, Trent Concrete Co., Warwick & Richardson Ltd., S. B. Moore Ltd.

Muskham Siding: *Newark Egg Packers Siding. Ransome & Co.'s Siding: Ransome & Marles Bearing Co. Ltd.

Tuxford North:
East Markham Public Siding.

Retford, Babworth Sidings:
A. J. Fisher; *J. Bibby & Sons.

Ranskill:
*Eric Fawcett Ltd., *Ministry of Supply (later WD) Sidings; *Courtaulds Ltd., *Kingsbury Concrete Co.

Bawtry:
Associated Quartzites Ltd., #Bawtry Coke Ovens & By-Products, *General Refractories Ltd., *Brick Marketing Co Ltd.; Oates Siding; South Yorkshire & Derbyshire Gas Co (later East Midlands Gas Board), Yorkshire Amalgamated Products.
Haworth Colliery Branch: Harworth Main Colliery; *Glass Bulbs Ltd.
Misson Siding: *Ministry of Works.

Doncaster–GN lines:
Branch from Rossington: Amalgamated Denaby Colleries Ltd, Rossington Colliery. Belmont Sidings: Arnold & Son Ltd., *Briggs Motor Bodies Ltd., British Ropes Ltd., Darlington Fencing Co. Ltd., *SPC Wagon Repairs Ltd. *Ford Motor Co. Ltd. Siding.
Carcroft line: Doncaster Corp. Highways Dept. Siding.

Doncaster–GC and Joint lines:
Allen & Orr's Siding, #Anglo-American Oil Co., *W.S. Arnold & Sons (executors, of) Siding; Balby Public Siding.
Bentley Colliery (GC & H&B Joint line): British Bemberg Ltd. Siding, Burnett's Wagon Works; Cherry Tree Lane Goods; Doncaster Amalgamated Collieries Ltd.
Bullcroft Colliery (GC & H&B branch): Doncaster Canister Co., Doncaster Cooperative Society Coal Siding; Doncaster Ice & Cold Storage Co.'s Siding; Doncaster Wagon Co. Ltd. Siding; Farmer's Co. Siding.
Marshgate Goods and branch:*East Midland Gas Board Siding; *International Harvester Co., S. Parkinson & Sons Ltd Siding.
*Wheatley Park Goods: *Bowser, Monks & Whitehouse, Stevens' Wagon Works.
York Road Goods and GC & H&B Joint Line: C. F. Booth Ltd., Doncaster Cooperative Society Siding; *J. Fowler & Co. (Leeds) Ltd.

Arksey:
Bentley Colliery; #Bentley Colliery Goods Siding.

Heck:
Yorkshire Amalgamated Products

Selby:
#Henwick Hall Siding (public).
Bell, Berry & Co.; Brayton Siding (public); *British Oil & Cake Mills Ltd., British Sugar Corporation Ltd.; Dent's Siding; E. M. Fawcett's Siding; Fletcher's Siding; *Kirby's (Selby) Ltd Flour Mills; #Olympia (formerly Selby) Oil & Cake Mills, Selby Flour Mill, Selby Gas Works (later NE Gas Board), Selby Urban District Council; Thorp Gates public siding (Leeds line); Yorkshire Dyeware Co.

York, including Foss Islands area and DVLR:
Anglo-American Oil Co.'s Depot & Siding; *W. Bridge Ltd.; Burton Coal Siding; *Carlton Street Siding; Corporation Siding; *Derwent Rubber Co. Ltd. Depot Siding; Holgate Dock; Leatham Flour Mills, Logan & Hemingway's, Skelton Bridge; Rowntree's Sidings; St Cuthbert Siding; Shell-Mex & BP Ltd, Layerthorpe; Station Hotel Laundry Siding; Waterworks Siding, Clifton; *Waterworks Siding, Layerthorpe; Workhouses & City General Hospital; York Gas Co.'s (later NE Gas Board).
Poppleton branch: British Sugar Corporation.

Raskelf:
Hodgson's Coal Depot.

Pilmoor:
#Moor Siding (public)

Thirsk:
Jackson's, later Calvert Scrap Metals, #Manor House Siding (public).
Thirsk Town Goods: Anglo-American Oil Co.'s Siding; Shell-Mex & BP Ltd. Siding; Strike & Sons Siding; J. Toser's Siding.

Northallerton:
#Logan & Hemingway's Construction) Siding.

Eryholme:
Rolling Stock Co. Ltd.
Croft Depot: Croft Gas Works (later Northern Gas Board).

Darlington, Bank Top:[3]
Alliance Boiler Works, Black Banks Chemical Works (Thos. Ness Ltd); Boyd's Siding; Cleveland Bridge & Engineering Co. Ltd.; *Darlington Cooperative & Industrial Society. Haughton Bridge Depots & (public) Siding:*R. Blackett & Son, Dawson, Forcett Ltd. Works, Grieveson & Whitwell Ltd., Haughton Road Brickworks, *L. Wynn-Williams' Works; North of England Maltings Siding; Burnip's Brickyard; W. Richardson & Co's Siding; J. Tinsley Engineering Works, Victoria Works; Wagon Repairs Ltd., Weardale Steel, Coal & Coke Co, J. Weeks & Co. Horticultural Engineering Works.

Darlington, Hope Town:
Albert Hill and Skerne Works & Sidings; Albert Hill Foundry, British Steel Tube Works, Darlington Gas Works (later Northern Gas Board) Albert Hill Works and Skerne Works, Darlington Wire Mills Ltd. Works; Goldsborough Patents Ltd., *A. R. Jolly, T. Oldham's Scrap Yard, Premium Radiator Co., Railway Appliances Works, J. Sherwell & Co. Ltd., Skerne Iron Works Ltd., J. Tinsley Engineering Works, Skerne; Brown's Saw Mills, Pearson's Siding; Chemical & Insulation Co., Darlington Corporation, Hunden's Lane Siding; Darlington Electricity Works (later CEA); Bunker, Manure & Cement Siding; Darlington Forge Co.'s Works, Darlington Railway Plant & Foundry Co.'s Siding; Darlington & Simpson Rolling Mills Ltd., Rise Carr and West Works; Dunwell Bros' Whessoe Brick Works; *Esso Petroleum Co. Ltd., Grieveson & Whitwell Ltd., Cockerton and Rise Carr Depots; Jubilee Siding; *Morley Bros., *NAAFI Sidings, Whessoe Lane; Nestfield Engine Works and Wagon Works; Northern Gas Board, Albert Hill Works; Northgate Coal Depots, #North of England School Furnishing Co. Scolastic Sidings; Patons & Baldwin's Siding (Fighting Cocks branch); Pease & Partners' Granary and Warehouse, Redline Glico Ltd., Rolling Stock Co. Ltd. Nestfield Works, R. P. Simpson & Co. (Alnwick) Ltd., North of England Maltings, R. Stephenson & Hawthorns Ltd. (Springfield) Locomotive Works; T. Summerson & Co.'s Foundries, T. W. Ward Ltd.; Whessoe Lane Siding, *Russell & Wringham, Whessoe Ltd. Foundry and Siding; H. Williams Ltd., Railway Appliance Works.

Aycliffe:
Aycliffe Lime & Limestone Co. (later Gjers, Mills & Co.), Ord & Maddison's Lime Works.

Ferryhill (to Tursdale Junction):
Barker & Co.'s Slag Works (Coxhoe Junction); Coundon Depot (Leasingthorne branch); F. W. Dobson & Co. Chilton Limeworks & Quarry; Cornforth Basic Works; Earl of Eldon's Sand Tip Siding; Ferryhill North Slag Works; Ferryhill South Slag Works; Fishburn Colliery (branch from

Sedgefield); LNER Gas Works (later BR, NER; Mainsforth Colliery; *Mainsforth Lime Works; North of England Electric Co. (later CEA); Pease & Partners Ltd., Bishop Middleham Quarry; Steetley Dolomite Quarry Ltd.; #Thrislington Colliery, Coke-Ovens & By-Products Works. Tursdale Colliery & Coke Ovens (later NCB Central Stores, Leamside line). West Cornforth Chemical Works (Leamside line).

Plawsworth:
Kimblesworth Colliery.

Chester-le-Street:
Chester South Moor Colliery; Horner's Confectionary Works.

Birtley:
*AEI Ltd., #Bewick Main Colliery, Birtley Brick Co., Union Brick Works; Birtley Cartridge Case Factory (later ROF, Birtley), #Birtley Co.'s Siding, #Birtley Gas Works (later Northern Gas Board), #Birtley Grange Brick Works, #Birtley Iron Works & Gas Works; #Black Fell Siding; #Black Horse Siding; Blue Barns Manure Siding; #Blythe's Brick Works, Caterpillar Tractor Co. Ltd., #Durham Chemicals Group, #Eighton Banks Siding; #Goodall's (Disinfectants) Ltd., W. T. Henley (Telegraph Works) Co. Ltd., #Newcastle-on-Tyne Elec. Supply Co, Change of Frequency Stores (later CEA); #Newcastle-on-Tyne Zinc Oxide Co., #Ouston Colliery 'A' Pit and Gas Works, Ouston Colliery 'E' Pit (Birtley Colliery); #Ouston Grain Warehouse & Saw Mill, #Ouston Manure Depot; #Pelaw Grange Saw Mill, #Pelaw Grange Siding and Depots; *Ravensworth Ann Colliery, *Ravensworth Betty Colliery, *Ravensworth Brick & Tile Works, *Ravensworth Shops (NCB); *J. O. Scott, Pelaw Grange Brick Works; #Urpeth Colliery ('B' and 'C' Pits) & Coke Ovens; #White Hill Bank Head Siding; #Whithouse Siding.

Team Valley Trading Estate:
*British Road Services (Parcels) Ltd., *Cadbury–Fry Ltd., *De La Rue Developments Ltd., *Durham Steel Co., *Fusarc Welding Co. Ltd., *Huwood Mining Engineering Co., *NE Trading Estate Ltd., *Reed, Millican & Co. Ltd., *Team Valley Cold Storage Ltd., *H. Wood & Co. Ltd., Wright, Anderson & Co.'s Coulthards Lane Siding.

Gateshead:
Armstrong, Whitworth & Co.'s Close Works, *S. Bowran, Shipcote Works (Felling line); *Bramwell's Siding; #Carrick & Wardle, Redheugh Engine Works; Clark, Chapman & Co. Victoria Works; *Coronation Works (Allhusens branch); #Eagle Depot (E. S. Holdsworth & Co.); Gateshead Cooperative Society Depot, Gateshead Corporation Depots; Goodhall, Bates & Co.; #Hope & Co.'s Raby Depot; ICI (General Chemicals) Ltd. Works; *Jenning's Siding; Kirkpatrick & Barr's; Marple & Gillott, St James' Siding; Oakwellgate Public Siding; Park Lane Glass Works (Ferry & Son); #Redheugh Colliery; River, Bolt & Nut Co.'s Tyneside Works, Sowerby Ellison Glass Works.

Newcastle-upon-Tyne (excluding Blaydon, Jesmond Loop and Riverside line):
Forth (Goods):
English Steel Corp., Elswick Works; #Hawthorn, Leslie & Co., Newcastle Gas Works (later Northern Gas Board), Elswick Works; #R. H. Patterson & Co.; Railway Street Coal & Lime Depots; Robert Stephenson & Hawthorns Ltd., Vickers-Armstrong Ltd., Elswick Ord. & Eng. Works, and Wharf

Newcastle Central: #Benwell Colliery; Forth Cattle Dock, Forth Hydraulic Engine House, Forth Provender Store, Walker, Parker & Co. (later Associated Lead Manuf. Ltd.).

New Bridge Street:
Goods & Coal Depot, #Backworth Coal Depot & Siding; Caruthers' Granary, *Guinness & Co. Warehouse, *J. Heinz' Warehouse; Newcastle Corp. Elec. Gen. Sidings, Schweppes Ltd. Warehouse.

Quayside Branch:
*Cooperative Wholesale Society Grain & General Warehouse; Newcastle Corporation Sheds 1, 2, & 3; Newcastle Corporation Wharves Nos. 3 – 26; *Spillers Ltd, Tyne Mills.
Heaton Junction: *J. Arnott & Co.'s Siding; #H. Down & Co., Heaton Foundry Co. Ltd., Heaton Manure Loading Wharf, Heaton Junction Public Siding; *Hunter's Coal Depot, *Imperial Tobacco Co. Ltd., *Metal Box Co. Ltd., *Needlers Ltd.; Newcastle Cooperative Society Coal Depot; Newcastle Corporation Sidings; Nicholson Chemical Works. Dope & Varnish Works; A. Parsons & Co. Ltd., Heaton Works; F. Turnbull & Co.

Killingworth:
Baradon Colliery & Sidings; #Burradon Lizzie and Weetslade Pit; #Dinnington Colliery, Depot & Brickworks; *Havannah Colliery; Hazebrigg Colliery; #Hope Cottage Siding; Killingworth Colliery; Killingworth Saw Mill; Scorer's Manure Siding; Seaton Burn Colliery & Depot; *Weetslade Colliery & Washer.

Annitsford:
#Annits Village Siding; #Ann Pit; Cramlington Lamb Pit & Brick Works; Dam Dykes Siding; Dudley Colliery & Depot; #Hartford Colliery (Scott Pit); Shankhouse Colliery (Amelia Pit); #Wrightson Colliery.

Cramlington:
Cramlington Coal Co. Siding.

Stannington:
#W. Slater; #W. Younger.

Morpeth:
J. R. Temple's Siding; *Shell-Mex & BP Ltd. Siding.
Pegswood: Bothal Park (or Ashington Junction) Siding; *Longhirst Public Siding; Pegswood Colliery & Siding.

Widdrington:
Burn Fireclay Co.; Stubswood Colliery & Siding; #Widdrington Old Colliery.

Chevington:
Amble Junction Siding.

Warksworth:
South Shillbottle Colliery; Shortridge Farm Siding; #Southside Colliery.

Alnmouth:
Shillbottle Colliery.

Little Mill:
*Howick Whinstone Quarry & Pipe Works (later Trollop & Colls Ltd), *Littlehoughton Concrete Pipe Works, Little Mill Lime Kilns; #Little Mill Whinstone Quarry.

Christon Bank:
#Christon Bank Tramway Station Siding; #Fallodon Siding & Depot.

Bedford:
Appleby's Siding; Craigmill Siding; *Craig Drier Siding.

Scremerston:
#Billingdean Colliery; #Scremerston Colliery.

Tweedmouth:
Allan Bros., *J. T. Dove Ltd., Johnson & Darling's; McCreaths'.
Tweed Dock: Esso Petroleum Co., *Fisons', *Northern Gas Board, *Roofing & Building Supply Co., H. O. Short & Sons, J. P. Simpson's Maltings.

Berwick-on-Tweed:
Berwick Auction Mart Co.

Reston (Chairnside Branch): Auchencrow Public Siding; Billiemains Public Siding.

Dunbar:
Thomas Allandale & Sons Ltd., #Battlebent Siding; Beltenford Public Siding; British Malt Products Ltd., Westbank Mills; Oxwellmains Limestone Siding; Associated British Portland Cement Co.; Oxwellmain Public Siding; West Barns Siding.

Drem:
Ballencrieff Public Siding.

Longnididdry:
#Longniddry West Siding.

Prestonpans:
Meadowmill Mine (on Branch); #Morrison's Haven Siding; Northfield Siding; Ormiston Road Coal Depot; Prestongrange Colliery; Prestongrange Brick & Fireclay Works; Preston Links Colliery; Seton Siding; Summerlee Iron Co. Ltd.
Tranent (including colliery branches): #Bankton Colliery; Kingslaw Siding; Myles' Siding; Tranent Public Siding; Tranent Mains Siding; #Wester Windygoul Siding; Windygoul Siding.

Inveresk:
Inveresk Paper Co., Musselburgh; *NCB Siding, Wallyford Colliery.

Niddrie: *Edinburgh Corp. Water Dept., Pipe Works; Newcraighall Colliery; Niddrie Sanitary Fireclay Works; Woolmet Colliery.

Portobello:
Buchanan & Co. Wagon Repairs; Joppa Saw Mills; J. & P. Cameron Corn Store; #Craigentinny Gas Works (later Scottish Gas Board); #Edinburgh Corporation Refuse Bank; LNER (later BR, ScR) Materials Store; Meadowbank Siding; Palace Brewery, Rose Lane; Portobello Bottle Works; Westbank Power Station (later South of Scotland Electricity Board); Woods Park Repair Depot.

Edinburgh:
Abbeyhill–Piershill Loop: *Bruce & Sons, Central Fruit Co., Lindsay & Sons & Scarlett; Lochead (Moray) Siding (W. Younger & Co.); #London Road Foundry (Miller & Co.); Rankins' Siding; Scotsman Siding: A. S. Clarke & Co., #Ormerod, Wood & Co., M. Ritchie & Co., Veital, Moore & Erskine.

N.B.: Not listed above are a large number of sidings in the Greater Edinburgh/Leith area, amounting to over 100 entries in the *RCH Handbook*. These came under the jurisdiction of various stations on the branches from Portobello or on the South Suburban line (including the St Leonards branch), some being worked jointly from LMSR stations.

Appendix F

Specific wartime locomotive workings

Unfortunately it seems that hardly any STNs or movement orders giving details of the scheduling of wartime special trains have survived, let alone records of the locomotives used. The following is a tantalizingly short example of details.

The 'Convoy' coal trains caused a lot of trouble, partly due to frequent breakdowns of grease-lubricated private-owner wagons on the long journeys, and a sample report on 'Convoy' coal trains running during the Blitz winter of 1940–41 is intriguing. It cites the progress of a sample of five actual block coal trains from Co. Durham on Friday and Saturday 14 and 15 March 1941.

No. 1—left West Hartlepool at 11.55 on 14th March for Westbury, arriving 02.35 16th March; it had O4 No. 6574 to Normanton (via York), LMS 4F No.4337 on to Branston, LMS 4F No. 4171 on to Stoke Gifford, then GW 'Saint' No. 2951, with assisting engine from Bathampton.

No. 2—left West Hartlepool at 17.02 on 15th March for Ferme Park, arriving 21.10 on 16th March; it had O4 No. 6193 to York, where it was delayed two hours waiting for an engine, that turned out to be A1 No. 2579 which took the train on to New England, where O1 No. 3468 took over.

No. 3—left Stella Gill at 09.05 on 14th March for Brimsdown, arriving at 10.50 on 15th March; it had Q7 No. 907 to Doncaster, O4 No. 5400 on to Whitemoor, then J20 No. 8274.

No. 4—left Whitburn Junction at 14.25 on 14th March for Hartford Exchange Sidings, arriving 18.00 15th March; it had V2 No. 4825 to York, then O4 No. 6235 right through to Northwich, assisted by J6 No. 4173 from Wath to Dunford Bridge, plus O4s Nos. 6500 and 6224 from Wath to West Silkstone Junction (Worsborough Incline).

No. 5—left West Dunston at 20.35 on 15th March for Heywood, arriving 16.40 on 17th March (having been held over the Sunday at Rochdale); it had Q6 No. 1131 to Normanton (via York), then LMS 7F No. 9519 to Rochdale.

Appendix G

The impact of the Air War on the ECML

Damage and Disruption Due to Enemy Action on the ECML and Some Connecting Lines
No account of the railway scene during the war can suffice without an attempt to recount the various episodes of damage and disruption caused by enemy action. In fact, on the LNER the ECML came off relatively lightly. Considering that it was virtually impossible at any time for a bomber to hit a specific railway target at night, the list of damage and disruption given below is actually an impressive indication of the intensity of the air raids. Nonetheless, in any account of air raids in Britain in the Second World War, it is salutary to remember how minor was the damage done by the Luftwaffe in this country compared with the devastation meted out later in the war by the Allied Air Forces, both as a result of area bombing and when the railways of Germany and of occupied France, Belgium, Holland and Luxembourg were subjected to a campaign of targeted interdiction in 1944–45. For example, on the night of 14 October 1944 alone Duisburg in the Ruhr received as many tons of bombs as did all the British targets during the worst month (September 1940) of our Blitz.

What follows here relates primarily to the ECML, and the reader should bear in mind that other railways—and many other places in Britain—suffered much more severely from air raid damage, and at one time or another incidents of some kind due to enemy action occurred in almost every part of the country. The indirect effects, for example, of raids on London, Hull, Leeds, Glasgow and other places connected with the ECML were often as great as the direct damage on ECML centres. The first significant damage inflicted by the enemy on the LNER was a bomb on the Down Goods line between Barnetby and Brocklesby in the early hours of 13 June 1940. Other bombs fell in Humberside that night, and it is well known that Hull and Grimsby suffered severely during the Blitz and later. The LNER's property in the area was heavily damaged, as it was in Norwich, Yarmouth, Lowestoft, Nottingham, Leeds, Sheffield, Middlesbrough, West Hartlepool, Clydebank and elsewhere. There is not space here to describe the damage done at all these places, and reference is made to only a few of the numerous incidents that happened on the lines branching off the ECML. Moreover, it was far from just direct damage by blast or fire that was suffered: traffic could be interrupted for hours or days by the mortal danger from delayed-action (DAB) or unexploded bombs (UXB). When a high-explosive (HE) bomb—or worse, one of the hefty land-mines that were dropped by parachute—failed to explode accidently or deliberately, it could often cause more disruption than if it had, for until it did explode or was defused its mere presence on or near a line necessitated the closure of that line and diversion of all trains. Often UXBs were found hours or days after a major raid, and lines had to be closed for longer than it took to repair actual damage. Anti-aircraft (AA) shells were inclined to shower shrapnel on people on the ground, and if the shells failed to explode they were also a menace. For example, in 1940 unexploded AA shells at New Barnet on 20 September and at Ferme Park on 29 December each caused interruption of traffic for over three hours.

In the initial, violent and almost continuous phase of the London Blitz, in September–November 1940, a number of incidents of serious damage on or near the ECML occurred, and these are listed below. However, compared to the damage done on many other lines in London this was not so very disruptive. The main effects of the Blitz on the ECML were indirect. Thus, from the first heavy daylight raids early in September 1940 to the end of the Blitz in May 1941, the passage of the heavy mineral and freight traffic on to the SR from the Ferme Park yard *via* the Widened Lines and over Blackfriars Bridge was interrupted directly by the destruction of adjacent buildings, including Farringdon Goods station, but also especially of bridges etc. on the SR lines. During September and October 1940, not only were the routes over Blackfriars Bridge and *via* either Herne Hill or London Bridge cut for prolonged periods, but there were also serious interruptions of the routes to the SR by the North London, West London and East London lines.

When bombs actually exploded on plain track, by dint of hard work it did not take many hours to restore traffic—if at first with hand-signalling, but when bridges and other major structures were hit it was a different story. Right from the beginning of the Blitz in September 1940 the SR suffered many serious incidents of this kind, and as a result when the direct route to the SR *via* the Widened Lines was out of action on several occasions there was a great build-up of traffic in the ECML yards. For example, on 14 September no fewer than 1,791 wagons were held up at Ferme Park and another 2,300 at East Goods, Clarence and King's Cross yards, and the LNER expected to be able to clear only about 1,350 in the next 24 hours. It was therefore diverting coal traffic to south London all the way round through Bletchley, Oxford, Basingstoke, Eastleigh and Chichester.

Bridges and locomotive sheds were prime targets, but hard to find and hit. The enemy could hardly fail to hit the vast Stratford complex, but the damage they did to King's Cross, South Blyth and York engine sheds was probably incidental, as was that to York shed—where on 9 July 1940 the first LNER railwayman was killed. However, raids on Louth shed on 19 February 1941 and on Tweedmouth shed on 10 February 1942 were well directed, the first virtually destroying the little depot, killing one man and injuring two others.

Air-raids themselves obviously could have dire consequences, but it must be remembered that the most serious delays and disruption were caused in the dark stages of the war by trains being stopped or slowed to a crawl simply because there was an air- raid warning in force, and also by the difficulties of operating in the Black-Out. Until November 1940 it was ruled that after the sounding of the 'Alert', all passenger trains must be stopped and warned by a signalman—and the passengers given the opportunity to detrain at the next station. The trains then had to crawl at 15 mph (10 mph for freight trains) until the 'All Clear' had sounded. After October 1940 the speed-limit in Alerts was raised to 25 mph in daylight but remained at 15 mph in darkness, but the delays caused havoc with timetables and with the rostering of men, locomotives and stock, and trains—more especially freight trains—often had to be controlled on an *ad hoc* basis. Fortunately these restrictions were soon recognised to be impractical and unnecessary: even if drivers went very slowly they still might run into an obstruction or fall into a crater in the dark—as did happen several times. Therefore from February 1941 all trains were allowed to run at normal speeds during Alerts in daylight or at 30 mph during black-out hours, and the order to stop to inform passengers of an Alert was rescinded because few people took any notice. At night trains still had to be stopped for the driver to be warned of an Alert—also the guard, who had to turn off the train lighting—until December 1944; who told the train-crew when the 'All Clear' had sounded is not clear. During the V1 flying bomb emergency in London and the south-east in 1944, in daytime signalmen put out white boards with a black upward-pointing arrow to warn drivers of Alerts. The heavy air-raids on London led to the practice of having expresses call at a major suburban station to help passengers keep away from main termini; on the ECML Up expresses stopped at Finsbury Park if an Alert was on, to let passengers transfer to the Tube there if they wished.

For some reason best known to the Germans, virtually the only city on the ECML to be bombed heavily was London. Newcastle-upon-Tyne, in spite of its prime importance as an industrial target, had only two major raids throughout the war, on the nights of 9 and 25 April 1941, and these were widely dispersed over the Tyneside area, bombs falling mainly well downstream from Newcastle. Peterborough and Darlington each had several incidents, none doing grievous harm to the railways. Grantham town was struck no less than twelve times in the last three months of 1940 and in one raid 39 people were killed, but the railway was little affected. Doncaster, on the other hand, was fortunate to escape, for on 21 December 1940 a major—but accidental—fire at the Carriage Works (which began in the paint shop and burnt out the carriage body and joiners' shops) attracted a number of enemy bombers whose sticks entirely failed to explode.

It could have been that the failure of the enemy to bomb major railway centres on the ECML (and elsewhere) was to a certain extent thanks to the installation of decoy lighting (QL sites) and fires (QF sites), which in addition to smoke-screens were employed to mislead the German bomber crews. In November 1940 QL sites were set up at Loversall near Doncaster; to represent the lights of Decoy (!) Yards, and at Eye to represent New England Yard; in November 1941 one was brought into use at Upper Poppleton, south-west of York, but it confused RAF crews approaching nearby Rufforth Airfield and was abandoned two years later. There were of course several decoy sites in other parts of the country.

As described later, the railway installations at York were the most unfortunate on the ECML, receiving a pasting in one of the relatively small-scale *Baedeker* raids in 1942. Edinburgh, Britain's second capital, never had a major raid; the only recorded railway damage in the Edinburgh area occurred in minor incidents at Leith LMS on 18 July, at South Leigh on 22 July and at Portobello on 4 August 1940, and at North Leith and Junction Road stations on 7 April 1941. In London, by far the greatest damage in the Blitz was done in the City and East End, and therefore on the LNER it was the Great Eastern section that was most affected. London also was the prime target of the flying bombs and rockets in 1944–45, and again the LNER suffered principally in the East End. Indeed one in seven of all V2s (German rocket weapons) that fell in Britain damaged LNER property.

The earliest reported incidents on the ECML itself were at Darlington, where on 27 June 1940 minor damage was done to signal and telephone wires—cutting communications with Tees-side for a few hours, then at Newcastle on the night of 2 July 1940 one bomb fell near the station, one near the High Level Bridge and another at Gateshead West, causing minor damage and interruption of block working.

London Area

The London Blitz had begun with a vengeance on 7 September 1940. Havoc in the East End was so widespread that the LNER stopped all traffic in the Stratford District that night—a Saturday, and for the first time of many to come the SR stopped all inter-company exchange traffic. From then on London was bombed almost every night until the end of November. The first incident on the ECML itself occurred in the early hours of 9 September, when the potato market at King's Cross was severely damaged, and several bombs fell in the Top Shed area. One in particular landed next to the main-line shed, destroying one wall and the roof over two stabling roads. Stores buildings were damaged, the glass of the Suburban shed blown out and the dividing wall with the LMSR brought down; a water main was burst, the coaling-plant put out of action and telephones cut. Several locomotives were damaged (notably O1s Nos. 3462 and 3473 and N1 No. 4571), but in all this only five men were injured—none seriously, and engines still came and went. A bomb struck the Shed area again on 23 October and an AA shell hit it on 21 December.

King's Cross was again affected on the night of 17 September, with debris and damage on the Down main and slow lines to Belle Isle, delaying but not interrupting traffic for several hours. And it was not only bombs: on the evening of 20 September an AA shell exploded in the station forecourt, killing two and injuring 27. On 9 October York Road station was hit, although traffic was not affected. At King's Cross Goods, UXBs disrupted working on 2, 11 and 21 October (when Outwards traffic had to be diverted to the Inwards shed), and then on the morning of 9 November major damage was suffered there, with 28 people being killed and 102 injured. Further extensive damage was sustained by the Outwards shed and No. 1 Office in raids on 13 and 15 November, and on 30 January 1941—nine people being injured on that occasion.

On the night of 17 April 1941—in London's worst raid of the war, Farringdon Goods station was destroyed in the fires, but apart from relatively minor damage suffered on 15–16 November 1940, 12 January and 17 April 1941, King's Cross passenger station was spared (although bombs fell in the Milk Yard)—until the night of 10–11 May. At 03.15 on that night, HE smashed about 75 feet of the west side of the main station roof between the booking-hall and the footbridge, killing five staff and eight soldiers in the RTO's office. On No. 10 platform, the booking office and its entire stock of tickets—but not the cash, secure in a safe—buffets, stores and many headquarters offices were all destroyed. One engine (N2 No. 4761) and fifteen vehicles on No. 10 and the adjoining track were damaged. Roof girders fell across platform lines 6, 7, 8 and 10, and more of the west wall was in danger of collapsing, but the station was partially reopened in 24 hours; it took two weeks to effect repairs sufficient to allow platforms 7 and 8 to be used. A temporary booking-office was established in the Georgian tea-room, and the latter substituted by a buffet car at the buffers of platform 10. The great hole in the roof was not repaired until over a year after the end of the war, and while this was being done the roof was again extensively damaged—by a fire. Traffic on the Widened Lines and/or to Moorgate was suspended for many hours or days—even weeks—on many occasions during the Blitz, by bombs, debris, fires, also flooding and derailments. Indeed, Moorgate and Aldersgate stations were so completely destroyed that the suburban service from Moorgate was suspended from October 1940 for the duration of the war. King's Cross Metropolitan station was struck on 9 March 1941, and on the night of 10 May bombs penetrated through the St Pancras main station down to the Midland connecting line to the Metropolitan, and others also severely damaged the Circle line just west of King's Cross. As a result it was 2½ months before any LMSR trains could run through on to the Widened Lines, and almost five months before the Circle line was reopened through from Euston Square.

Broad Street station was closed when the viaduct between Shoreditch and Dalston Junction was severed in a raid on 13 October 1940, followed on the next night by further damage at Canonbury. Broad Street station was out of action until 11 November, but all lines were not restored until February 1942. All services, except those to Poplar, had been restored progressively by mid-January 1941, but the LMS steam suburban trains to the GN suburbs were never reinstated. The terminus was again isolated for a few days after bomb damage to the viaduct at Haggerston on the night of 16 April 1941.

At Holloway, on the evening of 12 October 1940 much damage was caused to buildings, coaches and wagons in Clarence Yard; two men were killed, and the Down Goods and Carriage lines were blocked for 21 hours. Then on the evening of 14 October first the cattle pens were hit at 19.35, the bombs penetrating down to the Piccadilly line tunnel, and an hour or so later much damage was caused by HE that fell on an Up coal train, when also two passenger trains were damaged; two people were injured in the 19.30 from Hertford North as it passed and the debris blocked all Up lines. Most lines were cleared within 24 hours, but it took over a week to restore normal working. The Caledonian Road coal depot was struck on 8 November, and on the night of 11 January 1941 a DAB fell at Holloway South and all traffic—including that on the Piccadilly Tube line—was interrupted for 13 hours until the bomb had exploded; full normal working was not restored until nearly six days later.

Just down the line in the area of Finsbury Park there were a number of incidents. Firstly, at midnight on 26 September 1940 a land mine fell near the station without exploding and all traffic was suspended until the next evening. Next, on the evening of 29 September a bridge was damaged near the station and all lines were blocked for an hour, normal traffic not being restored for 11 hours. Then, in the evening of 8 October the station itself was struck at the north end of the Down side, damaging the 20.20 Down local from King's Cross standing at No. 8 platform. Five railwaymen and two others were killed and eight injured, and debris blocked Down Slow lines Nos. 1 and 2 for 36 hours. The station was further damaged early on 15 October. In the evening of 10 October a goods train was hit on the Down Canonbury line next to No. 1 Box, damaging the engine and blocking the line for 12 hours, and Ashburton Grove and East Goods Yards were closed on account of UXBs. On the night of 13 October, 25 wagons of meat which would normally have unloaded at Farringdon were hit in Clarence Yard. The Up Canonbury line was blocked by debris for seven hours on 8 November, and on the nights of 19 March and 10 May 1941 both Canonbury lines were blocked for 14 hours by overbridge damage. In the fire raid of 29 December 1940, apart from the Widened Lines once again being blocked by burning buildings all around, the Down Goods lines between Finsbury Park and Harringay were blocked for 16 hours by debris.

The Ferme Park/Hornsey area was struck several times. One night in October 1940 virtually all traffic was stopped for 12 hours after a DAB was found, while another bomb cracked the flyover viaduct. In the early afternoon of 3 November a bomb wrecked the footbridge at the north end of Hornsey station, forming a crater across all the Up lines, which were severed for 24–48 hours. Then at midnight on the following night a bomb fell in the Down yard, injuring three men, damaging an engine, and seriously impeding yard work for several days, while on 29 December the Down Slow line was damaged by an AA shell.

Further down the line, at Wood Green on 5 October a bomb fell at the 'Khyber Pass' a little before 11 p.m., causing the Down Slow, Goods and Enfield lines to be blocked for 20 hours. The station-master at New Southgate was bombed out shortly before noon on 27 October, then he was tragically killed (and four men injured) when working in the goods yard there on the morning of 16 November; a DAB exploded causing much damage to signalling and for five days trains had to be hand-signalled. A UXB fell by the line at New Barnet in the early hours of 20 September, suspending all traffic for three hours; early the next morning more were suspected between Potters Bar and Brookmans Park—and an empty train was sent along to investigate (!). The signal box at New Barnet was hit just after midnight on 18–19 March 1941, two men were injured and traffic was interrupted for 13 hours. On 19 October 1940 in the early hours, bombs nearby affected Hadley Wood North Tunnel—but trains were allowed to pass through after being diverted for three hours. Potters Bar station was damaged in the evening of 26 February 1941.

Strangely, traffic was interrupted—often for at least 12 hours—by enemy action more frequently on the Hertford Loop than on the corresponding stretch of the main line, there being no less than nine occasions during the nine months of the Blitz, and isolated ones later, Enfield Chase station sustaining extensive damage on 15 November 1940. The High Barnet, Edgware and Alexandra Palace branches were blocked for many hours on at least six occasions; on 25 September 1940 a bomb by the signal box at Finchley Central caused interruption of LPTB trains for four hours, and Cranley Gardens station was badly damaged on 15 November. On the evening of 19 April 1941 a bomb cracked the north end of the new Northern Line tube tunnel at Highgate, and then an hour later another bomb demolished the tunnel mouth. The branch was blocked again after HE landed at Park Junction in the late evening of 7 October 1943. Each of the other branches off the ECML in the King's Cross District was affected by bombing incidents at some time, the Hitchin—Cambridge line being hit and blocked on two occasions in September–November 1940. Down the ECML in Hertfordshire, bombs fell on or near the railway at Hatfield on 14 September 1940, but damage (if any) was not recorded. Welwyn Garden City had several incidents: traffic was interrupted by a UXB for eight hours on the morning of 3 October, and immediately after that a DAB exploded, damaging the signalling. Three days later all lines there were blocked by debris for 14 hours. Then on 30 October an exploding AA shell made a large crater in the Down Slow line, which took 12 hours to repair. Lastly, on 2 November three UXB's fell near the Up side, and Up and Hertford line traffic between Hatfield and Welwyn Garden City was diverted for some hours.

Early in 1944 the Germans attacked London again, albeit on a smaller scale, giving it what was called the 'Little Blitz'. The most important incident affecting the ECML occurred at Canonbury on the North London line in the early hours of 19 February, when HE caused a blockage that took no less than 58 hours to clear. There were four occasions when traffic on the Hertford loop was interrupted for several hours. Damage on the SR halted freight exchange on several occasions, whereas on the ECML itself there were few incidents. On 22 January, incendiaries on the line at Hadley Wood interrupted traffic for an hour then a UXB caused interruption of passenger trains (freight went on running at 5 mph) for 36 hours. Two UXBs fell in the area of King's Cross shed and goods yard on 19 February but did not cause much disruption, and there was a certain amount of damage at New Southgate on 20 February and at Wood Green tunnel on 25 February. Our defences were now very powerful, and from the AA barrage one shell blocked the exit from Hornsey engine shed on the night of 22 February, and another on 1 March destroyed the offices at the King's Cross Potato Market.

German Flying Bomb (V1) and Rocket (V2) Offensives (June 1944–March 1945)

The GN section of the LNER bore its share also during this later time. Although the damage caused was considerable, disruption of traffic was a good deal less than in the Blitz, when there had been so many UXBs to deal with and also the exigencies of yard work at night when the lights were turned off in 'Alerts'. With South London receiving so many of the V1s, as in the Blitz the SR lines were cut several times, causing problems with interchange freight traffic. Individual incidents on the ECML and its branches were as follows.

On 26 June 1944 at lunchtime, buildings at King's Cross Goods were damaged. On 4 July in the evening, a V1 blast near Finsbury Park station caused interruption of signalling on the Down line to Harringay, but this was restored by midnight. On 14 August at 07.00 a V1 fell in St Pancras Junction coal bays, causing extensive blast damage at King's Cross Goods, six men and a horse being injured. On 10 October in the early morning, a V1 near Hatfield station damaged No. 3 Box and interrupted signalling to Welwyn Garden City; trains had to be hand-signalled for over three hours. On 26 October the Hertford line was blocked by a V2 that exploded at the end of the Up platform at Palmers Green—just as the 18.20 Finsbury Park–Hertford North train was about to leave. Eleven passengers were injured and the line was blocked for 24 hours, local passenger trains being cut back with shuttles between Hertford and Winchmore Hill, and Wood Green and Palmers Green, the gap being covered by buses. On the morning of 10 November, a V1 at Hornsey goods yard severely damaged buildings, but there was no interruption of traffic. On 1 December in the early evening, a V2 rocket exploded close to Muswell Hill station, doing extensive damage and blocking the Alexandra Palace branch, which was not reopened until 48 hours later.

On 13 January 1945 in the early hours, a V2 rocket exploded right on the main lines 200 yards south of Wood Green. All lines except No. 2 Down Slow were blocked. The station, four signal-boxes and 55 carriages in the sidings were seriously damaged. Before mid-morning No. 1 Down Slow was repaired and used for Up traffic, which was sent over to the Up by the flyover at Ferme Park, Up night expresses suffering massive delays as a result. Down Suburban services were cancelled and Up local services reversed at New Southgate or Bowes Park. Six of the eight running lines were back in use before the evening rush, and suburban services were reinstated from King's Cross starting with the 17.35 (this was a good example of the efficiency and hard work that was normally shown by the Engineering Department staff in the war to restore normal working as quickly as possible). On 17 January about midday, a rocket landed in the vicinity of Moleswood Tunnel and was followed soon after by a second explosion: although no damage to track was done, No. 2 control circuits were cut and all telephone communication between Hertford North and Watton-at-Stone was severed. On 25 January at first light, a rocket explosion damaged Gordon Hill station. Finally in Central London, the rocket that landed on the crowded Farringdon Market in mid-morning on 8 March, caused great carnage, seriously damaging the Goods station and retaining wall, and the depot was closed for two weeks.

York

On the night of 28 April 1942, as one of their retaliatory *Baedeker* raids, which were not on the scale of the Blitz and involved less than 100 raiders, the Luftwaffe went to York. They not only caused great damage in the city, but also this time turmoil on the railway. At about 02.30, the station was struck by HE smashing through the roof of platforms 2 and 3, and showers of incendiaries fell, starting major fires that destroyed the booking, telegraph, parcels and stationmaster's offices. Unfortunately, the 22.15 King's Cross–Edinburgh 'Night Scotsman' was in the station, and the middle six of its 20 carriages—an unremarkable length in those days—were burnt out, together with stock at adjoining platforms. The 'Night Scotsman' had been in the station for some seven minutes before it was hit, and there had been time for passengers to take shelter—although many did not. Courageous and prompt action by the station staff enabled the other 14 coaches to be drawn clear, and for much valuable property to be saved from the fires.

Clifton carriage sidings were severely damaged, Leeman Road coal depot was wrecked and the Civil Engineer's shops were set on fire, as were also the stables—but the horses were saved. Last but not least, at the main locomotive depot, No. 4 shed received a direct hit that ravaged A4 No. 4469 and B16/1 No. 925 quite beyond repair. (O4 No. 6283 was also badly damaged, and J39 No. 3095 less severely). The damage extended to Nos. 1 and 3 sheds, and 20 locomotives were damaged in some way and 50 imprisoned. Fifteen coaches at York were destroyed and 220 damaged. Human casualties on the railway (passengers and railwaymen) were 4 killed and 81 injured. On top of all this, the main line to the north and the Harrogate branch were blocked at Skelton Junction.

No traffic was able to pass through the station until the morning of 30 April, when platform 8 was available for Down trains. Freight was stopped entirely and passenger traffic was diverted *via* Church Fenton and Harrogate to/from Thirsk, until 18.00 on 29 April. After that just one Down and Up line were made available on the Goods lines, by which time most of the passenger trains and half the normal freight trains were passing York—by the Goods lines. In spite of the great damage—and six UXBs remaining on Railway property, immense hard work and improvisation enabled traffic to move again fairly freely in a remarkably short time, normality being restored by 3 May. Later in 1942, on 17 December, damage was done by bombs to the power supply at Foss Islands Goods depot—but this may have been accidental, from 'one of ours'.

Restoration of the buildings destroyed in the April raid naturally took time: it was a year before temporary (flat) canopies were put up over platforms 8 and 9. Initially, refreshments were served in the former left-luggage and parcels offices, then a combined dining/tea room was restored and the former tea room converted to a staff canteen. As soon as possible a temporary parcels office (with electric hoist from the subway) and left-luggage office were built, and the telegraph office was rehoused in the HQ building. After the war, in 1948, the roof spans were repaired, rather than being demolished, and so remain today.

Newcastle Area

The first serious damage to the LNER in the North-East during the war had been at Sunderland, where the station was largely destroyed in a sharp raid on 6 September 1940. In 1941, on the night of 9 April considerable damage was done at North Shields, Monkseaton, Jarrow, South Shields and Tyne Dock between 22.00 and midnight, electric stock being severely damaged, lines blocked and services interrupted. On the night of 25 April, Sunderland and the Tyneside towns below Newcastle were heavily attacked, but serious damage was done to the railways only at South Blyth, where the station and shed were largely destroyed; a bomb fell in the yards at Heaton, the Blyth & Tyne was blocked between Seghill and Seaton Delaval, and damage was done at Tynemouth then—and on several other occasions. Then again, on the night of 30 September, the passenger and goods stations at North Shields were severely damaged—albeit fortunately with no casualties, and on the night of 2 October South Shields had a sharp raid and damage was done to the railway there, at other places on the coast, at Wallsend and between Benton and Backworth. Relatively minor damage, including at St Peters on the Riverside line, was done in small raids on the nights of 29 December 1941, of 30 April 1942, and again on the night of 12 March 1943. Sunderland station was hit again in small raids on 14 March and 16 May 1943. Also off the ECML itself, the Coast line was blocked at West Hartlepool on both 4 and 8 May 1941, while Middlesbrough station (and V1 class No. 416 on an empty train) were badly damaged in a brief daylight raid on 3 August 1942, with two people killed and 13 seriously injured.

The railways in Newcastle itself suffered most on the night of 1 September 1941 (from 22.15 until 23.00), when a sharp raid by a mere 28 German bombers caused disproportionate damage. The large New Bridge Street Goods warehouse was hit, and it was completely destroyed by an enormous fire that burned fiercely for three days; 5,200 tons of goods, including 2,000 tons of flour, were consumed by fire, and four people killed and three injured. They managed to save 33 wagon loads, containing 'bicarbonate, potatoes, Horlicks product, biscuits, oil etc., packages of hams, Andrews' salts, syrup and glass, and two trailer loads of tobacco and apples.' At least one of several courageous and resourceful men received official commendations for their actions that night. Temporary repairs were undertaken in 1943, to enable the Goods depot to be of use again for 'smalls' traffic in case Forth Goods was bombed—which fortunately it was not. The New Bridge Street Depot was not fully restored after the war, its pre-war traffic having been principally from Newcastle Quayside and the amount of trade through there remained restricted after the war.

Meanwhile on 1 September a bomb at Argyle Street badly damaged the signal box, and other bombs damaged the signal box and the platforms at Manors North. A UXB at Manors North put all lines north and east from Central out of commission until the evening of 2 September, when two of the four lines towards Heaton were reopened. Some ECML traffic was then able to go north to Morpeth *via* Tynemouth. In addition Jesmond station was badly damaged and the line blocked, as was the Riverside line at Carville for four to five days. Manors North reopened at 18.00 on 3 September, and traffic was running normally by the evening of 5 September. On 2 September, 16 passenger and 27 freight trains on the ECML to or from Edinburgh were diverted *via* Carlisle—and also *via* North Wylam for 10½ hours until debris had been cleared at Blaydon. Between 2 and 4 September four Up passenger trains and five Up and seven Down freight trains were diverted *via* Carlisle and the LMSR (Settle & Carlisle line to the Leeds area, and/or Caledonian routes). The LNER was singularly unlucky in such an otherwise small raid, and the congestion was cleared only by the evening of 8 September.

Miscellaneous Enemy Attacks on or near the ECML

From the outset, coastal towns were particularly susceptible to 'tip-and-run' raids, as was the ECML. These began once the 'Phoney War' was over in the summer of 1940. The initial incidents at Darlington and Newcastle have been mentioned, and these were followed by similar ones at Ferryhill on 6 and 7 July 1940, between West Monkton and Backworth where bombs slightly damaged the track on 8 July, and at Portobello on 4 August. Thereafter, there were many relatively minor incidents throughout the war on or near the ECML, as follows.

1940: On the night of 24 August, bombs fell close to the ECML at Highdyke, causing slight damage. During the night of 29–30 August, UXBs were reported near the ECML at Stannington and traffic was diverted *via* Backworth and Newsham. On the night of 13 October, HE landed on the Up side at Everton Box (near Sandy), and the Up lines were blocked for six hours. On the afternoon of 23 October, an overbridge was damaged and a water main burst at Spitalgate (Grantham), blocking all lines but only for 20 minutes after which the Up Goods line was usable, normal working being restored in four hours. In the evening of 27 October, all lines at Alne were blocked after a bomb landed on a York–Newport special goods train; all traffic was diverted *via* Ripon and Church Fenton for over six hours. On 4 December in the afternoon, a DAB exploded in Grantham, causing damage to sidings and killing a platelayer.

1941: On the evening of 5 January, several bombs at Darlington caused extensive damage to Stooperdale Boiler Shop, Faverdale Wagon Works, and to the paint and other shops; there was also a problem at the Works with UXBs. On 15 January at 22.45, in a minor raid on Peterborough, bombs fell on the main line between New England North and Werrington Junction, causing interruption of traffic on the Down Main, Goods, and Engine lines for over three hours. The south end of New England locomotive yard was also hit, two large cranes and a locomotive were derailed and three locomotives damaged, and the mineral office was badly damaged. In the yards 112 wagons were damaged, and the locomotive and empties yards were blocked for 42 hours; Wisbech Sidings Box was also heavily damaged by a bomb. In all that night one railwayman was killed and 14 injured. ECML trains were diverted *via* the Joint line for about four hours, and access to New England locomotive depot was restored by the evening of 16 January. The Peterborough area also received attention on 30 January, when the M&GN line was completely blocked by HE at Eye Green, and only restored after four days.

Late on 15 January, the Up Main and Goods lines between Grantham and Great Ponton were cut by HE, for nine hours. In the afternoon of 19 February, HE hit a stationary goods train (of chocolate from Rowntree's to Faslane Military Port) at Sessay Wood, causing blockage of the Down lines for six hours. As there was then only one Up line at that point, much traffic had to be diverted—and this was also the time of the Great Blizzard. On 7 March in the early afternoon, the South Junction Box and the station at Newark suffered some damage, but traffic was not interrupted. On 8 March, following a 'sneak' raid at lunchtime, traffic on the main line was interrupted by a UXB at Longhoughton; for five hours traffic was diverted to other lines, but at least one main line express was diverted at Alnmouth on to the Alnwick and Wooler branch and so to Tweedmouth *via* Coldstream. On 15 March, Langford Box (near Biggleswade) was damaged and communication cut. On 1 April, Christon Bank Box was damaged by blast, but was repaired in 44 hours and traffic was not interrupted. On 8 April in the very early hours, the Up and Down Main and Up Independent lines were blocked at Annitsford for three hours and trains diverted on to the Blyth & Tyne. On 10 April in the early hours, during the fairly major raid mainly affecting the North and South Shields areas, the station at Low Fell was set on fire, delaying traffic. On 16 April, the 07.20 York–Pickering local was derailed when its engine fell into a bomb crater at Coxwold; three staff were injured, and the line was blocked for 14 hours. On 25 April in the late evening, debris blocked the main and electric lines at Heaton for two hours, and electric stock was damaged; an electricity sub-station was destroyed by a bomb on the same night at Benton. On 4 May just after midnight, seven wagons were damaged at Gateshead; soon afterwards a bomb fell near the High Level Bridge and traffic had to be diverted for five hours. Towards midnight on 2 May, HE fell close to the line at Barnby (near Newark), cutting communications and forcing diversions for a few hours. On 9 May in the very early hours, Retford station suffered slight damage; on 10 May a UXB was found at Burnmouth in the morning and traffic had to be diverted for 8 hours *via* Kelso or *via* Carlisle. On 3 June, slight damage was caused at Tweedmouth shed in the early hours. On 14 June in the early morning, traffic was interrupted at Northallerton and at Pilmoor for several hours by damage to the signalling. Early on 9 July, the lines were blown out at Honington, and Colwick–Whitemoor traffic had to be diverted on to the ECML. Two days later, HE landing between Werrington Junction and Essendine caused damage to signalling and some interruption of traffic, while on 15 July Grantham also received some attention but damage then was slight. On 13 August, the Down Main at Alnmouth was severed by HE during the morning, and UXB was suspected for a while and traffic disrupted. In the afternoon of 17 August machine-gunning at Innerwick damaged a bridge, the main line was blocked for six hours and traffic diverted *via* Carlisle; one workman was killed and seven injured. In the early hours of 13 September, a goods train ran into a bomb crater near Knitsley on the Durham–Consett line; the line was blocked for nine hours. In the late evening of 7 November, a bomb landed near the line between East Linton and Dunbar, severing the telegraph. Lastly, on the morning of 21 November, bombs exploded on the line at Goswick, severely damaging the signal box. In addition, the locomotive (C7 No. 2207) and first coach of the 06.45 Newcastle–Berwick were damaged; three passengers were injured, and on account of suspected UXBs traffic was diverted *via* Coldstream or *via* Carlisle for a time.

1942: On 4 January, Tweedmouth station and signal box were severely damaged by HE; three men were killed and four injured, but the main line was not blocked and normal working resumed within 24 hours. Again, on 10 February in the evening, bombs partially demolished Tweedmouth engine shed, damaging five locomotives and other buildings, and blocked the main line by hitting an overbridge; seven locomen were injured and one shunting locomotive standing near Billingdon

Bridge was damaged. In the early hours of 30 June, incendiaries landed on railway property at Peterborough, setting fire to the Great Northern Hotel and engineer's stores, and on 24 July a bomb landed at midnight at Peterborough East but only damaged cables. On the morning of 2 September, UXBs were discovered at Doncaster station and Decoy Yard; traffic was disrupted until they were made safe.

1943: At Warthill on the York–Hull line, on the night of 23 September, several canisters of anti-personnel bombs were dropped by the enemy close to the station. Most of the bombs failed to explode, but the line had to be closed for nine days for all the bombs to be found and disposed of.

1944: On 22 January in the early morning, as the 21.40 Leeds–Kings Cross express emerged from Potters Bar tunnel the crew saw incendiaries falling on the line. They stopped and picked them up! However, UXBs were also reported, so trains had to be diverted *via* Hertford North for 26 hours.

Attacks on Moving Trains

Almost throughout the length and breadth of the country but mainly on the eastern side, there were occasions when lone German aircraft attempted to bomb or machine gun moving trains, especially during the first half of the war. Indeed there were also instances when British or Allied aircraft shot up trains, or even dropped bombs—presumably accidentally. Incidents on the ECML included the following.

In the afternoon of 31 October 1940, the locomotive (O4 No. 6364) of the 06.44 Worksop–New England freight was shot up at Warrington Junction; damage was confined to puncture of the tender tank, but the driver had to be taken to hospital. On 23 December 1940 between Essendine and Little Bytham, the 08.00 Newcastle–King's Cross and the 'Flying Scotsman' (hauled by A4 No. 2510—which suffered a punctured smoke-box) were almost simultaneously gunned; one passenger (a soldier) was killed. On 20 January 1941, the 16.08 Hitchin–King's Cross was attacked (without harm being done) between Hitchin and Stevenage, while near St Neots V2 No. 4801 was shot up and its tender holed. On 1 April 1941, B16 No. 1384 sustained minor 'gunshot wounds' on a freight at Christon Bank. In the early hours of 7 May 1941, a freight train was gunned at Tuxford North and slightly damaged. In the afternoon of 3 June 1941, a freight was shot up at Alnmouth and the guard injured. Very early on 14 July 1941, the 18.55 Newcastle–King's Cross was gunned at Langley (near Knebworth); damage was slight, but three servicemen were injured, also damage was done to two ambulance trains (Casualty Evacuation) stabled in the sidings. In the evening of 10 November 1941, between Marshall Meadows and Burnmouth, V2 No. 4886 and D49/2 No. 247 on the 09.50 King's Cross–Edinburgh suffered fairly minor damage from aerial gunning, although one of the drivers was injured. Next day the Up 'Flying Scotsman' was machine-gunned at the same place, but suffered little damage and no serious casualties. Finally, on the night of 3 March 1945, the Luftwaffe had their 'last fling'—*Operation Gisela*, sending 70 fighter-bomber intruders ranging widely over airfields in the east and Midlands. In the course of the operation, the 22.25 Newcastle–King's Cross was gunned near Temple Hirst soon after midnight, receiving little damage and no injuries. Shortly afterwards, the 00.25 empty stock train from Helmsley to York was gunned between Husthwaite Gate and Sunbeck Junction, killing a relief signalman travelling on it, and at Northallerton 45 minutes later, a freight for Newport Yard was gunned—twice in 15 minutes while taking water—and damaged, as were wagons and buildings in the goods yard.

Aircraft Crashes and related Incidents on or near the ECML

During the war huge numbers of aircraft crashed in Britain, the great majority of which were 'ours'—especially bombers taking off or landing in the eastern half of the country, and it is not surprising that some of these crashes affected Railway Company property. While crashes right on the tracks were not infrequent, more often either the line had to be closed while UXBs from the crashed aircraft were dealt with or the aircraft cut the telecommunication equipment. Sometimes bombs jettisoned by Allied aircraft fell on the lines, and Allied planes even occasionally shot up trains. Such pranks were normally forbidden, but at one site on the ECML—Goswick, on the Northumberland coast, superannuated locomotives and coaches in a special siding were officially used for practice in the art of 'train busting', which proved very profitable before and during the Liberation of Europe in 1944.

Barrage balloons proved very susceptible to storms, and when they broke loose they sometimes landed on the railway or more often trailed their cables across the telegraph wires. At Finsbury Park on 11 May 1940, a balloon fell on the roof of the station and in February 1944 one floated down on the roof of King's Cross.

The following is a compilation of all known incidents on or directly affecting the ECML and of the more serious incidents on its branches, the majority of crashes being at points close to a military airfield. The few cases where the aircraft have been identified here from other sources provide a small sample of the circumstances involved:

1940: In the afternoon of 30 July, a crashing RAF plane cut the telegraph at Baldock. During the night of 16–17 August all lines were blocked between Baldock and Ashwell by a crashed RAF bomber. In the night of 16 September, balloon cables brought down telegraph wires between Doncaster and Arksey, and on 15 October a balloon came down between Escrick and Naburn and blocked the ECML for four hours. 1941: Very early on 8th April, all lines at Little Bytham were blocked for 3½ hours after a Hampden bomber on a training flight was shot down on to the railway by a German night-fighter intruder.

1942: On 25 April, an engine ran into a parachute (believed to be carrying explosives) at Tempsford and remained entangled for 95 minutes. In the afternoon of 12 November a plane crashed into the embankment at Stukely, causing interruption of the telegraph. Early on 18 November, the Richmond branch was completely blocked by an RAF plane between Scorton and Moulton. On 20 December, a Spitfire crashed on the Clifton fish stage at York, setting it and three coaches on fire. The pilot was courageously rescued by driver Imeson; traffic was not affected.

1943: On 8 January at 12.40, between Eaglescliffe and Dinsdale, the 11.30 Saltburn–Darlington local (hauled by A8 No. 1519) ran at over 45 mph into the burning wreckage of an RCAF 427 Sqn. Wellington on transit, which had overshot the runway at Middleton St. George Airfield and crashed on the line. To save the passengers, driver Barber although badly burned drove on and then with fireman Blunt—who was killed—jumped, and the engine overturned. Yet the line was cleared in 45 minutes. On 26 January at 23.00 hrs a 466 Sqn Wellington bomber, bound from Leconfield to Lorient, suffered engine failure and crashed at Barnby Moor & Sutton station, but no railway damage was reported. On 29 January shortly before midday, a 51 Sqn Halifax on test and coming into land at Burn Airfield crashed on the ECML, between Heck and Temple Hirst, killing in their hut one platelayer and injuring three. In the early hours of 5 April, between Alne and Raskelf, the locomotive of the 20.20 Edinburgh–King's Cross picked up in its water-scoop a

---

container of incendiaries believed to be from an RAF bomber; the bombs burned out under the engine and the train was able to continue. On the morning of 10 April, at Temple Hirst—again, a plane crash on the ECML cut the telegraph for five hours. Soon after midnight on 14 April, a plane crash on the ECML at Saltersford (Grantham) blocked all lines for several hours. At noon on 17 May a plane crash near Beningbrough station cut the telegraph for three hours. On the morning of 22 June, a loaded RAF bomber crashed close to the line from Grantham at Bracebridge Brick Siding near Lincoln; the signal box was evacuated and the line closed for three hours until it was safe. On 29 June in the early hours, an RAF plane crashed in flames on the Up line 30 yards from the signal box at East Fortune. In the afternoon of 2 October, two planes collided and fell on the track near Market Weighton station, blocking all lines. In the late evening of 22 October, the Church Fenton–Harrogate line was blocked for 11 hours between Tadcaster and Newton Kyme after a 427 Sqn Halifax from Leeming aborted a raid on Kassel and crashed on the Up line, then the other line was blocked by a fire-tender that attended the incident but broke down. Very early on 20 November, a plane crash on the Selby–Market Weighton line at Bubwith blocked the line for 14 hours.

1944: In the afternoon of 20 January, a plane crashed on the ECML between Westwood (Peterborough) and Werrington Junction, blocking both main lines for 10 hours, but traffic was able to pass over the goods lines. In the morning of 23 February at Haxby (on the York–Scarborough line), a plane crashing into pylons brought them down on to the railway. On the night of 15 April, a Halifax on taking off (probably from Topcliffe Airfield) on a night training flight hit the bridge over the ECML at Sowerby (a mile south of Thirsk) then struck and severely damaged lineside cottages recently rebuilt in connection with the ECML widening and buried one of its engines in the Up Goods line; apart from the crew of five, three people on the ground were killed. On 7 June, UXB from an RAF bomber held up traffic at Goswick for some hours. From soon after midnight on 17 June, the Selby–Goole branch was closed for 2–3 days while a number of UXBs from a crashed Allied aircraft were blown up near Airmyn & Rawcliffe. On 12 August in the morning at Alne, a bomber crashed on fire by the ECML; no bombs exploded, but the telegraph was cut, and all traffic was interrupted and diverted *via* Starbeck until safety from explosions was assured. Early in the evening of 27 August, a fully-laden bomber crashed near the Northallerton–Eaglescliffe line at Welbury; traffic had to be diverted on to the ECML for 19 hours until the area was deemed safe. Early in the evening of 9 October at Heck, a fully-laden bomber crashed into wagons in a siding; traffic was diverted *via* Knottingley for five hours. In the morning of 18 December, a plane crash blocked one line on the Grantham–Lincoln branch between Caythorpe and Honington. On 24 December in the morning, a USAAF B17 bomber, fully laden with fuel and bombs, crashed on the ECML between Connington and Holme; a signal box was damaged and the line blocked totally for two hours until UXBs were removed, signalling not being restored for 16 days.

1945: On 9 February late in the afternoon, a crashing plane cut the telegraph for 8 hours between Connington and Holme. On 24 February early in the afternoon once again at Heck, the telegraph was cut by a low-flying plane. In the late afternoon of 5 March, two planes crashed near the ECML at Dringhouses (York); UXBs were suspected on the Down side so for four hours trains were run only on the Doncaster lines. Shortly before midnight on 14 March, Heck witnessed a crash near the ECML; trains were diverted until the line could be declared safe. Finally, in the afternoon of 25 October—after the war was over—a plane crash blocked both lines for several hours between Dunbar and Innerwick.

An incident that caused immense disruption on the railway but no actual casualties was the explosion in a bomb store at RAF Snaith at 13.35 on 19 June 1943. The explosion was caused by 'airmen disregarding regulations on the handling of explosives in the open', when they were setting fuses. There were a number of Service casualties. The windows of Heck signal box were blown out, and the ceilings came down in the stationmaster's house. Because much ordnance was left in a 'pre-activated state' and the dump was only 500 yards from the ECML Shaftholme Junction–Selby section, the LNER had to divert all passenger traffic *via* Knottingley or Hull for 10 days (albeit goods traffic for only 36 hours), with consequent congestion and delay. From 16.00 on 28 June until 05.30 on the 29 June, all traffic had again to be diverted while the RAF deliberately exploded further bombs every 45 minutes. The result of this accident was an extended fuss about the location of bomb dumps near enough to railways to cause damage to trains if the ordnance blew up, and afterwards much more severe restrictions on the siting of bomb dumps were imposed. Nevertheless, subsequently there were several instances across the country of exploding ordnance affecting the railways. Associated with the ECML were the following.

At 17.10 on 8 September 1943, Hexham station had to be evacuated after the accidental explosion of small arms ammunition—which killed three soldiers engaged in loading it. Much heroism was shown by railway staff who coupled up and removed wagons to comparative safety in case they blew up. The goods station and engine shed were extensively damaged, and trains were not allowed through until midnight.

Just after 16.00 on 4 February 1944, Catterick Bridge station was wrecked by an accidental explosion of bombs. Eight people were killed (including the stationmaster and two women clerks), and 88 injured (10 staff).

Great heroism was displayed at Moulton on the same branch at 05.40 on Sunday 25 March 1945. Fire broke out on the 05.00 Darlington–Catterick Camp goods, loaded with bombs. Driver T. McLoughlin set the train back to the platform, and he and fireman J. C. Northcott, guard M. Campbell, and (female) porter D. Rowe tried to put out the fire with buckets then took the wagons to a safe place. There was no explosion.

A very nasty incident occurred at Gascoigne Wood Yard at 19.35 on 18 April 1945—very near the end of the war. Driver T. H. Stainton and fireman J. Talbot, on J21 No. 1513, were working a goods from Selby which included—next to the engine—12 wagons of 50 lb bombs for RAF Wheldrake (on the Derwent Valley Light Railway). On passing Hag Lane Box they noticed that the eighth wagon was on fire, and pulled up. Helped by Inspector T. H. Popplewell—and all aware of the bombs, they uncoupled the front seven wagons and drew them forward into the reception sidings. But the burning wagon and two others exploded, 98 bombs (13 tons of TNT) going up. There was first a small explosion—which allowed the men to take cover, followed by a massive blast that unfortunately killed the fireman on another locomotive (J6 No. 3522) standing nearby, and produced a crater 50 feet deep and much damage to surrounding wagons and buildings. Driver Stainton was awarded a George Medal, and Taylor and Popplewell received Commendations.

Appendix H

Accidents on the ECML,
September 1939 to December 1959

Serious Accidents, until the end of 1959

Accidents can be separated broadly into three classes: (A) those due to human operational error, (B) those caused by mechanical failure, and (C) those caused by 'Acts of God'. On the railway, (A) can be divided between errors of signalmen and others 'on the ground'—here designated 'Aa'), those of train drivers ('Ab'), and those due to wrong-doing by other staff or members of the public ('Ac'). Mechanical failures can be divided broadly again, into defects on locomotives or rolling stock ('Ba'), and defects of track or signalling ('Bb'). Logically, category 'C' would include accidents due to HM's Enemies, to terrorists or to vandals while—unlike in more recent times—there were only two instances of vandalism causing trouble on the ECML during the period covered, and one of those caused no accident as such.

Below are lists setting out the accidents of which the authors are aware, occurring on the ECML alone between September 1939 and December 1959, in summary form and in chronological order, with classifications as above in so far as they can be discerned. (Significant accidents not quite on the ECML are in parentheses).

The list is of accidents that were relatively serious in terms of casualties and/or damage. Full description of them all would fill another volume, and the list cannot be vouchsafed to be complete, especially as records of incidents not resulting in fatalities may not have survived. During the war official reports to the Minister of War Transport were limited by decree to generalities, except in the case of accidents involving death or serious injury or extensive damage to rolling-stock. (The most comprehensive summary accounts appear to be in the *Daily Situation Reports* of the REC to the Ministry of Transport. Other accounts are in the Ministry's own Reports, and for the LNER in the *Monthly Reports* of the Working of the Railway by the Chief General Manager).

Considering the amount of traffic it carried, serious accidents to trains on the ECML during this twenty-year period seem to have been relatively rare, and few were very disastrous in terms of the number of people killed. The last is, however, usually a poor index of an accident's severity, although there was a rather justifiable public outcry in the immediate post-war years when accumulated arrears of maintenance to track and rolling-stock led to a spate of derailments at speed. It should be borne in mind that the ECML had an extensive number of level-crossings for a trunk route, and they were the scene of several accidents. Their replacement by the now almost universal automatic lifting-barriers began soon after the first such barrier was installed in November 1952 at Warthill on the York–Hull line.

Less Serious Accidents, until the end of 1947

Far outnumbering the relatively serious accidents there were numerous mishaps that did not involve injury, loss of life, or major damage to rolling stock or track—a criterion that is admittedly rather subjective. It would be tedious to enumerate these mishaps individually, for between September 1939 and the end of 1947—that is during the period of the REC—there were over 200 recorded on the ECML in addition to the 'serious' ones listed. Regrettably, the authors have not discovered records of 'less serious' accidents which occurred after Nationalisation.

In this modern age of motorways and an endless choice of alternative road routes, it seems trivial that it was a serious matter if a mishap involved a few hours of interruption of traffic, its diversion to other routes or just the imposition of single line working (SLW). In the railway age—and in the war in particular—such occurrences were indeed serious, because of their knock-on effect on the normal, never-ending flow of traffic on a trunk route such as the ECML.

During those eight years or so there were at least 60 occurrences when all traffic was interrupted on some section of the ECML between London and Edinburgh for at least an hour, and trains had to be diverted to other routes to keep traffic flowing. (Local passenger traffic was usually dealt with in these cases by the hiring of buses). A similar number of mishaps blocked one line on a two-track section, but the traffic was continued by resort to SLW on the other line and perhaps some diversions. In about 20 instances on multi-track sections the extra tracks could be used, but as these were at the same time the busier sections anyway the disruption of traffic flows could be just as bad. For example, on at least seven occasions mishaps at the north end of York station necessitated the re-routing of passenger trains on the freight lines past York Yard and reversal in and out of the station at the south end. Again, at King's Cross on 15 to 20 occasions—including as well as derailments the flooding of Gas Works tunnel or a fire in the temporary roof over the main train-shed—when part of the station was blocked, local trains were cut back at Finsbury Park and goods trains on the Widened Lines were held up.

On the ECML generally there was usually an alternative and roughly parallel route that could be used, although in the war all routes were so fully occupied these diversions caused considerable inconvenience. The principal alternatives were: the Hertford Loop; *via* March and Cambridge—perhaps also up to Liverpool Street; the Joint line *via* Sleaford or Boston and Lincoln; the Knottingley or Gascoigne Wood–Church Fenton route—combined with Starbeck–Ripon if York was blocked; *via* Bishop Auckland; the Leamside line; the Jesmond–Benton NW curve route; all the way round *via* Carlisle and the Waverley route; and the Kelso–St Boswells line. There were also some occasions when accidents blocked other routes and traffic had to be diverted on to the ECML, e.g. the GN & GE Joint Line, Northallerton–Eaglescliffe, etc. During the night of 11–12 February 1942, there were extensive diversions off the GC main line on to the ECML following the tragic accident near Beighton Junction, when a displaced girder on a freight train in Holbrook Colliery Sidings ripped into a passing troop train, killing 11 soldiers and injuring 36. There were also other occasions when the ECML was used for WCML traffic when the latter was blocked for some reason. This occurred more frequently after Nationalisation, such as after the Harrow disaster of 8 October 1952, but during the war some LMSR traffic was occasionally passed to the LNER, for example when an express collided with a barrow at Wembley on 13 October 1940 and the main lines into Euston were totally blocked.

Derailments of a few defective wagons were the commonest mishap, but there were numerous collisions involving two freight trains. When no injuries were recorded, presumably these were slow-speed occurrences, but they must have been due to lapses on the part of drivers or of signalmen. Collisions involving one freight train only were common, resulting from a 'snatch' causing the division of the loose-coupled train followed by the rear portion catching up with the front portion. Occasionally coaching stock also became divided, and apart from those already listed as 'serious', there were a further 15–20 derailments or minor collisions on the ECML involving coaching-stock trains. Frequently—and especially towards the end of the war and shortly afterwards, there were many major locomotive failures, when big ends, coupling-rods or other main components broke and the engine was totally immobilised and/or damaged the track, and because it could not be moved without the breakdown gang it completely blocked the line. There were also several occasions when single-line working had to be instituted for some hours while a broken rail was replaced. Sometimes a passenger train was derailed at catch-points when after being stopped on a bank (e.g. several times at Egmanton, south of Retford), the train was allowed to run back while restarting was being attempted.

Lastly and most poignantly, there were at least two instances of traffic interruption due to a trespasser being knocked down and killed, and when the communication cord was pulled because it was thought that someone had fallen from the train ahead. (In that instance, the locomotive was detached and went forward in the dark to search the line).

Not included of course in the above are the traffic interruptions caused by enemy action, nor are aircraft crashes on the line. During the war, there were also often problems caused by barrage balloons and their cables, and not a few by road vehicles—most often military—driving or falling on to the railway.

Serious Accidents

27/11/39 16.48—Hitchin. The engine off the 15.05 local from King's Cross collided with the 16.45 to King's Cross. Two coaches were derailed, and both crew of the light engine were injured. The Up lines were blocked until 04.30 28/11. (Ab?).

16/12/39 c.19.30—Barlby, Selby. A succession of derailments: three vehicles of the 18.30 Doncaster–York, then the leading and rear vehicles of the 16.00 King's Cross–York (hauled by A4 No. 4485), later causing damage to the locomotive of the 19.55 Leeds–Hull, one vehicle of which was also derailed. No further details. (Bb).

2/2/40 02.17—Holloway. The engine of an empty stock train ran into Holloway North Down Box, injuring the signalman; the Down Slow line was blocked for nearly seven hours.

13/6/40 c.10.30—Hett Mill, between Ferryhill and Durham. Three platelayers were knocked down and killed by the 08.45 York–Newcastle express.

2/1/41 19.08—Haywoods Crossing, Askern. A troop train collided with an Army lorry, killing two of its occupants and injuring another. Rail traffic delayed only 1½ hours. (Ac).

28/4/41 15.40—Westborough Box, near Claypole. Fire broke out in the second-to-last coach of the second portion of the 12.45 King's Cross–Newcastle express, hauled by V2 No. 4779. The coach was occupied by boys of Ampleforth College (near Gilling) who were returning to school for the summer term, and the fire was started by boys flicking lighted matches. On account of the draught caused by the speed of the train, the fire was fanned so rapidly that in the 90 seconds it took for the train to stop after the communication cord had been pulled the coach was engulfed in flames. It then spread to the third-to-last coach so quickly that the front of the train could only be uncoupled ahead of that coach, and the last three vehicles were burnt out. In the awful mêlée of fire and smoke, six boys died and seven were seriously injured. All trains were diverted off the ECML *via* Bottesford, Lincoln, and Retford or the Joint line until 19.00 (Ac).

17/9/41 21.53—Hitchin. The 18.30 Highbury Vale–New England empties collided with the 20.44 King's Cross–York parcels, derailing the engine of the latter and also several wagons. Most lines were blocked until 18.00 18/9; Cambridge trains were diverted to Liverpool Street.

18/12/41 22.35—Tweedmouth Junction. On being diverted on to the Kelso branch on account of a mishap at Dunbar, the first four coaches of a Pacific-hauled express were derailed when a rail shattered to pieces. (The rail was laid in 1890 and had been thoroughly worn by locomotives slipping).

14/2/42 03.18—Sessay. The 22.15 King's Cross–Edinburgh express collided with a freight train, and the locomotive was derailed. There were no casualties. All lines—including the new Down Slow that had only been opened two weeks before—were blocked until 13.30, and trains were diverted *via* Starbeck and Sinderby. (Ab?).

28/3/42 03.50—East Linton. The 19.05 King's Cross–Edinburgh express was derailed completely, due to fracture of a connecting-rod, but the locomotive and all the coaches remained upright and there were no injuries. Both lines were blocked however until 21.15, with diversions *via* Kelso and Carlisle and some freight over the Border Counties line.

31/8/42 early hours—Between Hougham and Claypole. The 23.15 King's Cross–Edinburgh express, loaded to 20 coaches, became divided, and the last two coaches of the front portion of 15 and all the last five coaches were derailed. Both lines were blocked until 18.00 and the Down line until 20.00.

18/9/42 22.58—Selby. The first coach of the 19.00 King's Cross–Edinburgh derailed; main lines blocked until 07.00 19/9.

4/11/42—Between St Neots and Tempsford. One Up coal train ran into another, blocking all lines for an hour, and all Up lines for much longer.

28/11/42 evening—Peterborough North. An Up train, hauled by V2 No.4879, ran into the back of a Grimsby train, telescoping the last van.

19/12/42 16.25—Newcastle, High Level Bridge. The 15.57 local EMU from South Shields collided with a light engine (a D17/2) at the north end of the bridge. There were several injuries, and the bridge was blocked until 20.00.

2/1/43 18.40—Egmanton Box, near Retford. On restarting from a signal stop, the fourth coach of the 15.30 King's Cross–Newcastle express became derailed on catch-points. The driver continued for 1,000 yards before he realised, and the track was much damaged. The ECML was blocked until 04.35 3/1/43. (A scenario repeated several times).

10/1/43 17.00—Newcastle Central. An electric parcels car collided with empty stock in No. 4 platform, telescoping two vehicles; the motorman was injured.

25/1/43 09.57—Newcastle, High Level Bridge. The 08.20 Middlesbrough– Newcastle collided with an electric parcels car. The locomotive and two coaches of its train were derailed, and all lines were blocked until 16.30. Up lines until 17.30.

29/1/43 13.09—Christon Bank. The 10.40 Edinburgh–King's Cross, held at a signal, was run into by the runaway rear portion of a freight train that had divided. The locomotive was derailed, and all lines blocked until 18.55 (22.30 for Down lines). (Ba?).

30/1/43 12.25—Newcastle Central. The 10.05 passenger train from York collided with a station pilot, and a wagon was derailed blocking platforms Nos. 7-10.

20/3/43 20.44—Werrington Junction. The locomotive of a Down freight derailed and overturned. All lines blocked until 03.00 21/3.

10/6/43 13.19—King's Cross. The 08.40 express from Cleethorpes (hauled by A4 No. 2509) collided with the buffer-stops of platform 8. Minor injuries to 27 people. (Ab).

13/6/43 18.22—Manors Junction (gantry) signal box burned down, due to an electrical fault. Lines blocked by debris until 20.00 (to electric trains until 02.40 14/6). Normal working from 17/6, but trains had to be hand-signalled until a temporary Box was installed.

8/7/43 17.27—Between Peterborough North and Spital Junction. A coach caught fire on a King's Cross–Newcastle express, but it was removed and no-one was hurt.

8/8/43 14.12—Church Fenton. The 10.15 (Sun.) Liverpool–York LMS train was derailed and divided. Several passengers were severely shocked and bruised. All lines except the Down Leeds were blocked until 18.55 10/8, and trains were diverted *via* Gascoigne Wood and Selby.

13/8/43 16.40—Lincoln Road Box, between Tuxford and Retford. The 13.25 King's Cross–Hull express was in collision with a lorry that crashed the gates. Three were killed and four injured in the lorry. All lines were blocked, but only until 17.25. (Ac).

20–21/8/43 Midnight—Tuxford North. The locomotive of the 22.05 Doncaster–King's Cross parcels train was derailed after a glancing collision with the 23.30 Ranskill–Mansfield munition workers' train. There were no casualties, but all lines were blocked until 02.25 and trains were diverted *via* Lincoln.

21/8/43 14.15—Carlton-on-Trent. A van on the 07.23 King's Cross–Doncaster train came off the rails—but the train was not stopped for another two miles. All lines were blocked and trains diverted *via* Lincoln until 15.55.

11/10/43 07.13—Middle Road Crossing, near March. The 22.20 Edinburgh–Colchester express collided with a car in dense fog, killing three and injuring two. (Ac).

28/10/43 06.15—Hitchin. A light engine collided with an empty stock train, causing derailment of both and blockage of both Down lines until 14.10.

1/11/43 15.33—Connington. Collision of a special stock train with a lorry on a crossing—no casualties.

2/11/43 01.25—Tweedmouth. An Edinburgh–King's Cross parcels train, hauled by A3 No. 2795, collided with the rear portion of a divided freight train. The locomotive overturned and five coaches were derailed; the fireman was injured. All lines were blocked until 03.05 3/11.

15/11/43 09.27—York. A special forces leave train from Thirsk collided with the buffers in platform 12. Several men were slightly injured. (Ab?).

30/11/43 19.30—Selby South. The 18.30 Leeds–Hull collided with a pilot engine. One person was injured. All lines were blocked for 12 hours, and ECML traffic was diverted *via* Knottingley and Church Fenton. (Ab?).

4/12/43 05.50—Newcastle Central. An EMU from Benton collided with a light engine, injuring the driver. All lines were blocked until 08.00. (This occurred just seven hours after the 22.45 Newcastle–South Shields EMU ran into a light engine at Gateshead East, two coaches being telescoped but causing only minor injuries).

17/12/43 22.00—Finsbury Park No. 6 Box. The driver of the empty stock for the 22.25 Down Sleeper ran into a light engine.

1/1/44 17.40—Biggleswade. The leading coach of a King's Cross–Doncaster relief train caught fire, but it was detached, and there were no injuries.

16/1/44 16.03—Hatfield. A local train from King's Cross collided in fog with a light engine on the wrong line. Twelve people were slightly injured. (Ab?).

13/3/44 09.50—Newark. The 08.45 Doncaster–King's Cross express, hauled by V2 No.4844, was derailed by a piece of cast iron on the track and then by distortion of a check-rail on Newark Dyke Bridge. The ECML was blocked until 21.30, with buses and/ or diversions and SLW until 16.15 on 14/3.

2/5/44 07.22—Essendine. Two freight trains collided. All lines except the Down main blocked until 11.45.

29/5/44 16.40—Between Skelton and Beningbrough. The rear coaches and five fish vans of the 14.30 Newcastle-Leeds were derailed. One person was injured and several shocked. All lines were blocked until 18.10–21.45, and trains diverted *via* Ripon.

31/7/44 00.46—Christon Bank. Both lines were blocked for five hours after the collision of a Down special fish train with the 02.11 Little Benton–Meadows empties whose driver had overrun signals. Then, after restoration of the Up line, the engine and front coach of the first train through—the late-running 22.00 King's Cross–Edinburgh express running wrong line—became derailed because staff had failed to clamp the facing points. All lines were blocked until 10.25; all cleared at 16.40. (Ab, Ac).

5/8/44 Midnight—King's Cross. The locomotive leaving on an express for Edinburgh became derailed. The recovery breakdown-train was then also derailed, and platforms 8–10 and the Suburban lines were also blocked until 11.00.

21/8/44 16.29—Wood Green. The engine (A4 No. 2512) and 10 coaches of the 16.00 King's Cross–Leeds derailed at the junction of the Down Main and Down Slow No. 1, the engine coming to rest in the station: three people were injured. The Down lines were blocked and Up traffic was affected by cranes working from the Up Main; all not fully clear until 21.05 22/8. (Ab?).

29/8/44 17.30—Wood Green. The 17.22 Finsbury Park to Gordon Hill (with N2 No. 2675) derailed on the flyover, because the driver was going too fast; the first coach ended up on top of the engine. Six people injured. Normal working restored 12.15 30/8. (Ab).

13/9/44 16.36—Doncaster, Marshgate Junction. The 10.15 Edinburgh–King's Cross express collided—at slow speed—with the Newcastle–Hornsey stock train, derailing its last vehicle. Two passengers were slightly injured. SLW was imposed from Arksey on the Down line.

12/10/44 11.53—Yaxley. The 22.20 King's Cross–Leeds freight train derailed because a bale of cloth fell off. Considerable damage was done to track, bridge and gantry. Most lines were blocked until 21.30.

8/11/44 20.51—Grantham. The 17.30 Leeds–King's Cross express overran signals and collided with a Colwick–New England freight crossing from the Down to the Up side. Damage was minor, but all lines were blocked until 03.25 9/11. (Ab).

3/12/44—Tweedmouth. A Down freight while being propelled to the Up line to allow another to pass was run into by an Up freight that overran a signal. No injuries, but some diversions (Ab).

24/12/44—Pilmoor. The 01.00 express parcels York–Newcastle became divided and partly derailed. All lines blocked, but Up Slow available within the hour.

31/12/44—Edinburgh Waverley. The 22.30 to Colchester on leaving collided with an empty stock train whose driver disobeyed signals. Several coaches of both trains derailed, but no casualties. Disruption was caused for 10 hours.

4/2/45—King's Cross. Due to partial failure of the locomotive's steam sanders, the 18.00 express to Leeds/Bradford, consisting of 17 coaches hauled by A4 No. 2512, stalled in Gas Works tunnel, and—without either the enginemen or the guard being aware of it on account of the smoke and noise ran back 200 yards. The signalman was unable to switch the points in time and the last coach was derailed, killing two and injuring 26. It was common for these heavy trains to stall in Gas Works tunnel, and inadvertent reversal had happened before—but this was serious. The derailment also brought down part of the signal-gantry and bridge next to the signal box, and the resulting chaos lasted three weeks because the breakdown gang cut the otherwise intact cables and the area was devoid of power signalling. Hand-signalling, and the use of Finsbury Park as the terminal for local trains went on until 23/2. Following the Accident Inquiry, lights marked with the distance into the tunnel were placed at 50-yard intervals, and stricter rules about the use of banking engines instituted. (Ab).

9/3/45 04.50—Barlby North Junction, Selby. On colliding with an engineers' train, the locomotive of the 23.15 King's Cross–Newcastle was derailed. All lines were blocked and trains diverted *via* Church Fenton.

15/9/45 20.00—Newcastle Central. Due to a signalman's error the 19.17 EMU from Monkseaton *via* Riverside running into platform No.2 was struck by a light engine. Only one injured, despite considerable damage to train. Up and Down Main and Platforms 1–3 blocked; all cleared by 16.20 16/9. (Aa).

6/10/45 16.23—Newcastle Central. The 16.00 from North Wylam running into platform No. 13 collided with a light engine just derailed. Engine and train derailed. Slight injuries to 20 people.

22/10/45—York. Due to a signalling fault, as the 18.40 to Sheffield was leaving Platform No. 3, a shunting engine proceeding from No. 2 struck the fifth coach, causing derailment. No injuries.

31/10/45—Carcroft & Adwick-le-Street. A 12-coach express (hauled by K2 No. 4633 and B4 No. 6098) was derailed shortly after leaving the ECML, due to failure of a connecting-rod big-end on the K2. (Ba).

5/1/46 05.40—Browney Box, south of Durham. The 03.40 Low Fell–Doncaster freight, hauled by B16/1 No. 842, divided on account of a coupling snatch after surmounting the 'hump' at Relly Mill. The signalman at Browney stopped the front half of the train, which was then run into at speed by the rear half. He also set all his Down line signals to danger, but one of the derailed wagons caught the wires and pulled them 'off ' again. The approaching 23.15 King's Cross–Newcastle express (hauled by V2 No. 4895) therefore ploughed into the resulting wreckage at 50 mph. Ten people were killed and 29 injured in the consequent pile-up. Trains were diverted *via* Bishop Auckland and Leamside until 22.35 6/1, and again on 7–10/1 to allow clearing of wreckage. (Ba, + C?).

29/1/46—Grantham South. A King's Cross–York parcels train ran into the rear of the 22.10 King's Cross–Edinburgh. Two passengers and the guard were slightly injured. (The Southern Area Passenger Manager, C. G. G. Danbridge, was on board).

10/2/46—Potters Bar. Due to a signalling error, the 21.32 Hatfield–King's Cross local, hauled by N2 No. 2679, was derailed and the engine ran into the buffer-stops. The 21.45 King's Cross–Edinburgh (hauled by V2 No. 4876) then collided at speed with the coaches of the local. After that the 17.00 Bradford/Leeds–King's Cross (hauled by V2 No. 4833), which was nearly but not quite able to stop in time, ran at 5–10 mph into the first V2. Two people were killed and 11 injured. All trains were diverted *via* Hertford North for the next 48 hours, and a push-and-pull with F2 No. 7106 operated between Wood Green and Potters Bar. (Aa).

24/2/46 20.48—Thirsk. The driver of the 18.50 Newcastle–Bristol express, hauled by V2 No. 4878, failed to observe a speed restriction over newly relayed track and derailed his train. Almost all trains were diverted *via* Ripon and Starbeck, but the Up slow was used by some freights. Normal working resumed 17.30 on 25/2. (Ab).

15/7/46 19.30—Red Hall, south of Hatfield. Faulty track was thought to have been the cause of the total derailment at 60 mph of the 19.05 King's Cross–Aberdeen (hauled by V2 No. 3645). The engine broke loose and was derailed 50 yards ahead of the train. Eleven people were injured. Trains were diverted *via* Hertford for 24 hours. (Bb).

The recovery operation is in full-swing after the high-speed derailment of Thompson A2/1 No. 60508 *Duke of Rothesay* at New Southgate. *Picture: B. W. L. Brooksbank*

10/11/46 22.35—Marshmoor Box, south of Hatfield. Yet another V2, No. 905 (ex-4876) in its second accident in nine months, on the 16.45 Newcastle–King's Cross was totally derailed on faulty track. There were only seven injured, none seriously. All lines were blocked and trains suspended or diverted *via* Hertford, until 11.30 on 11/11 for the Down and 18.00 for the Up. This was the last straw for H.M. Inspector, and after that part of the blame for these successive derailments of 2-6-2s was attributed to the design of their pony-truck suspension. This was urgently altered on some of the class, but track maintenance improved anyway, and there were no more of these derailments.

30/12/46 11.20—Doncaster Central. The 09.05 Ripon–King's Cross express, running 'permissively', collided with the rear of the 09.40 Hull–King's Cross express in platform 1. The driver of the Ripon train had been given a green hand-signal by the signalman, but 'failed to control his engine adequately'. Several coaches were derailed and damaged, and the Up lines were blocked until 17.30—partly because further coaches were derailed when moved. There were 40 injured, four seriously. (Ab).

8/7/47 15.14—King's Cross. The 09.05 express from Ripon again—collided with the buffers. Three coaches were damaged and 26 people were injured (two badly). (Ab?).

31/7/47 01.05—Balderton–Barnby Boxes (south of Newark). A tyre came off the wheel of the fourth coach of the 22.15 King's Cross–Edinburgh; it passed through the floor and roof without hurting anyone. The coach was re-railed several hours later. (Ba).

9/8/47 16.41—Doncaster, Bridge Junction. A terrible mistake by a signalman during the confusion of the changeover from semaphore to colour-light signalling, on a very busy summer Saturday,

Two men survey the damage caused by the collision between Bridge Junction and Balby Junction, Doncaster, on 9th August 1947.

resulted in the 13.25 King's Cross–Leeds express (hauled by V2 No. 936) colliding at 40 mph opposite Sand Bank Box with the 13.10 King's Cross–Newcastle (hauled by A3 No. 50), which was held at Bridge Junction awaiting entry to the station. Four coaches of the front train were smashed, 18 people were killed and 120 injured (76 of them seriously). (Aa). Traffic had to be run over the goods lines for the ensuing 25 hours—but on the summer Saturday two weeks later a locomotive derailment at Retford Crossing blocked the ECML completely for two hours.

26/10/47 (Sunday) 12.47—Goswick. Another occasion when a driver ignored a temporary speed restriction, in this case at a crossover connection to the Down line, by taking it at 65 mph. The train was the 11.15 Edinburgh–King's Cross, hauled by A3 No. 66. The train derailed, and 28 people lost their lives, 65 were injured (many of them seriously). All lines were blocked for 15 hours and trains were diverted, principally *via* Carlisle. (Ab).

1/3/48 01.00—Connington North Box. A light engine collided (in fog) with a lorry at a level crossing. The lorry was carrying ten German ex-prisoners-of-war, one of whom was the driver; five were killed and the others seriously injured. Subsequently, at 17.26 on 16/10/48, at the same crossing a man was killed in his car by an Up empty stock train hauled by a Pacific. (Ac? + Aa). As a result of these accidents, Connington North Box was moved in 8/54—bodily—to beside the crossing, so that the gates could be controlled directly from the Box.

9/7/48—Little Bytham—Essendine. The right-hand injector blew out on V2 No. 943, working an Up fish train. Although badly scalded the driver stayed on the footplate to stop the train.

17/7/48 c.06.00—New Southgate. Bad track was the cause of the derailment at 70 mph of the 19.50 Edinburgh–King's Cross express (hauled by A2/1 No. 60508). The engine parted from its train, slipped along the track for 100 yards and ended up on its side. The fireman was killed, but as only one coach overturned only one passenger lost his life. (Bb).

29/1/49—Holloway. In dense fog, the Up 'Aberdonian' (18.45 Aberdeen–King's Cross, hauled by V2 No. E924) collided with an empty stock train. The locomotive was extensively damaged, but there were no casualties. (Ab?).

16/2/49—York. LMS Class 5 No. 4781 on its way to the shed collided at the main crossover at the north of the station with J25 No. 5656 working a freight from Foss Islands. Both engines were derailed, but the lines out of the station were only partially blocked.

19/2/49—North of Wood Green Tunnel. The 05.25 King's Cross–York parcels, hauled by A3 No. 60107, ran into the rear portion of a Down freight that had divided. The A3 was derailed and the lines blocked for several hours, with diversions *via* Hertford, partly because the King's Cross crane fell over while clearing wreckage. (Ba? + Aa).

23/6/49 20.40—Penmanshiel Tunnel, between Cockburnspath and Grantshouse. Fire, probably due to a lighted match in a corridor igniting inflammable cellulose lacquer paint, in one minute engulfed the last two coaches of the 10-coach 19.30 Edinburgh–King's Cross express (hauled by A3 No. 60035). It was a fine evening and many windows were open. The train, travelling at speed, was brought to a stand by the action of the guard in a little over a minute after the fire started, with the burning coaches only just outside the tunnel. However, the fierceness and rapidity of the fire forced some of the passengers to have to escape by smashing windows, and seven were hurt, two of them seriously. The first eight coaches were soon taken on to Grantshouse, and after the other surviving passengers had walked there or had ridden by car, the train proceeded at 22.30, only 105 minutes late. No sign of the fire had been seen by the Cockburnspath signalman or by a railwayman passenger who passed through the coach a few moments before the fire broke out. In addition, an asphyxiating gas was produced, and the consequences would have been even worse if the whole train had stopped a second later—entirely in the tunnel. (Ac).

5/6/50 14.32—Tollerton. In a heat-wave the track became distorted. The previous train merely suffered a shaking and minor damage, but the rail broke as the 12.15 Newcastle–York (hauled by A1 No. 60153) derailed at 45 mph and nine people were injured. Traffic on the ECML north of York had to be diverted *via* Starbeck and Sinderby. (Bb).

8/9/50—Selby. The 18.30 York–Swindon, hauled by B1 No. 61250, was derailed on entering the station. Trains had to be diverted *via* Church Fenton and Knottingley.

c. 21/10/50—Peterborough. Within a few days, there were two runaways and a collision, all of light engines. In the first, J52 No. 68789, un-manned, pushed J52 No. 68866 (also without a crew) off New England shed and up the main line to near the North station, where they collided with J3 No. 4128 on a ballast train. Secondly, J3 No. 4123 took the wrong line out of Eastfield Yard and collided with and derailed an Austerity 2-8-0. Lastly, J6 No. 4191 set off without a crew from New England shed and ran to Werrington Junction before it was derailed. (Ab or Ac).

16/3/51 10.09—Doncaster, Bridge Junction. Owing to track defects, the 10.06 Doncaster (08.45 Hull/09.15 York)–King's Cross, hauled by A2/2 No. 60501, was derailed as it was leaving Doncaster. Four people were killed and 29 injured. Main line trains had to be diverted *via* Darnall and Retford. (Bb).

14/7/51 17.00—North of Huntingdon. Fire, believed to be caused by an ember from an engine, destroyed the second coach of the Down 'West Riding' (15.45 King's Cross–Leeds/Bradford), hauled by A3 No. 60058. Unfortunately, the coaches involved were a crowded articulated twin from the pre-war 'West Riding Limited' and egress was possible only at each end of the set. Therefore passengers had difficulty in escaping and there were 23 injured. The guard, believing smoke reported earlier was merely coming from a hot axle-box, had tried to have the train stopped by throwing a message attached to a potato to a signalman,—but without success, and the train was brought to a stand by a passenger pulling the communication-cord. (As this was a summer Saturday, there must have resulted much chaos on the line, trains presumably being diverted from Peterborough *via* Cambridge). (C).

17/8/51 10.36—Newcastle Central. The motorman of the 10.35 EMU to Tynemouth *via* Wallsend departed on the guard's authority without checking the signal—a common mistake—and collided with the incoming EMU from Tynemouth *via* Benton. Three people were killed and 41 injured. (Ab).

21/12/51 17.05—Piershill Junction, Edinburgh. Due to a signalman's error, an Outer Circle local from Leith Central (hauled by V1 No. 67630) collided with a light engine (A4 No. 60018). (Aa).

22/1/52—King's Cross 'Hotel Curve'. N2 No. 69569, running light, collided with and derailed the rear of the 09.54 King's Cross–Hertford North (hauled by N2 No. 69492), blocking the local line from Moorgate for several hours. (Ab?).

16/7/52 19.59—Ricall. Due to the gatekeeper reversing the signal and allowing a car to cross at Ricall Gates Crossing (on the Selby–York main road), two people were killed in the car by the Down 'Tees-Tyne' Pullman (16.45 King's Cross–Newcastle), hauled by an A4. The train was relatively unscathed, but the gatekeeper was sentenced for manslaughter. (Aa).

14/11/52 08.55—Three Counties. The 07.35 Clarence Yard–Doncaster semi-fitted freight, hauled by V2 No. 60880, became divided and the rear portion ran into the front portion at speed. All four tracks were blocked and trains were diverted *via* Cambridge and Ely until 16.00 (Ba? + Aa).

28/10/53—Goswick. The collapse of a big end on A2/1 No. 60509, hauling the 21.15 Glasgow–Colchester caused it to be derailed at points at 55 mph. Remarkably, little damage was done to the train and there were no serious injuries. (Ab).

17/12/53—Longniddry Junction. An obstruction that had just fallen off a Down freight derailed at 60 mph the 00.41 Edinburgh–King's Cross special parcels (hauled by A2 No. 60530). The engine crashed through the station, became detached from its tender and fell down the embankment. The fireman was killed and the driver seriously injured. Trains were diverted *via* Kelso. (Ac).

20/1/54 18.15—Thirsk. Electrical points failure caused the sudden change of 'clear' colour-light signals to 'danger' as the Down 'Heart of Midlothian' (14.00 King's Cross–Edinburgh, hauled by A1 No. 60126) was approaching at 75 mph. Although it was brought down to 20 mph it still left the tracks, but stayed upright and damage was slight, and there were no casualties. Trains were diverted *via* Starbeck and Ripon. (Bb).

10/4/54 early hours—Oakleigh Park. The driver of the 22.35 Ardsley–King's Cross fitted freight, on V2 No. 60861, was unaware that he was on the Up Goods line that ended there and ran at some speed through the sand-drag. (Ab).

3/9/54—Sessay. J27 No. 65827, on a Burdale–Thirsk goods, derailed when it ran at speed into the brake-van of the 07.00 York–Thirsk goods. The van had been left unprotected on a 'permissive block' line, but the driver of the York train averted a more serious accident by speeding his engine out of trouble. (Aa? + Ab).

19/4/55—Newcastle Central. Due to misreading signals by one of the drivers, two light engines (V2 No. 60968 and LMS 4MT 2-6-4T No. 42073) collided heavily at the diamond crossing at the east end of the station and were both derailed. (Ab).

21/6/55 03.34—Between Huntingdon and Offord. A Hull–King's Cross fitted freight (hauled by a V2) suffered division and derailment after travelling at 40 mph for two miles following derailment of one wagon due to a suspension defect. Both parts of the train were stopped and there were no injuries. (Ba).

1/9/55 17.23—Peterborough, Westwood Junction. The 15.50 King's Cross– Leeds/Bradford, hauled by W1 No. 60700 was derailed as it was leaving Peterborough North, due to failure of an engine bogie frame. The bogie design was subsequently modified. (Ba).

7/1/57 07.12—Welwyn Garden City. In this serious accident the 19.10 (Sunday) Aberdeen–King's Cross, hauled by A2/3 No. 60520, ran through adverse signals and collided at a closing speed of 30–35 mph with the 06.18 Baldock–King's Cross local (hauled by L1 No. 67741). One person was killed and 43 injured, mainly in the local although it was on the move, casualties in the express being minimised by the stronger steel bodies of its coaches. Although AWS was in operation, No. 60520 was not yet fitted for it. Soon after, on 8/3/57, the same train, hauled by A2/3 No. 60514 (also not fitted with AWS) overran the self-same signals; the 06.30 King's Cross–Welwyn Garden City narrowly escaped a converging collision. Drivers had already been complaining vehemently about the siting of the signals in question, and after this they were substituted by colour lights. (Ab).

27/2/57—Hadley Wood. The 00.35 Ferme Park–New England Class H broke in two and the rear part ran back through Potters Bar tunnel and collided with the 02.15 King's Cross-Grantham newspapers; there were no injuries. (Ba? + Aa).

3/5/58 09.26—York. A3 No. 60036, on the 07.32 from Sunderland, overran the buffers, demolished a kiosk and slightly injured 11 people. (Aa, or Ba?).

19/11/58 04.30—Hitchin. In thick fog, the 03.25 Ferme Park–New England freight (hauled by 2-10-0 No. 92187) passed an automatic signal at 'danger' and ran at 15 mph into the 02.28 Ferme Park–New England freight (hauled by another 2-10-0, No. 92145). Wagons were thrown across the Up lines and were struck firstly by the 22.35 Ardsley–Ferme Park freight (hauled by V2 No. 60885), which was derailed and tore up the track. Some of its vans were then smashed into by L1 No. 67785 running on the Up slow and this engine turned over, covered with wreckage. Casualties were confined to four train-crew slightly injured. All lines were blocked until 11.00, when just

Bridge Junction, Doncaster, looking north towards the station, on 16th March 1951 after the derailment. The third and fourth carriages were the first to leave the track and, unfortunately, this pier supporting Balby Road Bridge was in their path.

Thompson A2/3 No. 60520 *Owen Tudor* after the derailment south of Welwyn Garden City on 7 January 1957. The locomotive would enter Doncaster Works in seven days' time and return to traffic on 23 February. *Picture: B. W. L. Brooksbank*

a single line became available. Many Down expresses were cancelled, and there had to be major diversions of traffic, up the GE section from Peterborough (in one case, Sandy) and Cambridge to Liverpool Street. A complete embargo was put on all Up ECML freight south of Peterborough, and the most urgent Down traffic from London was diverted to the LMR. All lines were not cleared until 08.05 20/11 and certain overnight expresses were diverted once more to Liverpool Street. (Ab).

18/1/59—Newcastle Central. The 06.42 Long Benton–Newcastle EMU collided with an empty EMU outside the station. The driver was killed, and three passengers injured. Only the electric services were disrupted.

27/7/59—Benton Bank, near Heaton. A train of empties, hauled by Q6 No. 63399, collided with derailed wagons. The driver was killed and the fireman injured; all traffic had to be diverted *via* Jesmond and Benton NW Curve.

20/8/59 12.51—Between Relly Mill and Bridge House Boxes south of Durham. Fire destroyed the kitchen-car of the Up 'Elizabethan' (09.45 Edinburgh–King's Cross, hauled by A4 No. 60031). No one was hurt. The rear seven coaches of the train were reversed to Durham and continued on *via* Bishop Auckland.

15/9/59—Stobswood Crossing, near Widdrington. The 10.35 Alnwick–Newcastle, comprising a two-car Metro-Cammell DMU, collided at 50–55 mph with a lorry on a crossing that had been kept open (against the rules) by the crossing-keeper following the passage immediately beforehand of a Down mineral train. The DMU, which was running under clear signals, was derailed and eventually came to rest after smashing into a brake-van in a siding. The driver was killed, and five passengers and the lorry-driver were injured. All traffic was run on the Down line from 12.15 until 20.50. (Ac).

9/11/59—Finsbury Park. A goods empties, hauled by an N2, ran out of control down the branch from the Highgate direction and collided violently with empty stock in the station. The crew of the N2 were able to jump clear and no one was hurt, but there was much wreckage to be cleared from over the Seven Sisters Road. (Ab, or Ba?).

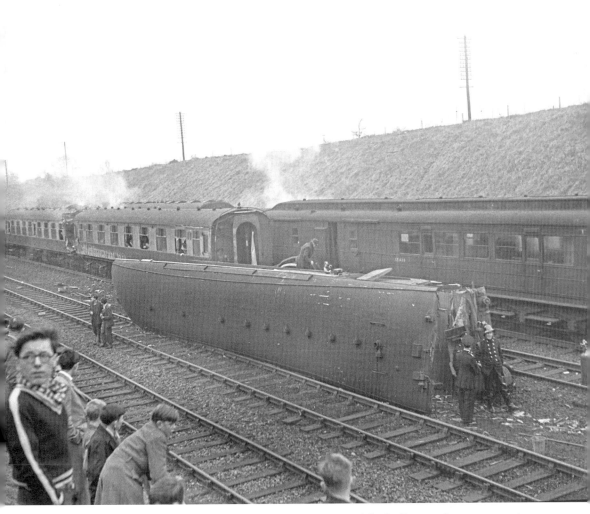

Two carriages are already back on the rails at Welwyn Garden City and this badly twisted one appears to be next. A number of local children are on hand to watch the operation. *Picture: B. W. L. Brooksbank*

Appendix I

Snow and floods on the ECML in the 1940s and 1950s

Snow on the line

The severe weather, with snowstorms and great frosts in several of the winters of the 1940s and 1950s caused widespread chaos due to failures of the block signalling system, and freezing of points, water-troughs, water-columns, locomotive injectors, and carriage-heating pipes—even brake-blocks. During the blizzards, ploughs had to be run over hundreds of miles of track and often failed to prevent snowdrifts blocking lines, derailments were common and of course ice and snow interfered with the running of third-rail electric trains—as on Tyneside. The problems caused by severe weather were especially serious under the conditions of intensive traffic during the war. In Britain as a whole, the worst problems of this kind occurred in the first winter of the war, even before enemy action was causing difficulties.

For about six weeks from the third week of January 1940 there was a period of the 'worst winter weather for a century', with prolonged frost and severe blizzards at times. It affected most of the country and many lines were blocked by snowdrifts—390 miles on the LNER alone. Work in many marshalling yards—already hampered by the Black-Out and fog, was brought to a standstill by ice and heavy snow. The snow-ploughs were first out on the Newcastle–Berwick stretch of the ECML on 16 January, the Ouse froze at York on 23 January, and the Tyne froze as far down as Dunston with the temperature in Newcastle falling to -4F. Yet, the ECML was in fact just kept open, although traffic was impeded by snow at Biggleswade and at Corby (Lincs.). Naturally punctuality suffered severely, the average lateness of ECML expresses declining to 40–100 minutes in the four weeks ending 3 February.

With most of the main lines over the Pennines impassable, including the Settle–Carlisle line, and also the WCML blocked by snowdrifts on 31 January not only in Scotland but also in the most unlikely places such as between Preston and Lancaster and at Golborne, the weather brought freight traffic to a virtual standstill in the northern half of Britain for days at a time. The result was a severe shortage of coal, and households were restricted to two hundred-weights a week. For a few days the Waverley Route was also blocked and all traffic in and out of Scotland had to pass over the ECML. In the last week of February 1940 widespread floods came with the thaw, and interrupted traffic at various places; for example, there was three feet of water in Gainsborough and flooding seems to have been the cause of a derailment at Newark.

In 1941 it was nearly as bad—and for the ECML worse. In the North-East there had been continuous frost for five weeks up to the beginning of February, and the water froze in Wiske Moor troughs—severely damaging them, with fog for 12 of the days. Up to a quarter of the staff were off sick. There were heavy falls of snow on 19 January and the ECML was blocked for two hours between Selby and Ricall. In the next three days many branch lines were blocked in Yorkshire and Lincolnshire and yards made inoperative. Constant use of snow-ploughs was needed, and the military were called in to assist, but there was still much congestion. More snow caused 'working difficulties' in East Yorkshire and Lincolnshire on 5–6 February, and possibly related to it, there was a serious derailment at Bawtry when five coaches of an empty stock train came off the rails in the early hours of 6 February and blocked both lines for over two hours (after which single-line working was operated), with trains being diverted *via* the Joint Line.

As far as the ECML was concerned the worst blizzards came on 19–21 February, with 56 hours of almost continuous snowfall—'the worst in living memory'. First, there was disruption in the Darlington area, and ECML trains had to be diverted *via* Stockton, Ferryhill and Leamside. Freight traffic north of Darlington was already suspended on 20 February, and then two feet of snow settled on the city of Newcastle, and even Newcastle Central became snow-and-ice-bound. The ECML was blocked by snow-drifts between Darlington and Ferryhill and at Forest Hall, as were the lines to Sunderland and to Carlisle; the Tyneside electric services had to be worked with steam engines or suspended entirely. Anglo-Scottish trains were diverted to the LMSR—although the Waverley route was also blocked by a derailment, and freight was virtually halted. The snow brought down miles of telegraph lines and they were strewn across the tracks. Block telegraph communication and telephones failed over the whole area, with District Controls completely out of touch, and the few trains that ran had to do so under a 'time-interval' system. There were numerous derailments to add to the chaos, one at Bishop Auckland blocking another alternative route to Newcastle, another between Darlington and Eaglescliffe; only the Coast line remained open—to Sunderland. Three expresses from London were 'lost' south of Durham, becoming snowbound, the passengers and crew having to be nourished with food brought partly by road and partly by foot through the snow. The passengers of the 23.30 from King's Cross of 19 February were finally detrained at Darlington at 03.00 on 21 February, after many adventures. Passengers for Scotland on trains that eventually got through to Newcastle—in over 24 hours—were put up for the night on the floors of the public rooms of the Royal Station Hotel.

To clear up the mess and restore all the communications took several weeks, and at times 300 extra men were so employed. Signalling repairs needed 10,000 new insulators, 4,000 miles of copper wire, and much help from men from the LMSR and the Royal Corps of Signals. Then, after the snow came the almost inevitable floods—and at Beamish a major embankment slip resulted in a J39 finding itself in a field. Block working was restored on the ECML by 23 February, but passenger services—which for Scottish traffic had been diverted to the LMSR Midland Division—were still restricted a week later, when only 160 miles of lines out of 600 in the North-East were back to normal block working. Normal traffic operations were not achieved until 10 March, and on the branches by 17 March. As the freight and coal traffic that was held up had first to be cleared, there was a total ban on acceptances in the NE Area north of Darlington for several days, being relieved gradually until 3 March. Only 50 'Convoy' coal trains moved during the week of the storm—compared to the normal of about 175, and the shortfall had to be made up from collieries further south.

The Divisional General Manager NE Area (C. M. Jenkin Jones) ended his report of the episode:

> We have experienced what is without question the greatest dislocation of railway facilities which have ever occurred in this country … Men voluntarily remained on duty as long as they could be of service—in many cases for thirty hours, in some cases for over fifty hours.… the staff of the Area by the determination and endurance with which they faced a great devastation have quickly brought it within manageable limits, and by their spirit of service to the public and to the country they have shown an example of the highest conception of the duty of railwaymen.

Nevertheless, in those days equal devotion and heroism was being displayed in other parts of the country under the Blitz, from the worst of which Tyneside was lucky to be spared.

In view of the even greater burden of traffic the railways were having to bear in the final three winters of the war, it was fortunate that there were no blizzards comparable to those earlier in the war. Still, in late January and early February 1942, a blizzard in the North-East and Scotland again brought freight traffic to a standstill. On 3 February the ECML was blocked by drifts between Dunbar and East Linton, also all four lines to Scarborough were blocked and so were all lines north of Aberdeen, but all were clear in two days on this occasion. Then, in the first week of March, severe weather caused some difficulties further south. In 1944, snow on 26–27 February did cause damage to signalling and consequent severe delays on lines in Lincolnshire and Nottinghamshire, the North-East and Scotland, and problems continued for a week or so in certain places. The ECML was spared, but had to carry traffic unable to pass on the Joint line. In January 1945, there was heavy snow again especially in Scotland, and blockage of various branches; on the ECML there were block failures but no actual interruption. On all these occasions the weather hold-ups forced very extensive embargoes.

Before the days of lines electrified with overhead wiring, gales were not such a hazard, but there was a widespread severe gale on 7 April 1943, indirectly affecting the ECML. A tree fell on the 10.15 York–Scarborough between Weaverthorpe and Ganton, injuring the guard and slightly hurting four passengers. On the same day a tree blocked the Border Counties line near Hexham, and near Darlington a signal gantry was swaying so badly that trains were suspended on the Bishop Auckland line.

The 'big freeze' of 1947 (for seven weeks from late January to the middle of March) was probably the worst. This and the ensuing floods when the snow suddenly melted, brought chaos to the country and privations—in terms of power shortages—unknown even in the war, with industry reduced for a period to a three-day week, mainly on account of the inability of the railways to move the coal from the pits to the power stations, gas works and docks. Colliery and other branches were so snowed up that many thousands of loaded wagons were stranded at the pits, and when they could be moved the cold was so intense that the coal was frozen solid in the wagons, while the Arctic weather hindered the movement of empty wagons to pits and of loaded ones away from them. On 12 February, the Cabinet decided that absolute priority must be afforded and emergency measures taken for the movement of coal—for 30,000 loaded wagons were now being held up. To save fuel, numerous passenger trains were cancelled, and severe limitations were put on the consumption of fuel for industrial and also domestic purposes. Given the priority for coal, there had to be extensive embargoes on merchandise traffic, although the effect of them was lessened by the fuel shortage causing a sharp drop in manufacturing output. Loaded wagons forwarded on the LNER fell in the first three months of 1947 by 15 per cent compared with the same period in 1946. The LNER cut loaded passenger train-miles by 27,000 from 22 February, then by 124,000 (the countrywide figure being 42,000) from 17 March, cuts which were not restored until the summer 1947 service began—belatedly, on 16 June.

Beginning in East Anglia, intense frosts came on 23 January and remained almost unbroken until mid-March, causing severe delays due to freezing of locomotives and their watering facilities. This was especially so in London on 29 January, when three ECML expresses were delayed an average of 4½ hours due to frozen locomotives.

Having already overcome trains down in Devonshire, snow came to the East on 28 January. Main lines and branches were blocked by snow-drifts on many occasions and for lengthy periods in the North and East of England, with several instances of even passenger trains having to be abandoned, the engine fires dropped and passengers marooned either in the unheated trains—or if they were lucky, in cottages or station-masters houses. The Darlington–Penrith/Tebay line was blocked for eight weeks, with a train abandoned near Stainmore for much of that time.

Helped by violent blowing-off of the locomotive of the 17.55 King's Cross–Hull, on 22 January the glass fell from the roof at Peterborough North on to the train. On 4 February, the roof of Grantham station partially collapsed under the weight of snow, blocking the ECML for some hours. The ECML was first completely blocked by snow-drifts on 21–22 February, between Newcastle and Berwick. Also the GN & GE Joint line was blocked at that time at Cowbit, forcing diversions on to the ECML. A worse snowstorm struck the North on 26 February, blocking many branch lines and the ECML itself once more between Newcastle and Berwick for 36 hours. Operations at York and Newcastle were brought almost to a standstill, and traffic was also interrupted by drifting snow near Retford and between Berwick and Edinburgh. Freight traffic in the NE Area had got back to 70 per cent of normal by 1 March, but further snowstorms on 27 February in Scotland and on 1 March in Co. Durham and in the Midland and Eastern Counties on 4–5 March brought traffic again almost to a halt. Finally, the worst storms of all in the North on 12–13 March blocked both of the LMS routes south of Carlisle and the ECML had to take the LMS traffic from Scotland. But then on 13–14 March both the ECML and the Waverley LNE routes became blocked in several places by drifts. However, on this occasion, after a block on the Newcastle–Carlisle line had been cleared, most ECML traffic could be diverted to the Settle–Carlisle route which by then had been reopened by the LMSR. On two successive nights 2,000 passengers were stranded at Newcastle, many off diverted expresses from St Pancras, and—as in 1941—they were bedded down in the Royal Station Hotel and in the refreshment rooms. Nevertheless, by running light engines and snow-ploughs and somehow keeping the traffic moving in spite of frozen signals and point-work, the ECML itself was otherwise kept clear in the blizzards of 1947—albeit with delays to ECML expresses of six to eight hours. Thanks to the herculean efforts of the staff, coal was kept moving and accumulations at the collieries did not exceed two days' output. Still, when a thaw came the LNER had to convey 170 extra coal trains a week up to London early in March. Locomotive shortages—and shortcomings, already serious owing to the number needing repair, were accentuated by so many being frozen up or needed to clear snow; the percentage availability on the LNER fell to 73 per cent in the period. Wagon stocks—another critical factor—were kept up for the military and other Government depots assisted in their repair.

After the great freeze came the great thaw, and lines became flooded in many parts of the country. The first were in the Lea Valley and Cambridge district, necessitating the diversion of GE trains *via* Hitchin and the new connection from Bowes Park to Palace Gates. After that there were floods in the Lincoln and Doncaster districts, and a hurricane-force gale in the south caused widespread disruption of telecommunications by fallen posts and trees. On 24 March the ECML was flooded between Selby and York, with part of the main-line embankment at Barlby north of Selby being washed away. Selby engine shed was put out of use—and 42 engines isolated, by the floods, fully until 28 March and partially until 13 April. Trains between Doncaster and York had to be diverted *via* Askern and Ferrybridge and those from Leeds *via* York. Various other lines were flooded, including that from York to Scarborough, on which the station and yards at Malton were inundated for several days.

All this caused the average delay to principal ECML expresses to rise from 50 minutes in January 1947 (also in January 1946) to 75 minutes in February and 87 minutes in March; these were figures typical of trains as a whole—and without taking account of complete curtailments of services. In the eight weeks ending 22 March, 75 per cent of King's Cross–Leeds trains were over

45 minutes late and the average lateness was 65 minutes. For trains through York and beyond, delays due to the floods varied between two and three hours. A general speed limit of 60 mph was imposed from 15 March until 19 May and even after that at certain points on the ECML, because of the effects of a general waterlogging of track that was already suffering from wartime arrears of maintenance. The upshot of all this severe weather in the first part of 1947 was that the public timetable was no longer worth the paper it was printed on.

The ECML did again succumb to the snow on some later occasions. In 1955, on 20 December at the height of the pre-Christmas rush, a blizzard in the north completely interrupted traffic at York. For some hours nothing could move at this great centre and diversions round the city had to be made *via* Knottingley, and Starbeck. Similar disruptions of services by snow occurred in 1958: on 8–10 February at Newcastle and down the ECML to Berwick trains were held up for hours by snowdrifts: although the main lines were never completely blocked, a freight train was abandoned in the snow right behind Newcastle Central station. Then on 25 February it was the turn of the south: the ECML was just kept open, but trains were cancelled or heavily delayed, and a Cambridge line train—hauled unusually by BR Standard Class 5 No. 73157—was marooned in a snowdrift between Ashwell and Royston.

The Deluge in the Borders in August 1948, and its aftermath

A natural calamity that radically affected the ECML was the disastrous flooding in south-east Scotland on 12 August 1948. The disaster was vividly described by George Dow in *Deluge over the Border* (1968):

> on 12 August the rain became a deluge, unabated for 24 hours, during which period it is estimated that over 200 million tons of water fell on the Berwickshire hills alone … Rivers rose between 15 and 20 feet, bursting their banks and sweeping all before them … On the railway between Dunbar and Berwick [*i.e.* the ECML] 11 bridges and culverts were washed away, three others were damaged and there were major landslides, washouts and slips at 14 different places.

The Berwick–Dunbar stretch was by no means the only one or the first to be severed. The ECML was first blocked a little to the south at Scremerston and at Goswick in mid-afternoon. Then: '… from 3.40 p.m. on August 12th until 5.25 a.m. next morning Edinburgh District Control Office received more than 80 reports of mishaps.' The line was blocked by extensive flooding between Cockburnspath and Grantshouse, Burnmouth station was under three feet of water, water poured in torrents through Penmanshiel Tunnel. There were landslides to the east of the tunnel, and later no less than seven bridges between Grantshouse and Reston were washed away—with in some places the tracks left hanging in the air. It soon proved useless planning diversions, for:

> At 9.00 p.m. the driver of the first northbound express to be diverted by the Waverley Route, the 9.00 a.m. from King's Cross, reported a landslide on the Down line between Borthwick Bank and Gorebridge and almost simultaneously another landslide blocked both Up and Down lines at Tynehead. Thus the Waverley Route became unusable for through traffic, and by the early hours of August 13th even its tributaries, the St Boswells–Reston and the St Boswells–Kelso–Tweedmouth lines, were partially out of action. There was no alternative left but to divert trains to the West Coast route *via* Carlisle, Carstairs and Haymarket West.

Apart from the main lines—the ECML and the Waverley Route, eleven branch lines of the former NBR in the Borders were affected by floods, landslides and bridge washouts, some so devastatingly that they were never reopened.

That night there must have been chaos, for two main-line trains, the 19.00 Carlisle–Edinburgh and the 10.05 King's Cross–Edinburgh (diverted on to the Waverley Route), and a St Boswells–Reston branch train, were isolated and their stranded passengers had to be rescued by buses—convoyed along the flooded roads by police. In addition, a number of freight trains and light engines were cut off. The 'Flying Scotsman' reached Edinburgh Waverley 10 hours late, having retreated from Alnmouth back to Newcastle, then over to Carlisle and up the Waverley Route as far as Hawick, and finally retreating to Carlisle again to come up to Edinburgh *via* Carstairs.

It was found that certain branches could be reopened without much delay, but not so the ECML between Berwick and Dunbar. The blockages in Northumberland were cleared quickly, but not even one line of the Waverley Route could be restored until 10.00 hr. on 15 August. All the essential passenger and freight traffic between Edinburgh and England had to be diverted *via* Carstairs and Carlisle, thence mainly up the WCML or the MR line *via* Leeds, the 'Flying Scotsman' for example running *via* Carstairs, Carlisle, Leeds and Selby. This diversion was very awkward because to reach the ex-CR line to Carstairs each train from Waverley had to be reversed both at Haymarket West and at Dalry Road Junctions, using a pilot engine between them. Carlisle could hardly cope with all this extra traffic for any length of time. At first all freight but perishables was cancelled, and this led to a huge backlog. In the meantime, while would-be passengers at Borders stations on the blocked main and branch lines could be collected by buses, lack of lorries in those days meant that freight at these stations had to wait many days before it was collected.

The complete destruction of so many bridges on the ECML between Berwick and Cockburnspath meant that the line would be out of use for months. The diversion of traffic through Carlisle *via* the reopened Waverley Route could only be a very temporary expedient for the reasons given. Therefore the somewhat revolutionary decision was made to send (from 16 August) all the ECML traffic over the (reopened) St Boswells–Kelso–Tweedmouth branch, in spite of its having an uninterrupted stretch of over 11 miles of single line. But the Gresley Pacifics were game—if often with a banker—for the first 10 miles of 1-in-70 facing Up trains on the Waverley Route from Hardengreen Junction to Falahill Box—the climb up to Falahill for Down trains being more gradual, and the bridges on the branch could take them. Nevertheless this diversion added 93 minutes to the London–Edinburgh express journey, and to prevent Newcastle passengers having to wait, extra expresses to London were added for them to the timetable. The 'Non-Stop' (the 'Flying Scotsman') now had to run 409 miles, which it did indeed manage on 17 occasions without stopping at all in spite of the extra 16 waterless miles between Lucker troughs and Edinburgh. However, by dint of hard restoration work on the Kelso line, the scheduled delay in the overall time was cut early in September to 70 minutes, and train times adjusted to allow the withdrawal of some of the extra trains from Newcastle.

The emergency schedules for diverted freight trains were prepared on the 'pre-deluge' basis of a thousand wagons each day in each direction between Edinburgh and Berwick, and with the knowledge that the Kelso route could take only ten express freight trains a day, so taxed was it already with passenger trains … after taking full advantage of the remaining capacity of the Waverley Route to Carlisle and the St Boswells–Kelso–Tweedmouth line, the balance of the freight traffic that would normally have been operated by way of Berwick and Dunbar was sent *via* Kilmarnock and Carstairs and, after passing through Carlisle, was distributed *via* Newcastle and *via* the Midland and Western Divisions of the London Midland Region to Eastern Region exchange points at Wakefield, Ashton Moss (near Manchester) and Peterborough. Intensive working was adopted at weekends, and, by running numerous freight trains on Sundays, congestion was avoided at any point.

Dow omits to mention, however, that considerable use was also made of the Riccarton Junction–Hexham line for freight diversions.

Thanks to a massive effort by the Civil Engineers using, for temporary bridge replacement, military type bridging on steel trestles with foundations protected by steel sheet-piling, and a labour force of up to 500, the diversion of ECML freight from the Berwick–Dunbar section was ended on 25 October. Passenger trains were restored on 1 November, although speed restrictions still made all trains between the Capitals slower by about 25 minutes. The permanent rebuilding of the bridges would take many months more, and the branch from Burnmouth to Eyemouth was not reopened until June 1949. The Reston–St Boswells branch was permanently severed between Duns and Greenlaw, and worked as separate branches from Reston and from St Boswells for a few more years—as long as the traffic justified keeping them open.

The Kelso line was used for diverted ECML trains briefly again in December 1953 after the crash at Longniddry, and indeed the ECML was breached once more by floods on 28 August 1956, but this time only the Pease Burn between Grantshouse and Cockburnspath was washed away at a culvert; trains were diverted to the Waverley Route (the Up 'Flying Scotsman' *via* Beattock) for a few days until a temporary bridge was built. In October 1954 a reverse situation occurred, when for two days both the former LMSR main lines between Glasgow and Carlisle were blocked by flood damage, and trains diverted through Edinburgh Waverley—mainly down the Waverley Route but also some by the ECML, bringing for the first time 'Duchesses', 'Royal Scots' and 'Jubilees' down to Newcastle.

Endnotes

Introduction

1 Passenger-miles are the product of passengers carried and the distance of their journeys; as these statistics are normally based on tickets issued, they are underestimated to the extent that fare-dodging is prevalent. Net ton-miles is the product of revenue-earning load and miles conveyed; thus the railways' internal goods, e.g. permanent way material, is not included, nor are empty wagons.

Chapter 1

1 Throughout this book, for the sake of clarity, tenses in the description are all in the past, even if the features described still exist.

2 To be precise, the end-on union was with the L&Y line to Knottingley, whence access was obtained to York by running-powers over the York & North Midland (later NER) through Ferrybridge, Burton Salmon and Church Fenton, until in 1871 the NER built its line down from York through Selby to connect with the GNR at Shaftholme Junction.

3 In practice the first two track stretch was at least 3¼ miles long, because passenger trains had to return to the main line at New Barnet, short of Greenwood box.

4 Throughout this book prices are given in modern decimal currency, although prior to 1971 it was of course £ *s. d.* Inflation from 1939 to 2017 was at a ratio of 61.7. Therefore £1.00 in 1939 equates to £61.70 in 2017.

5 Although second class accommodation had been provided on London (GN and GE) line suburban services, it was abolished in January 1938, and in 1939 it was used only on certain Continental boat trains to and from the packet ports, mainly to conform to the three (or occasional four) class practice in Europe.

6 The GN was also the innovator of the side-corridor coach, in 1882.

7 A bottle of Niersteiner cost 25p, a Volnay 1923 53½p, and various champagnes £1.00.

8 Except the 'Silver Jubilee', on which it was not practicable for the staff to serve meals all along the train from only one kitchen.

9 If you were 'in the know', you could also use the staff lift in the North British Hotel.

10 In the winter timetable, the 'Flying Scotsman' also had through carriages to Perth—with the locomotives still carrying the head board.

Chapter 2

1 But even in 1951 the speed limit for heavy lorries was 20 mph—which now seems incredible.

2 Soon after the war, an interesting report circulated by the Railway Clearing House in January 1946 was prepared by the four Railway Chief Operating Superintendents, and in 1946 also the

Railway Gazette published an official history (Bell, 1946). Each of the Big Four soon brought out their own accounts thereafter, the one on the LNER (Crump, 1947) probably being the best. The authoritative account of Inland Transport in the war is by Savage (1957). A popular account (John, 1945) was published directly after the war, and a more informed general survey (Nock, 1971) more recently; see also a book on the GWR by Bryan (1995).

3   Ministry of War Transport, from May 1941 after incorporation of the Ministry of Shipping.

4   The LNER moved this ammunition to dumps at Haxey (Lincs.) and Leadburn (Midlothian). Other emergency needs provided for by the LNER alone included 34 Casualty Evacuation Trains, and a contribution of 21 trains to the pool needed for mobilisation of the British Expeditionary Force, and also the establishment of railheads for the emergency stocks of coal, petrol, potatoes and fish.

5   See Part Two of this history, which hopefully will follow in due course.

6   Up to 20 per cent off standard rates for merchandise, 33 per cent for explosives—but in the First World War the railways had to carry Government traffic free of charge.

7   To the authors this seems still a very low figure, showing that the average passenger journey was nevertheless entirely a local one—say Knebworth to King's Cross, Thirsk to York, or North Berwick to Edinburgh. Still, in 1938 the average third class journey (on ordinary fare) was a mere 7.0 miles while the average first class one was 50.4 miles.

8   Harrogate, with its many hotels, was favoured for Government Departments evacuated from London, and so the relocation of these Departments entailed more traffic on the ECML in particular.

9   Ben Brooksbank considers himself fortunate, for he had a divided family and for much of the war he was away at boarding-schools. This gave him valid reasons for a good deal of travelling around the country—which he enjoyed. His secret, in order to get a better view out and see what was passing by, was to sit in the corridor on his bag, rather than in a stuffy compartment probably not even near the steamy and often partly netted-over windows.

10 Much of the Western Highlands of Scotland was already in this category.

11 For details, the reader is referred to the most interesting account written for the War Office in 1955 (available at the National Archives at WO277/17), *The Second World War 1939–1945, Army Movements,* by Major J. B. Higham and E. A. Knighton. For the American side, see *United States Army in World War II. The Technical Services. The Transportation Corps: Operations Overseas,* by J. Bykovsky and H. Larson: Office of the Chief of Military History, Department of the Army, Washington DC, 1957.

12 For military traffic on the ECML, the Movement Control District HQs were in Eastern Command at Cambridge and at Dunstable (from August 1941 and mainly concerned with stores), in Northern Command at York and (from June 1940) at Darlington and Nottingham, and in Scottish Command at Edinburgh.

13 Absent Without Official Leave.

14 European Theatre of Operations, United States Army.

15 The very first train left, in great secrecy, early on the morning of 1 September—over 48 hours before war was actually declared—for Glasgow, from London's Cannon Street station and went via Redhill, Guildford and Reading!

16 Military Port No. 1 at Faslane was later supplemented by Military Port No. 2 at Cairnryan near Stranrear.

17 In the NE Area of the LNER one of the two tracks of the Picton–Battersby and of the Tadcaster–Wetherby lines was used for this purpose.

18 The enemy was well aware of the disruptive effect of air raid warnings, and would send planes over in relays in order to keep a Red Alert in operation for hours on end.

19 Armoured fighting vehicles carried on 'Warflats' or on 'Warwells'. The big tanks (Cromwells, Crusaders, Churchills and Shermans) were so wide that they were slightly out-of-gauge, and trains of them were a great nuisance and had to be meticulously planned.

20 Savage (1957) says that 'Lavatory accommodation [at railway depots] for women was inadequate and canteens were often non-existent or very poor'—as if men didn't need lavatories.

21 Constituting the manual railway workers, so called after the Conciliation Boards set up in 1907 to allow negotiations between the Railway Companies and the men's representatives.

22 Fortunately, the Luftwaffe was by then incapable of sending over any significant force of bombers. Their 'mini-Blitz' of February 1944 was ineffective and the damage done to the railways by the Flying Bombs—in spite of the extraordinary fluke that one of the very first four fired by the Germans on 13 June 1944 cut the main line between Liverpool Street and Stratford—scarcely held up the great flow of *Overlord* traffic at all.

23 Lines of which passenger—and most normal goods—services were suspended included: Dalston Junction–Poplar, Palace Gates–Stratford–North Woolwich, and Didcot–Newbury–Southampton, also most services on the Kentish Town–Barking line.

24 Long Marston R.E. Stores Depot was the busiest, handling 10,027 wagons in its peak month of December 1944.

25 It has been asserted in some quarters that the then Labour Government used the Fund for other purposes, unconnected with railways.

26 These figures are of course miniscule compared to those suffered by the enemy and by our European Allies.

27 This figure was high partly because of the necessity to repair so many of the run-down antiquated former private-owner wagons in the 540,000 taken into public ownership at Nationalisation, but of the railway's own stock that of the LNER was the worst.

28 In 1959, under the Modernisation Plan, it was back up to 4.1 per cent—temporarily.

29 One of the first was built at Palace Gates, just off the ECML at Bounds Green in July 1958.

30 See *Report of the Royal Commission on Environmental Pollution*, 1994, Chairman Sir John Houghton.

31 Indeed Marples overruled a Central Transport Consultative Committee recommendation not to close the Westerham branch—which is now buried under the M25 motorway.

32 At 2.4 times Sir Brian's salary—shades of the 1990s privatisations.

33 The first one opened was at Thornton (Fife) in September 1957, and the only ones directly connected with the ECML—Millerhill near Edinburgh, Tees (Newport) and Tyne (Lamesley)—were not opened until the early 1960s.

Chapter 3

1 North Eastern Airways ran a daily service from London (Croydon) to Perth and Dundee, 'calling' at Doncaster and Newcastle. Connecting services flew from Doncaster to Hull, Grimsby, and Leeds, and by request(!) to Manchester and Liverpool. There was also a flight on many days from Newcastle to Glasgow.

2 However, in the plans for complete evacuation of the east coast towns, drawn up in case of a German invasion, the ECML was specifically excluded, to keep it clear for military traffic.

3 Cheap day returns were reintroduced almost right away in October 1939, only to be rescinded again in 1942.

4 Even one of these was taken off on 19 June.

5 Navy, Army and Air Force Institutes.

6 Railway Traffic Office(r).

7 For example, passenger trains took workers into the large RAOC depot at Barlow, on the Goole branch near Selby.

8 Officially, services from Moorgate were abolished on 6 January 1941 'to allow additional coal traffic to be carried by the Widened Lines'—*i.e.*, without restriction during the rush-hours.

9 But see the comment on bilking, made earlier.

10 Women's Voluntary Services.

11 The York canteen alone, during the 6 years and 10 months it was open, served 10 million customers. The Army Council Instructions specified precisely what refreshments should be available, and their price, for troops on the move (e.g. tea 0.25p a cup, sandwiches 1p each).

12 A plaque remains to this day at Retford station commemorating the serving by the WVS of '2,284,000 meals to HM and Allied Forces during the Second World War.'

13 Near York were some dozen bomber airfields, and the HQ of 4 Group at Heslington Hall (from April 1940) and of 6 Group (RCAF) at Allerton Park Castle; Grantham (St Vincents) was the HQ of 5 Group, until November 1943 when as Spitalgate it became the HQ of 9 Troop Carrier Command USAAF, 5 Group moving to Moreton Hall, Swinderby; HQ 2 Group was at Huntingdon (Castle Hill House) from October 1939, and later HQ 8 (Pathfinder) Group was near there at Brampton Grange—as was later the HQ of 1 Bombardment Division, USAAF: HQ1 Group was at yet another ECML location—Bawtry Hall. For the Army, York was the HQ of Northern Command and HQ Scottish Command was at Edinburgh.

14 The record claimed was 26 coaches—including some vans (estimated at a gross load of 850 tons), hauled from Peterborough to King's Cross on 31 March 1940 by V2 No. 4800.

15 The details of these trains, of those more 'innocent days' were actually documented—even the number of men and nature of stores conveyed, and can be studied in TNA AN2/1027. Most of the trains using the ECML were destined for Rosyth, Dunfermline or Leith, and the majority joined the ECML at York (having gone up the ex-GC main line) or else originated in the NE Area.

16 On 17 April no less than 400 empty coaches were sent up to Glasgow from the SR, and the peak day for dispatch of arriving overseas troops was on 19 April, when 82 specials were forwarded from all the ports.

17 11th Armoured, 3rd Infantry and 15th Infantry Divisions, with 8th and 27th Armoured Brigades and 6th Guards Tank Brigade.

18 The line from Hessle Road Junction, Dairycoates, to Riverside Quay was upgraded in 1946 for passenger train working.

19 About 20,000 passengers left King's Cross on peak summer Saturdays.

20 This trip was noteworthy in that on the return leg the locomotive collided with a crossing-gate near Balne—without serious damage to anything but the gate.

21 One of these B1s, No. 61379, was named *Mayflower*, because it passed through Boston, whence the Pilgrim Fathers had sailed.

22 Other overnight excursion trains were: one each from Aberdeen, Dundee, Edinburgh, Newcastle, East Boldon, Scarborough and Bridlington, Bradford, Cleethorpes and Lincoln, and Grantham, also there was a daytime one from Cranwell by the RAF branch to Sleaford. For the Coronation also many stations on BR enjoyed a much overdue repainting, and the frontage at King's Cross was cleaned and renovated.

Chapter 4

1 These were the 09.30 and 17.50 from King's Cross to Leeds (and back), noted in peacetime for their good meals, especially the 'Yorkshire Breakfast' served on the 07.50 up from Leeds.

2 In the Up direction, the Harrogate portion ran *via* York.

3 The 'Harrogate Sunday' Pullman ran *via* York before the war, but *via* Knottingley when reinstated in 1946—but only for a year, after which it—like the 'Queen of Scots'—went *via* Leeds.

4 Four on Saturdays and five on Sundays, as the 'Highlandman' and 'Aberdonian' were SX, and the 01.05 Edinburgh was SuX.

5 Five on Friday nights.

6 Convertible however, if necessary, to twins by opening communicating doors.

7 On at least one occasion—after the floods of 31 January 1953—the route taken to London was *via* South Lynn, the M&GN and Peterborough.

8 Water of doubtful quality was provided at Ballater on one occasion and complaints were made.

9 Sometimes, individual coaches were worked up *via* Willesden Junction and Canonbury.

10 Auxiliary Territorial Service.

11 A second 'Bayonet' coach was sent over in April 1945.

Chapter 5

1 To the LNER it was always 'goods' (or mineral), but 'freight' is used normally in this account as a generic term to cover all non-passenger-rated traffic or services.

2 That is not overnight Sunday–Monday, and in the summer timetable many did not run on Saturdays.

3 Several other wayside stations dealt with similar negligible quantities. Intermediate figures (tons respectively inwards and outwards) included: Acklington 460 and 3,810; Berwick 19,000 and 5,100; Cowton 940 and 620; Darlington 228,000 and 145,000; Morpeth 10,100 and 1,100; Northallerton 10,100 and 5,100; Selby 27,500 and 76,600; York 125,000 and 118,000.

4 Goods trains from Forth southbound on the ECML reversed out before proceeding to Newcastle Central, whence they went over the High Level Bridge, and conversely trains arriving at Forth reversed into the goods station. Otherwise these trains went *via* Blaydon Main and the loop to Norwood thence to the ECML at Low Fell.

5 Closed as early as January 1956, after which the spur for the banking pilot for southbound trains was moved to the King's Cross end of Farringdon station, the signalling and the system of communication between train-engine and banker drivers improved. Also, the limit on train lengths was raised from 30 to 50 wagons.

6 The Down Yard built at Connington during the war also had a hump, and Dringhouses acquired one in 1961.

7 Built near Blaydon for extra wartime traffic and opened October 1941.

8 One Down train stopped when required at Wiske Moor on Thursdays 'to leave groceries', and one Up train stopped at Danby Wiske and Cowton on Fridays 'to deliver wages bags'.

9 The train was routed *via* the Hertford loop.

10 'Not many people know' (perhaps) that Biggleswade—and also Crow Park, further down the ECML, were major sources of traffic in flowers.

11 While 773 20.30 to Deansgate and 774 21.00 to Huskisson (Liverpool) ran *via* Grantham, Colwick, then Annesley and the GC line through Sheffield and over Woodhead, 584 took

the ex-GN Leen Valley line to Brinsley Junction, then over to the LMSR Erewash Valley line at Codnor Park Junction and so to Manchester *via* the Hope Valley line. Only the Huskisson train ran after the war for a while, but the LMS route continued to be used until 1952 by a train in the former timings of the Deansgate train but it ran only from Colwick.

12 Connington to Leys, near Three Counties to Stevenage, and Hatfield to Marshmoor on the Up; Wood Green to Potters Bar, near Hatfield to Digswell, and Huntingdon to Leys on the Down.

13 Sleaford and Lincoln were both in fact bypassed by their respective avoiding-lines.

14 One of these trains waited three hours at Grantham before proceeding.

15 Trains to and through York from Hull impinged on the ECML going westwards to Selby before turning north at Gascoigne Wood Junction and approaching York *via* Sherburn-in-Elmet and Church Fenton. An exception was the nightly Express Fish train from Hull to Edinburgh which took the direct route through Market Weighton to York.

16 By mid-1942 there were 18 daily paths (including two *via* the Border Counties line)—and no less than 26 on Sundays, for freight trains on the Newcastle–Edinburgh route, although it is unlikely that all of them were ever used in practice.

17 This included 2-8-0 locomotives for the Middle East in February 1941—even though they could not negotiate most of the dock lines.

18 One notable shipment was a 75-ton transformer, which although quite out-of-gauge was brought along the ECML from Stockton, with great difficulty.

19 In June 1944, while Southampton received 248 special trains of stores for shipment, Hull dealt with no less than 303, Grimsby 66, Middlesbrough 38, Newcastle 10 and Leith 8. In the same period—many having used the ECML, London Docks received 223 trains and Tilbury 152. The total to all ports was 2,187.

20 One factory in Eastern Scotland dispatched 2 million jerricans in 4,000 wagons—presumably up the ECML—in the month before D-Day.

21 On a Thursday afternoon in November 1941—before the wartime widenings were carried out, the Ministry Inspector counted 17 Down and 14 Up freights on a run he made between Northallerton and Skelton Junction (28 miles) with a freight waiting at each of the nine colour-light signals on eight miles of the Down Slow between Northallerton and Thirsk, and five freights on the Up Slow with two more waiting in Thirsk Yard.

22 Overall, the distribution of freight traffic (in terms of wagons) at Northallerton at that time was roughly: Ministry of Mines 34 per cent, Ministry of Supply 24 per cent, Ministry of Food 7.3 per cent (excluding seed potatoes), War Office 2.7 per cent, miscellaneous 18 per cent, empties 14 per cent.

23 Only 1 per cent terminated at York, and southwards from York the distribution was 43 per cent towards Doncaster, 32 per cent to the Swinton & Knottingley line, and 24 per cent to the LMSR *via* Normanton.

24 Originating points of these coal trains were:—Blaydon Mineral, 1; Cliff House , 1 (Sunday); Heaton Mineral, 3; Percy Main, 4; Preston Colliery, 1; Tynemouth, 1; Washington, 6; West Hartlepool, 7. (In 1941 other starting points included Stella Gill, Whitburn Junction, and West Dunston).

25 Thus on 14 September 1940, a week after the real Blitz began in London, 12,224 wagons were on hand in LNER London yards and only 5,058 had been moved in the previous 24 hours; at Ferme Park the respective numbers were 1,797 and 1,200.

26 Perhaps not connected with the floods, a pilot engine was derailed at Newark and blocked the Up lines for three hours on 1 March 1940, and on the same day no less than four successive

derailments occurred on the Hotel Curve off the Widened Lines at King's Cross.

27 In the climax of the week ending 14 October 1941, when 215 'Convoy' coal trains were dispatched, 49 were from Northumberland collieries, 24 from Dunston area, 6 from around Bishop Auckland, and no less than 66 from mid-Durham and 70 from East Durham.

28 Much of this concrete was indeed recovered many years later—to provide hard-core for the Motorways.

29 Between mid-1942 and mid-1943 minerals traffic in East Anglia increased by 73 per cent and that of merchandise by 22 per cent, and severe congestion occurred at Whitemoor Yard.

30 See *The Second World War, 1939–1945. Royal Air Force: Maintenance*, Air Ministry, 1954.

31 It seems from the records that Admiralty depots, like many others, were unable to handle munitions at the rate they were supplied, and hundreds of wagon-loads accumulated up and down the country. One set of sidings devoted to them near the ECML was at Haxey on the GN&GE Joint.

32 On or near the ECML, such trains were allocated to: Finchley Central, Meldreth & Melbourn, Godmanchester, Bawtry (2), Catterick Bridge, Marston Moor, West Auckland (2), Shildon and Alnwick.

33 Loaded wagons forwarded by King's Cross District were down by 8.9 per cent and by Doncaster District down 8.3 per cent.

34 The Hull service—non-stop to Hougham—had to be worked by a B1 because the weight restriction of bridges beyond Doncaster prohibited not only Pacifics but V2s and K3s also.

35 Also a piped coal train from Mansfield to Temple Mills—not on the ECML.

36 Much was now brought, in hopper wagons, to a new coal concentration depot at Palace Gates, opened in July 1958, which was reached off the wartime link from Bowes Park.

37 In the late 1950s running on the ECML between Gateshead and Ouston Junction.

Appendix A

1 Merchandise classes 1–6 comprised minerals other than coal, classes 7–10 other bulk traffic requiring cartage by the Railway Company, and classes 11–21 merchandise requiring collection or delivery, in order of value, class 21 being the most valuable.

2 Of the Tyneside electric stock, one luggage motor composite and an articulated twin-set of open thirds were destroyed by bombing in the war, and not replaced. Of the total losses, 81 passenger stock and 442 wagons were lost during the Blitz (*i.e.* up to 17 May 1941), so the remaining majority may have been destroyed mainly by V-weapons.

3 The Annesley–Woodford 'runners' were the outstanding example.

4 Doncaster–Leeds, Darlington–Middlesbrough, and Newcastle–Sunderland were carrying rather more than 50k p/w.

5 Hawick–Carlisle had less than 5k p/w.

6 The rest of the GN&GE Joint Line down to March was conveying about 150k t/w.

7 Budgeted and started before the war.

8 Budgeted and started before the war.

9 Budgeted and started before the war.

Appendix D

1 In TNA file AIR 10/3960.

2 It is based mainly on an REC list of September 1942 and many amendments to the end of the war, in TNA file AN2/1045.

3   They are probably more complete than for any other service.
4   MU – Maintenance Unit; other abbreviations: MAP – Ministry of Aircraft Production; MoS – Ministry of Supply; PFF – Pathfinder Force; RE – Royal Engineers.
5   After the war most Cold Stores were taken over by National Cold Stores Ltd.
6   Rail-connected with LMSR at Wisbech Sidings.
7   Most Landing Grounds became Airfields later in the war, when they were provided with concrete runways and hard standings.

Appendix E
1   Extensive changes of ownership here between 1938 and 1956.
2   The LNER Workshops are not included here.
3   LNER Works and Sidings not included. Almost all other Works and Sidings came either under Bank Top or Hope Town and are listed here.
4   Not included are the many works and sidings coming under stations in the Gateshead and Newcastle area, close to but not on the ECML, such as Dunston-on-Tyne, and down the river towards Wallsend, North Shields, Jarrow and South Shields.
5   In 1938, rail-connected factories in the Team Valley Trading Estate came under Dunston-on-Tyne (not ECML).